The Law of International Financial Institutions

ELEMENTS OF INTERNATIONAL LAW

Series Editors

Elements of International Law represents a fresh approach in the literature of international law. It is a long series of short books. *Elements* adopts an objective, non-argumentative approach to its subject matter, focusing on narrowly defined core topics in international law. Eventually, the series will offer a comprehensive treatment of the whole of the field. At the same time, each individual title will be a reliable go-to source for practicing international lawyers, judges and arbitrators, government and military officers, scholars, teachers, and students engaged in the discipline of international law.

Previously published titles in this series

Occupation in International Law
Eliav Lieblich and Eyal Benvenisti

Arms Control and Disarmament Law
Stuart Casey-Maslen

International Law of Taxation
Peter Hongler

Jus Cogens
Dinah Shelton

The International Tribunal for the Law of the Sea
Kriangsak Kittichaisaree

International Law in the Russian Legal System
William E. Butler

The European Court of Human Rights
Angelika Nussberger

The Law of International Financial Institutions

Daniel D. Bradlow
University of Pretoria

OXFORD
UNIVERSITY PRESS

OXFORD
UNIVERSITY PRESS

Great Clarendon Street, Oxford, OX2 6DP,
United Kingdom

Oxford University Press is a department of the University of Oxford.
It furthers the University's objective of excellence in research, scholarship,
and education by publishing worldwide. Oxford is a registered trade mark of
Oxford University Press in the UK and in certain other countries

First Edition published in 2023

Published in the United States of America by Oxford University Press
198 Madison Avenue, New York, NY 10016, United States of America

British Library Cataloguing in Publication Data

Data available

Library of Congress Control Number: 2023942626

ISBN 978–0–19–286283–9 (pbk.)
ISBN 978–0–19–286282–2 (hbk.)

DOI: 10.1093/law/9780192862822.001.0001

Printed and bound by
CPI Group (UK) Ltd, Croydon, CR0 4YY

Series Editors' Preface

Elements of International Law represents a fresh approach to the literature of international law. It is a long series of short books. Following the traditional path of an international law textbook, *Elements*, rather than treating the whole of the field in one heavy volume, focuses on more narrowly defined subject matters.

There is nothing like *Elements.* It treats particular topics of international law much more extensively and in significantly more depth than traditional international law texts or encyclopedias. As each book in the *Elements* series has a relatively narrow focus, it provides a comprehensive treatment of a specialized subject matter, in comparison to the more limited treatment of the same subject matter in other general works.

Like a classic textbook, *Elements* aims to provide objective statements of the law. The series does not concern itself with the academic niches filled ably by doctoral theses, nor include works which take an argumentative point of view, already well done by the OUP *Monograph* series. Except in length and integration, *Elements* is for substantive topics comparable to OUP's *Commentary* series on individual treaties. Each book is exhaustively footnoted in respect of international legal practice and scholarship, including treaties, diplomatic practice, decisions by international and municipal courts and arbitral tribunals, resolutions and acts of international organizations, and commentary by the most authoritative jurists.

Elements adopts an objective, non-argumentative approach to its many subject matters and constitutes a reliable go-to source for practicing international lawyers, judges and arbitrators, government and military lawyers, and scholars, teachers, and students engaged in the discipline of international law.

Mark Janis
Douglas Guilfoyle
Stephan Schill
Bruno Simma
Kimberley Trapp

Acknowledgements

This book has been a work in progress for many years. I have been working on the international legal issues relating to the international financial institutions for most of my academic career. In the process, I have benefitted from many thought-provoking discussions, collaborations, and exchanges of information with many colleagues in academia, at the international financial institutions, in government, and in civil society organizations. They have all educated, stimulated, and challenged me to work harder on this important topic and, in the process, have enriched my thinking and research of these institutions. While some of them may not agree with me, collectively they have also convinced me that, despite all their shortcomings and the harm that they may have caused, multilateral financial institutions are an essential element in the international development finance ecosystem. We therefore cannot afford to shut them down. Instead, we must keep trying to reform their governance and improve their operations. It is my hope that this book will contribute to these efforts.

The list of people with whom I have interacted on these issues is too long and the risk of omitting some colleagues too great for me to list them all. I hope they will accept this general expression of gratitude as sufficient and will understand how grateful I am to all of them for what they have taught me and shared with me. Nevertheless, there are some colleagues who have played such critical roles in my development as a scholar working on the topic of the international financial institutions that I would be remiss if I did not explicitly acknowledge them. They include my former colleagues at American University Washington College of Law, the Center for Human Rights, University of Pretoria, in the International Economic Relations and Policy Department, South African Reserve Bank, and in the Independent Review Mechanism, African Development Bank. In addition, there are some colleagues who have been both wonderful sources of information and inspiration over the years and who helped in various ways in connection with this book. Thank you: Charles Di Leva, Jo Marie Griesgraber, Claudio Grossman, John Head, David Hunter, Andria Naude Fourie, Stephen Park,

Vikram Raghavan, Andres Rigo Sureda, and Herman Schwartz. Thank you also to Marie-Louise Aren, Gina Noval, Nthope Mapefane, and Magalie Masamba for their excellent research assistance with the book.

Finally, a very special thanks to my family for all their years of love and support without which I would not have been able to write this book.

Contents

List of Abbreviations

ADB	Asian Development Bank
AfDB	African Development Bank
AIIB	Asian Infrastructure Investment Bank
AMF	Arab Monetary Fund
AMRO	ASEAN + 3 Monetary Research Office
ASEAN	Association of Southeast Asian Nations
BIS	Bank for International Settlements
BRICS	Brazil, Russia, India, China, and South Africa
CAF	Corporación Andina de Fomento
CAO	Compliance Advisor Ombudsman
CATDM	Committee for the Abolition of Illegitimate Debt
CMIM	Chiang Mai Initiative Multilateralization
CRA	Contingent Reserve Arrangement
EBRD	European Bank for Reconstruction and Development
EDs	Executive Directors
EIB	European Investment Bank
GAB	General Agreement to Borrow
GATT	General Agreement on Tariffs and Trade
GDP	gross domestic product
GNI	gross national income
IBRD	International Bank for Reconstruction and Development
ICJ	International Court of Justice
ICSID	International Centre for Settlement of Investment Disputes
IDA	International Development Association
IDB	Inter-American Development Bank
IFC	International Finance Corporation
IFI	international financial institution
ILO	International Labour Organization
IMF	International Monetary Fund
IsDB	Islamic Development Bank
ITO	International Trade Organization
MDB	multilateral development bank
MIGA	Multilateral Investment Guarantee Agency
NDB	New Development Bank
PCIJ	Permanent Court of International Justice

PRGT	Poverty Reduction and Growth Trust
SAARC	South-East Asian Association for Regional Cooperation
SDRs	Special Drawing Rights
SUNFED	Special United Nations Fund for Economic Development
UDHR	Universal Declaration of Human Rights
UN	United Nations
WBG	World Bank Group
WHO	World Health Organization

Introduction

It is widely acknowledged that the International Monetary Fund and the World Bank have been influential and controversial actors on the global stage for much of their history. They have been active participants in the governance of the global economy and the international financial system and have played prominent roles in the management of many international economic, financial, and monetary crises.[1]

Their supporters praise them for providing their member states with the funds they need to finance their development and to help deal with balance of payments and other financial and economic crises. They maintain that these institutions, in addition to being important sources of international finance, provide their member states with high-quality policy advice and technical capacity development support. They also extol these organizations for being the source of first-rate policy-relevant research on the functioning of the global economy and the challenges of development, and for providing reliable and detailed data on the state of the global economy. Finally, they applaud their capacity to promote international monetary and financial cooperation.[2]

The organizations have also attracted intense criticisms from a diverse group of opponents. For example, the US financial community initially opposed the creation of the IMF on the grounds that it would undermine US

[1] The extensive literature on the history of the two institutions is too voluminous to be accurately reflected in one footnote. They have made an effort to record their own versions of the history. See, for example, MG de Vries, *The IMF in a Changing World: 1945–85* (IMF 1986); JM Boughton, *Tearing Down the Walls: The International Monetary Fund 1990–99* (IMF 2012); A Viterbo, *The International Monetary Fund* (3rd edn, Kluwer International Law 2019); E Mason and R Ascher, *The World Bank Since Bretton Woods* (Brookings Institution 1973); and D Kapur, JP Lewis, and RC Webb, *The World Bank: Its First Half Century* (Brookings Institution 1997). For more critical views of their history see, eg, B Rich, *Mortgaging the Earth: The World Bank, Environmental Impoverishment and the Crisis of Development* (2nd edn, Island Press 2013); E Toussaint and D Millet, *Debt, The IMF and World Bank: Sixty Questions and Answers* (Monthly Review Press 2010); and N Woods, *The Globalizers: The IMF, the World Bank and Their Borrowers* (Cornell University Press 2006).

[2] See Chapters 5 and 6 and the sources cited therein.

sovereignty and US financial institutions.[3] During the Cold War the institutions were often criticized for being instruments of leading Western states. Some later critics condemned them as being ideological and promoting a neo-liberal economic model.[4] Still other critics have complained that their operations serve elite and large corporate interests and cause significant harm to poor and vulnerable communities. They also maintain that they have failed to pay adequate attention to the environmental impacts of their operations and, as a result, have contributed to serious social and environmental problems in some of their member states.[5]

Given their history, it is not surprising that these institutions have been the subjects of many studies, books, and articles.[6] However, they have received relatively less attention from international lawyers.[7] This may be because public international law, historically, has not focused on these institutions' specialized areas of international financial and monetary responsibility. It may also be because they are international organizations and their international legal status, their privileges and immunities, and their rights and obligations are similar to those of other international organizations like the United Nations. Consequently, purely in international legal terms, they are perceived to be relatively less interesting than these other international organizations, whose work focuses on seemingly more challenging international legal problems like peace and security and human rights.

[3] See Chapter 2 and sources cited therein.

[4] See Chapters 5 and 6 and sources cited therein.

[5] See, eg, Rich, Mortgaging the Earth (n 1), and Chapters 5 and 6 and sources cited therein.

[6] As indicated above, there has been an extensive literature, consisting of both academic and polemic books, articles, and pamphlets on these institutions. This focus of this literature has tended to be on the economic, political, and international relations issues and impacts of the structure and function of these institutions. In addition to the sources cite in n 1, see eg S Kosak, G Ranis, and JR Vreeland (eds), *Globalization and the Nation State: The Impact of the IMF and the World Bank* (Routledge Press 2007); and A Buria (ed), *The IMF and the World Bank at Sixty* (Anthem Press 2006). Both institutions have also attracted the attention of anthropologists. See, eg, G Sarfaty, *Values in Transition: Human Rights and the Culture of the World Bank* (Stanford Series in Human Rights 2012); and R Harper, *Inside the IMF: An Ethnography of Documents, Technology and Organizational Action* (Academic Press 1998).

[7] The most prominent exceptions to these statements are the extensive writings by Sir Joseph Gold, former general counsel of the IMF (1960–1979) and by Dr IFI Shihata, former general counsel (1983–2000) of the World Bank. See, generally, Sir Joseph Gold Collection, at Southern Methodist University, available at <https://www.smu.edu/Law/Library/Collections/Sir-Joseph-Gold-Collection>; for some of Shihata's writings on the World Bank, see <https://www.worldbank.org/en/archive/history/exhibits/Remembering-WBG-General-Counsel-Ibrahim-Shihata>. In addition, there is an extensive literature on specific aspects of the operations of the IFIs and their social and environmental impacts, their impacts on human rights, and the conditionality attached to their operations. There is also some literature on their privileges and immunities. For more information on this literature, see Chapters 4, 5, and 6 and the sources cited therein.

The result is that, at least in English, there are relatively few general studies of the IMF and the World Bank as subjects of international law and of their international legal rights and responsibilities.[8] This is unfortunate because they are unusual international organizations that raise interesting international legal issues. For example, unlike the United Nations, their governance arrangements are based on a weighted voting system rather than on one sovereign member state one vote. This means that on issues that are decided by voting, a minority of their member states can compel the organizations to adopt policies, procedures, and take actions with which the majority of their member states disagree and which can have profound domestic impacts on the dissenting member states. It also means that the richest and most powerful member states can have a disproportionate influence over the policies guiding their operations. As a result, for example, the IMF may condition access to its financing on the recipient states taking various actions that limit the state's policy space and push it to implement politically unpopular economic policies. In fact, the IMF's policy conditionalities have contributed to the downfall of governments in its member states.[9] To cite another example, the projects that the World Bank funds may require the involuntary resettlement of people. It may condition its finance on the member state providing these people with compensation that complies with its policies rather than the domestic law in its member states. This can result in people adversely affected by a World Bank funded project receiving more compensation than those who are adversely affected by a purely domestic project.[10]

In short, therefore, the operations of the IMF and the World Bank can pose difficult questions about the *de facto* power of and the international legal responsibilities and obligations of international organizations. They can also raise interesting international legal issues relating to the relationship between these organizations and their member states. Their operations can also present important problems about how international legal topics, such as international human rights law, should be applied in particular projects or transactions. Sometimes, these problems are cases of first impression.[11] In this case, as discussed in more detail in Chapter 5, the

[8] ibid. See also D Bradlow and D Hunter (eds), *The IFIs and International Law* (Kluwer International Law 2010); and N Lichtenstein, *A Comparative Guide to the Asian Infrastructure Investment Bank* (Oxford University Press 2018).

[9] See Chapter 6 and sources cited therein.

[10] See Chapter 5 and sources cited therein. See also, for example, the cases of the World Bank Inspection Panel, available at <https://www.inspectionpanel.org/panel-cases>.

[11] ibid.

international financial institution in question will be establishing the first precedent on the particular issues and thereby helping to make the international law on these issues.

This book seeks to fill this gap in the international legal literature. It focuses on the international legal implications of the structure, functions, and operational history of these international financial institutions. It should be of interest and use to academics, legal practitioners, national officials, officials in international financial institutions, and law and international political economy students. It seeks to inform them about the relationship between the IMF and World Bank and international law.

The book, however, is not purely about international law. Given the complex and varied operations of these institutions and their relatively long history, it is necessary to provide information on their structures and functions and how these have evolved over time. As a result, the book contains substantial information that is not strictly speaking legal but is essential to understanding the context in which these entities operate and the challenges that they face both as actors in global economic governance and as institutions that are active players in the global financial system.

The book consists of eight chapters. The first chapter is an overview of the state of international organizational law and the international law applicable to international financial transactions in the inter-war years. One of its goals is to demonstrate how innovative and important the creation of the IMF and the World Bank were. The second chapter focuses on the Bretton Woods Conference at which the treaties establishing the IMF and the International Bank for Reconstruction and Development (IBRD), commonly called the World Bank, were concluded. The third chapter discusses these treaties—the Articles of Agreement of the IMF and those of the IBRD—in more detail. Its purpose is to provide information on the governance arrangements, mandates, and operating principles that their respective Articles stipulate for each of the organizations. The fourth chapter discusses the international legal status of these two financial institutions, their rights and obligations, and their privileges and immunities. The fifth chapter discusses how the structure, functions, and operations of the World Bank have evolved since its establishment. The sixth chapter covers the same issues for the IMF. The seventh chapter looks at the regional development banks and the regional financial arrangements that were created after the IMF and World Bank were already operating. The IMF and the World Bank were the models for many of these organizations and entities. The eighth and final chapter looks at the challenges that these institutions are currently facing and the contributions that international law can make to help the organizations successfully meet these challenges.

1
International Finance and International Law before Bretton Woods

The International Monetary Fund (IMF) and the International Bank for Reconstruction and Development (IBRD), now part of the World Bank Group (collectively the Bretton Woods Institutions) have both been important actors in the governance of the global economy over the past seventy-five years. During this time, they have influenced the development policies of many countries around the world and have played prominent roles in the management of international financial and monetary affairs. The IBRD has also influenced the debates about the international law applicable to international development projects and to the environmental and social responsibilities of transnational banks and corporations engaged in the financing and construction of these projects. In addition, these institutions have served as models for the design, structure, and operations of the regional development banks and regional financial arrangements that were established in the years after the end of the Second World War.

Given their dominant position in the institutional arrangements for global economic governance since the Second World War, it can be difficult to recall how innovative their creation at the Bretton Woods conference in 1944 was. In order to appreciate their original significance, it is useful to have some understanding of the governance arrangement for, and the international law applicable to, international financial and monetary affairs prior to the Bretton Woods Conference.

The purpose of this chapter is to provide this perspective. The chapter is divided into five sections. It begins with a brief historical overview of those aspects of the pre-Second World War economic situation that provided the historical context for the Bretton Woods conference. The second section describes the law applicable to international finance during this period. It focuses on the situation of sovereign borrowers. There are two reasons for this. The first is that the primary borrowers of the multilateral financing institutions that are the subject of this book are sovereigns or public sector entities with sovereign guarantees.[1] The second is that prior to Bretton Woods sovereign states were the only subjects of international law that borrowed on international financial markets.[2]

The third section concentrates on international monetary relations. The fourth section discusses the efforts to establish institutions of global economic governance prior to Bretton Woods. The fifth section looks at how the environmental and social impacts of large projects and key macroeconomic policies were handled in international law at the time. This is relevant because of the important controversies relating to these environmental and social issues that have shaped the international law regarding the operations of the international financial institutions in the past few decades.

The historical context

The period between the end of the First World War and the onset of the Second World War was a turbulent time for the global economy. The following data points give some sense of the difficult conditions that prevailed during this period. Some countries, such as Germany and Austria, experienced hyperinflation. In October 1923, German inflation peaked at 29,500 per cent, which meant prices doubled every 3.7 days.[3] In the case of Austria, inflation increased from 149 per cent in 1919 to 2877 per cent in 1922.[4] On the other hand, wholesale prices in the United States, United

[1] Today, multilateral development banks, either directly or through affiliates, do fund private companies. For more discussion of these activities, see IU Delikanli, T Dimitrov, and R Agolli, *Multilateral Development Banks: Governance and Finance* (Palgrave Macmillan 2018) 17–28; and 'MDB Task Force on Mobilization', *Mobilization of Private Finance 2018* (third report) 12–26. See also see discussion on the World Bank in Chapter 5 and the regional development banks in Chapter 7.

[2] Prior to the Second World War, it was not clear if there were any subjects of international law besides states. The precise international legal status of international organizations such as the League of Nations was a matter of debate. See, eg, LF Oppenheim, *International Law: A Treatise, vol. I Peace* (2nd edn Longmans, Green and C 1912) 32, 108–116; and J Crawford, *Brownlie's Principles of Public International Law* (8th edn OUP 2012) 392, 467–471.

[3] P Toscano, 'The Worst Hyperinflation Situations of all Time' (*CBNC*, 29 January 2014) <https://www.cnbc.com/2011/02/14/The-Worst-Hyperinflation-Situations-of-All-Time.html> (accessed 17 June 2020).

[4] See C Beer, E Gnan, and MT Valderrama, 'A (not so brief) history of Inflation in Austria' (2016) Monetary Policy and the Economy, Austrian Central Bank.

Kingdon, and France fell by 25–30% between 1926 and 1932.[5] World exports fell from USD33 billion in 1929 to USD12.7 billion in 1932 and had only grown to USD 22.7 billion in 1938.[6] The world price of commodities collapsed at the end of the 1920s. According to Arthur Lewis, 'From 1929 to 1930 the average price of wheat fell by 19 per cent, cotton 27 per cent, wool 46 per cent, silk 30 per cent, rubber 42 per cent, sugar 20 per cent, coffee 43 per cent, copper 26 per cent, tin 29 per cent; the index of prices of commodities entering world trade fell from 1929 to 1932 by 56 per cent for raw materials, 48 per cent for foodstuffs, and 37 per cent for manufactures.'[7] Unemployment in eleven countries in Europe and North America ranged from 0.9 per cent in Belgium to 19.2 per cent in Norway in 1928 and by 1933 it ranged from 14.1 per cent in France to 37.6 per cent in the United States across the same eleven countries.[8] The number of countries on the gold standard, which meant that they fixed the value of their currency in terms of gold, increased from five in 1920 to forty-three in 1929 and then fell to five in 1936.[9]

The causes of these volatile and difficult conditions are complex and multifaceted.[10] For current purposes, the two most pertinent are the breakdown of the gold standard and the beggar-thy-neighbour policies that helped cause the collapse in international trade in the 1930s.

The gold standard served as the basis for reasonably stable international monetary and trade relations before the First World War. It required countries to fix the value of their currency in terms of gold and make every effort to maintain that value for their currency.[11] The gold standard meant that holders of a currency, who were concerned that the issuing government was following policies that might force it to change the value of the currency, could convert their holdings into an equivalent amount of gold

[5] See DA Irwin, 'The French Gold Sink and the Great Deflation of 1929-32' (2012) 2 Cato Papers on Public Policy 1 31.

[6] 'The Statistical Office of the United Nations', *International Trade Statistics 1900–1960* (Draft Paper MGT (62)12) <https://unstats.un.org/unsd/trade/imts/Historical%20data%201900-1960.pdf> (accessed 17 June 2020).

[7] B Eichengreen and R Portes, 'The Interwar Debt Crisis and its Aftermath' (1990) 5 The World Bank Research Observer 69–94, p 76.

[8] See B Eichengreen and T Hatton, 'Interwar Unemployment In International Perspective' (1988) IRLE Working Papers <https://www.irle.berkeley.edu/files/1998/Interwar-Unemployment-In-International-Perspective.pdf> (accessed 17 June 2020).

[9] Id p 8

[10] See RN Gardner, *Sterling-Dollar Diplomacy in Current Perspective: The Origins and the Prospects of Our International Economic Order* (3rd edn Columbia University Press 1980).

[11] See B Eichengreen, *Golden Fetters: The Gold Standard and the Great Depression, 1919–1939* (OUP 1995) 70–83.

with the issuing country's central bank. This would happen, for example, if the country's economic policies were resulting in a trade deficit. This would lead to a decline in the demand for the country's currency, thereby causing downward pressure on the price of the currency. This in turn could lead to a differential arising between the currency's market price and its stipulated value in terms of gold. If the differential became large enough, more holders of the currency would find it profitable to convert their currency holdings into gold and use the gold to settle their foreign liabilities. This action would reduce the gold available to support the deficit country's currency. In order to maintain the gold value of the currency, the country would be forced to reduce the quantity of currency in circulation. This, in turn, would force downward adjustments in prices, including wages, in the domestic economy. The resulting deflation would make exports more competitive, which would ultimately lead to a reduction in the trade deficit and to increased gold flows into the country. This would then allow the quantity of money to increase, prices to rise, and the domestic economy to start growing. The reverse would happen in countries with a trade surplus.

The gold standard forced countries to have as their monetary policy priority the maintenance of the stipulated value of their currency. The fact that all stakeholders could rely on governments fulfilling this commitment provided stability and predictability for international trade, investment, and financial transactions. It also facilitated the free cross-border flow of capital, thereby supporting payments for international trade. It was also believed to promote the most efficient use of capital and other resources around the world. It should be noted, however, that the gold standard also depended on the fact that workers in most countries had limited rights at this time. Consequently, the ability of workers in the deficit countries to object to the gold standard forcing down their wages was constrained.[12]

After the First World War, countries tried to reactivate the gold standard regime by re-establishing the pre-war value of their currencies in terms of gold.[13] However, despite their concerted efforts, the costs of the war and the turbulence that many of the First World War combatants experienced in their domestic and international economic relations ultimately made it impossible for them to maintain the pre-war values of their currencies. In responding to this situation and its consequences, some countries decided

[12] ibid.

[13] See L Ahamed, *Lords of Finance: 1929, The Great Depression, and the Bankers who Broke the World* (first published 2009, Windmill 2011) 10–28, 570–609.

to substantially devalue their currencies so that they would gain an advantage in international trade. This set off a round of competitive devaluations and what became known as 'beggar-thy-neighbour' policies. The adverse impacts of these monetary developments were exacerbated by the protectionist policies adopted by some countries.[14]

The policymakers in the allied countries who worked on establishing the post-Second World War economic order viewed these efforts as an important contributing cause of both the Great Depression and the Second World War.[15] Consequently, they were determined to make sure that the world would not have the same experience after the Second World War. They therefore worked hard to design and then establish the institutions and global economic governance arrangements that they believed would protect the world from this outcome.

The 1944 Bretton Woods conference, which established the IMF and the IBRD and which is discussed in Chapter 2, was the first step in this process. Later conferences would lay the foundation for the establishment of the United Nations and the International Trade Organization.[16] The latter organization, which was expected to establish the rules for all aspects of international trade, did not come into being. Ultimately, it was replaced by the General Agreement on Tariffs and Trade, which only dealt with trade in goods.[17]

International finance transactions and municipal law

During the inter-war period, a number of states raised funds on international markets in order to finance their war debts, their budget deficits, and their current account deficits. They did so by issuing bonds on major

[14] See D Rothermund, *The Global Impact of the Great Depression 1929–1939* (Routledge 1996) 6–11.

[15] Gardner (n 10), 24.

[16] For a history of the founding of the United Nations (UN), see, for example, MN Shaw, *International Law* (6th edn Cambridge 2008) 30–31. For a history of the attempt to establish the International Trade Organization, see, eg, M Herdegen, *Principles of International Economic Law* (2nd edn OUP 2016) 16.

[17] For more on the history of the General Agreement on Tariffs and Trade (GATT), see, eg, R Hudec, *Enforcing International Trade Law: The Evolution of the Modern GATT Legal System* (Butterworths Legal Publishers 1993); and G Marceau (ed), *A History of Law and Lawyers in the GATT/WTO: The Development of the Rule of Law in the Modern Trading System* (World Trade Organization 2015).

international financial markets.[18] A number of these sovereign borrowers also defaulted on their debts during the inter-war years.[19]

Since these transactions were between a sovereign state and private investors, they did not qualify as international agreements under international law. Consequently, they were structured as private contracts that were subject to the domestic law of the state in which the bonds were issued. As the Permanent Court of International Justice (PCIJ) said in paragraph 86 in *France v Yugoslavia*, a case involving Serbian debts: 'Any contract which is not a contract between States in their capacity as subjects of international law is based on the municipal law of some country'.[20]

This meant that if the borrowing state defaulted on its obligations, the creditor banks or bondholders would have to try and enforce their contractual rights in the national court of either the borrowing state or one of the creditors. The law that would govern the dispute would be determined either by the terms of the debt contract or by the rules of private international law.[21] As a result, the creditors could find it challenging to convince a court that it should hear their case. First, pursuant to the law in the key creditor jurisdictions, the sovereign debtor would have immunity from suit.[22] Second, it was unclear if the sovereign debtor's home courts would have jurisdiction over the case. The sovereign might also have immunity in its own jurisdiction. Alternatively, the courts might determine that the debts were

[18] The primary financial markets at the time, like today, were those in London and New York.

[19] Capital flows during the inter-war period were through central bank cooperation and the issuance of short-term credits and longer-term securities. See M Flandreau, C-L Holtfrerich, and H James, *International Financial History in the Twentieth Century: System and Anarchy* (2003) 1–17. See also M Cecco, 'Central Bank Cooperation in the Inter-War Period: A View from the Periphery' in J Reis (ed), *International Monetary Systems in Historical Perspective* (1995) 113–134; G Balachandran, '"Finance Orientalism"? Britain, the United States, and India's Wartime Currency Crisis, 1914–1918' (1993) 16(2) South Asia: Journal of South Asian Studies 89–106; and A Ritschl, 'The German Transfer Problem, 1920–33: A Sovereign-debt Perspective' (2012) 19(6) European Review of History: Revue europeenne d'histoire 943–964.

[20] Case Concerning the Payment of Various Serbian Loans Issued in France, Case 14/29 *Fr v Yugo* [1929] PCIJ (ser A) No 20. <https://www.icj-cij.org/sites/default/files/permanent-court-of-international-justice/serie_A/A_20/62_Emprunts_Serbes_Arret.pdf> (accessed 20 June 2023).

[21] See M Waibel, *Sovereign Defaults before International Courts and Tribunals* (CUP 2011) 19–21.

[22] Most sovereign bonds were issued in London. See WMC Weidemaier and MG Gulati, 'Market Practice and the Evolution of Foreign Sovereign Immunity' (2018) 43 Law & Social Inquiry 496 for a discussion of the applicable law regarding state immunity in London. See R Jennings and A Watts, *Oppenheim's International Law: A Treatise, vol. 1 Peace* (first published 1905, Longmans 1992). The sovereign borrower would have comparable immunity in the courts of New York. See Weidemaier and Gulati, ibid.

outside their jurisdiction on other grounds, such as the location of the debt or the terms of the contract.[23]

The creditors' other option would be to seek one or more of their home state's support in upholding their rights. To this end, they would form committees of bondholders to negotiate both with the borrower and with their own sovereigns. In the case of the latter, they would seek to convince their own sovereigns to take up their case and advocate for their interests either through diplomatic channels or through other means.[24]

In principle, the creditors gained an additional possible way to enforce their claims following the creation of the PCIJ in 1920.[25] This court could hear disputes between sovereigns. Consequently, if the creditors could convince their governments to take on their case, they could have the case heard in the PCIJ.

In this case, their sovereign would be arguing that the defaulting sovereign debtor had violated the international legal principles dealing with the state's responsibility to treat foreign investors and foreign citizens within its jurisdiction fairly and equitably.[26] This meant that the state should not interfere with the foreigner's property and should not act towards the foreigner in a discriminatory or unfair or inequitable manner. However, if the state violated these principles, for example by defaulting on its debts it would incur international responsibility. This responsibility was towards the foreigner's home state and was for the injury caused to that state through the injury to its citizens. This meant that the PCIJ, in fact, would be assessing the injury to the creditor's home state rather than to the creditor

[23] See M Waibel, *Sovereign Defaults before International Courts and Tribunals* (CUP 2011).

[24] In an earlier age, the creditor's sovereign might resort to 'gunboat diplomacy'. This euphemism meant that the sovereign would use force to uphold the creditor's rights. See M Tomz, 'Enforcement by Gunboats', Chapter 6 in M Tomz, *Reputation and International Cooperation: Sovereign Debt Across Three Centuries* (Princeton University Press 2007)), for a history of gunboat diplomacy. See also KJ Mitchener and MD Weidemaier, 'Super Sanctions and Sovereign Debt Repayment' (2005) NBER Working Paper No w114725. The use of gunboat diplomacy resulted in 1907 in the Dargo–Porter Convention that prohibited states from using force to enforce debt contracts except in limited circumstances. For more on the Drago doctrine and the Convention, see LM Drago and HE Nettles, 'The Drago Doctrine in International Law and Politics', 8 The Hispanic Historical Review 204–223 (1928). <https://www.jstor.org/stable/2506116> (accessed 29 June 2023).

[25] See 'Statute of the Permanent Court of International Justice 1920', <https://www.un-ilibrary.org/content/books/9789210559096s003-c002#:~:text=The%20Statute%20of%20the%20Permanent,390%20(Statute> (accessed 14 March 2023).

[26] R Jennings and A Watts (n 22) 206–210 discussing the international law of state responsibility in the inter-war period.

itself. It also meant that if the creditor could not convince its own state to take on its case, it would not have a justiciable claim under international law.

As indicated above, France agreed to bring cases in the PCIJ on behalf of its citizens against Brazil and Serbia which had defaulted on their obligations in particular debt transactions.[27] These two cases, which were the primary international law cases in this period dealing with international financial transactions, confirmed the proposition that financial transactions involving sovereign debtors were governed by domestic law.

In these cases, Serbia and Brazil had issued bonds before the First World War that were held by, amongst others, French investors. These bonds specified that the borrower would meet its obligations in French currency, which at the time had a specified gold value. After France went off the gold standard, the nominal value of the French franc, which remained legal tender in France, declined in terms of gold. The borrowers therefore were able to pay back their debts in devalued currency. The bondholders persuaded the French government to take up their case and bring an action against the debtor countries in the PCIJ. The French state accused the debtors of causing injury to France by not paying the full value of their debts, as determined by the value of the gold content of the French franc specified in their contracts, and thereby breaching their contractual obligations.

In both cases, the PCIJ found in favour of the debtors. It ruled that the question of how to interpret the payments' related contractual clauses depended on the governing law specified in the contracts or as determined by the applicable private international law rules. The court in the Brazilian case, citing the Serbian case, explained that it was a 'generally accepted principle that a State is entitled to regulate its own currency'.[28] Consequently, the state was free to alter the value of the currency and to expect the new nominal value of the currency to be respected as legal tender in settling all outstanding debts.

It is also important to note that even if these agreements had been governed by public international law there would have been few principles available to resolve the dispute. In addition to the principle of state responsibility, the only international legal principles that arguably were relevant to these disputes were such general customary international law principles as

[27] See *F v Yugo* (n 20) and Payment in Gold of Brazilian Federal Loans Contracted in France, Case 15/29 *Fr v Braz* [1929] PCIJ (ser A) No 21. <https://www.icj-cij.org/sites/default/files/permanent-court-of-international-justice/serie_A/A_20/64_Emprunts_Bresiliens_Arret.pdf> (accessed 20 June 2023).

[28] *Fr v Braz* (n 27) at para 74.

pacta sunt servanda, clausula rhebus sic stantibus, and the principle of necessity. *Pacta sunt servanda*, which means that all agreements must be kept, is a general principle of all legal systems, and of customary international law.[29] In the context of international finance, the principle means that both parties to the contract must perform their contractual obligations as agreed. Consequently, it helps the creditor enforce the debt contract against the defaulting sovereign debtor. However, the principle is qualified by the principle of *clausula rhebus sic stantibus*. This principle means that both parties to an agreement may be excused from performing their contractual obligations because of a fundamental change in circumstances..[30] Given that in financial contracts, the creditors usually provide the debtor with all the agreed funds before the debtor is expected to meet its obligations to repay the debt, the principle would have been of little help to defaulting sovereign debtors during the inter-war period—or even today.

The principle of necessity, in some circumstances, may have offered a defaulting debtor some relief. This doctrine justifies a state in committing an international wrongful act, including a breach of its agreements, if it deems it necessary to protect its essential interests in a situation of grave and imminent peril.[31] Whenever it invokes this doctrine, the debtor would have the burden of proving that its situation had deteriorated to such an extent that it was facing an extreme peril and needed to default on its debt obligations in order to deal with the existential threat confronting it. Since the doctrine was not designed specifically for financial transactions and that debt contracts often were drafted with sufficient detail to cover most circumstances, the debtor would have had to overcome a high bar in order for the defence to be successful.[32]

[29] See JL Kunz, 'The Meaning and the Range of the Norm Pacta Sunt Servanda' (1945) in 39(2) The American Journal of International Law 180–197.

[30] See Kunz, ibid. Following the Second World War, the principle was made more flexible and has come to be an international law version of a more general change in circumstances clause. See, eg, M Panizzon, *Good Faith in the Jurisprudence of the WTO: The Protection of Legitimate Expectations, Good Faith Interpretation and Fair Dispute Settlement* (Hart 2006) 27–28.

[31] See R Boed, 'State of Necessity as a Justification for Internationally Wrongful Conduct' (2000) 3 Yale Human Rights & Development Law Journal <https://digitalcommons.law.yale.edu/yhrdlj/vol3/iss1/1> (accessed 17 June 2020).

[32] It should be noted that in more recent times, sovereign debtors have raised the necessity defence to justify their failure to perform their contractual obligations in specific economic transactions. They have met with mixed success, see Case No ARB/02/1 *LG & E Energy Corporation, LG & E Capital Corporation and LG & E International, Inc v Argentina* [2006] (Decision on Liability 2006) 21 ICSID Rev 155. See also Case No ARB/02/16 *Sempra Energy International v Argentine Republic* [2010] (Decision on the Argentine Republic's Application for Annulment of the Award 2010) p 198.

During the inter-war period, one other possible defense emerged. This was the doctrine of odious debt. According to this doctrine, a state should not be responsible for the debts of a predecessor government which had incurred the debt for purposes that were oppressive to the people of that state. The doctrine was originally proposed by Alexander Sack following the Russian Revolution and the Soviet Union's refusal to pay the debts of the former Tsarist regime.[33]

During the inter-war period, German war reparations payments were the one sovereign debt case that did receive significant international legal and diplomatic attention.[34] These payment obligations arose from commitments that Germany had accepted in the Treaty of Versailles in 1919.[35] The amount of the country's obligation were establishing at a meeting in London in 1921.[36] Since the German commitment was based on an international treaty, these financial obligations were established in international law. Germany's subsequent failure to meet its obligations, therefore, raised international legal issues and resulted in an international legal resolution.

Germany's failure to pay the expected reparations and its claim that it could not afford to make these payments led to two international agreements. The first agreement established the Dawes Plan for resolving the issue.[37] This plan involved the creditors placing an agent in Germany to assess the validity of the German claim that they could not pay, to determine what payments it should make and to ensure that the payments that it did

[33] See MG Gulati, S Ludington, and AM Weisburd, 'A Convenient Untruth: Fact and Fantasy in the Doctrine of Odious Debts' (with 'Response: Reflections on "A Convenient Untruth"')' (2007) in Duke Law School Legal Studies Paper No. 174 <SSRN: https://ssrn.com/abstract=1024824> (accessed 17 June 2020). See also MG Gulati, LC Buchheit, and RB Thompson, 'The Dilemma of Odious Debts' (2007) in 56 Duke Law Journal for a detailed discussion of the doctrine. While the doctrine has generated much interest, it has not met with great success in litigation or in negotiations about sovereign debts either during the inter-war years or since. It also has not played a prominent role in the operations of the international financial institutions and so will not be discussed in detail in this book.

[34] See TW Guinnane, 'Financial Vergangenheitsbewältigung: The 1953 London Debt Agreement' (2015) in 880 Yale University Economic Growth Center Discussion Paper for a history of German war reparations. See also E Toussaint, 'Why the 1953 cancellation of German debt won't be reproduced for Greece and Developing Countries' (CATDM, 27 March 2020) <https://www.cadtm.org/Why-the-1953-cancellation-of-German-debt-cannot-be-reproduced-for-Greece-and> (accessed 17 June 2020).

[35] Guinnane, ibid, 2–7.

[36] ibid, 9–20.

[37] See P d'Argent, 'The Conversion of Reparations into Sovereign Debts (1920–1953)' (2017) <https://ssrn.com/abstract=3258297> or <http://dx.doi.org/10.2139/ssrn.3258297> (accessed 17 June 2020) for details on the Dawes Plan.

make were distributed to their intended recipients, the countries to whom it owed the reparations.

The failure of the Dawes Plan to resolve the matter led to a second agreement and a new plan to deal with the payment of the reparations. This second plan was the Young Plan.[38] It led to the creation of the Bank for International Settlements (BIS).[39] The BIS, acting as the agent of the recipients, was expected to receive the reparations payments from Germany and transfer them to their intended recipients. In the event, Hitler's rise to power and Germany's subsequent refusal to make these payments meant that the BIS did not perform this function.[40] It is important to note that the BIS was also expected to play a role in global economic governance. This aspect of the BIS's functions is discussed later in this chapter.

The international monetary order during the inter-war years

One noteworthy feature of the inter-war period was the efforts that countries made to re-establish the gold standard.

The chief attractions of this standard for investors were its predictability and its automaticity. These features suggested that the gold standard was apparently operating outside the effective control of governments and was governed purely by market dynamics. However, the apparent automaticity of its operation was subject to the prerogative of each participating sovereign state to adjust the value of its currency and to specify what counts as legal tender in the state.[41] This meant that each sovereign state, in principle, could decide to take its country completely off the gold standard or it could decide to change the value of its currency by changing its gold content. However, either of these actions carried a high price. If a government decided to change the relationship between its currency and gold, it would affect expectations about the prices of both domestically produced and internationally traded goods and the value of outstanding debts. Thus, its

[38] ibid for the Young Plan.

[39] See 'Statutes of the Bank for International Settlements 1930', <https://www.bis.org/about/statutes-en.pdf> (accessed 14 March 2023).

[40] It is important to note that the German obligations survived the Second World War and were finally addressed in the 1953 agreement for dealing with German debts. The final payments on this agreement were made only in 2010. See d'Argent (n 37).

[41] See J Gold, 'Legal Models for the International Regulation of Exchange Rates' (1984) in 82 (5 and 6) Michigan Law Review 1533, 1534–1536.

actions could lead to unpredictable economic consequences. It would also have an adverse impact on the credibility of the state, which would have broken its promise to maintain the value of its currency in terms of gold.

There are two other relevant features of the pre-First World War gold standard that need mentioning. First, as indicated above, the gold standard was incorporated into financial transactions through gold clauses which stipulated that the borrower would pay back its debts either by paying the amount of currency equivalent to the stipulated amount of gold or by delivering the stipulated amount of gold. This meant that the risk of changes in the value of the currency was expected to be borne by the borrower.

However, the First World War had substantially altered the economic fortunes of the major European countries. As a result, their economies could not operate effectively at the pre-war value of their currencies. They also could not easily afford to pay back debts incurred at these pre-war values. This suggested that countries, wishing to go back to the gold standard, would need to devalue their currencies, which meant reducing their value in terms of gold. Unfortunately, there was no clear agreement on the size of the adjustments that each country should make in order to restore a sustainable gold standard. If countries devalued too much, they would gain an unfair advantage in international trade, thereby impoverishing their trading partners. If they set the value too high, their exports would become relatively too expensive, thereby impoverishing their own economies.

Second, the fact that the gold standard worked by forcing changes in prices, including wages, on deficit countries, meant that it could only work as long as workers were unable to effectively oppose downward adjustments in their wages. In other words, it could only function in states with limited democracies.[42] However, after the war, workers were becoming more organized and were more able to use the political system to make demands on the country's economic and political leadership. This meant that they were better able to resist the adjustment pressures associated with the gold standard. As a result, it was much harder for governments to impose the adjustments required by the gold standard on their populations.

The result, as indicated above, was that throughout the inter-war period, countries experienced bouts of economic instability. They adopted beggar-thy-neighbour policies to protect their economies and make their exports cheaper. They also, ultimately, decided to withdraw from the gold standard.

[42] See Eichengreen (n 11) 5–11.

In fact, by the outbreak of the Second World War, all the major powers were no longer on the gold standard.[43]

One other relevant feature of the gold standard was that, because it ostensibly operated automatically, there was no need for explicit international legal principles or rules to govern international monetary relations. In addition, at least as long as the gold standard operated effectively, there was not much need for states to meet to discuss international monetary affairs. In fact, at this time any interactions between states regarding international monetary affairs was largely limited to occasional interactions between central banks regarding movements of monetary gold.[44] Any agreements reached between these central banks did not qualify as inter-state agreements. Consequently, they did not implicate international law.[45]

The need for international meetings to discuss international monetary relations increased as the gold standard began breaking down and states began adopting policies that were mutually harmful. Consequently, during the inter-war period, there were efforts to organize international economic conferences.[46] However, at least in regard to monetary arrangements, these conferences did not result in any binding international agreements or any international legal principles that could replace the gold standard as the basis for international monetary relations.

Global economic governance

During the inter-war years there was no international organization that was specialized in international monetary or financial affairs. However, there were two efforts to promote global economic governance that influenced the outcomes of the Bretton Woods Conference.

The first was the establishment of the Bank for International Settlements (BIS). As indicated above, the BIS was created in 1930 as part of the agreement to deal with German reparations. It was envisaged that it would be owned by the central banks of the states that participated in the conference

43 ibid 19–24.

44 ibid 3–6.

45 See Ahamed (n 13) 19–20.

46 See P Clavin, 'The Fetishes of So-Called International Bankers: Central Bank Co-operation for the World Economic Conference 1932-3' (1992) 1 Contemporary European History 281–311. See also S Edwards, 'The London Monetary and Economic Conference of 1933 and the end of the Great Depression: A "Change of Regime" Analysis' (2017) 23204 NBER Working Paper 3-15 <http://www.nber.org/papers/w23204> (accessed 17 June 2020).

that led to the Young Plan. In the event, two states, Japan and the United States, decided that private banks rather than their central banks would become the holders of their shares in the BIS. Importantly the BIS was established under Swiss law rather than under international law. However, the Swiss government agreed to give immunity to the BIS and to treat it, in effect, like an international organization albeit one established under Swiss law.[47]

The BIS was established with two objectives. The first, as discussed above, was to act as the agent for the settlement of German reparations payments. The plan was that the Germans would make the agreed payments to the BIS who would then distribute the requisite amounts to each of the recipient countries, primarily France, Belgium, and the UK. Unfortunately, because the Nazi regime refused to pay the German debts, the BIS did not, in fact, play this role.

The second objective was to facilitate cooperation between central banks. As a result, the BIS hosted regular meetings between the member central banks until the outbreak of the Second World War. The bank also acts as a banker to central banks. In this capacity, it was expected to perform its services in a neutral and technical manner. It continued to perform this function throughout the war. This meant that it provided services to the German central bank throughout the war.[48]

The BIS was the first independent legal entity to play a role in international financial and monetary affairs. It continues to play an important international monetary role today by fostering cooperation between central banks. It has also taken on additional roles as an important source of information and analysis on the operation of the international financial and monetary systems and in supporting international financial regulatory cooperation.[49]

The second example of incipient global economic governance during the inter-war years was the role played by the Economic and Finance

[47] See DJ Bederman, 'The Unique Legal Status of the Bank for International Settlements comes into Focus' (2003) 16 Leiden Journal of International Law 787; see R Auboin, 'Essays in International Finance: The Bank for International Settlements, 1930-1955' (1955) Essay No 22; see also MP Hughes and C Palke, 'The Bank for International Settlements: An Evolutionary Institution' (2019) 15(1) Journal of Business Case Studies 19–23.

[48] ibid. MP Hughes and C Palke, 'The Bank for International Settlements: an Evolutionary Institution' (2019) Journal of Business Case Studies 15(1), 19–28.

[49] ibid. For more information on the BIS, see also: <https://www.bis.org/> (accessed 14 March 2023).

Organization, which was established by the League of Nations.[50] This entity established financial, economic, fiscal, and statistical committees to try and support economic recovery in its member states. For example, it played an oversight role regarding the financial support that was extended to countries like Austria to help them deal with the effects of the economic and financial crises that they were facing.[51] The League, operating in cooperation with the states providing the finances, determined that Austria would have to satisfy certain conditions in order to access all the available funds. The approach of the League, thus, informed the conditionality approach later adopted by the IMF. Interestingly, some of the personnel who worked for the Economic and Finance Organization of the League later became senior officials at the IMF.[52]

It should also be noted that the US government provided general economic support bilaterally to the governments of Cuba and Colombia at around the same time. In these cases, the United States sent experts on missions to the countries to study the problem and help the governments concerned develop policies to deal with the challenges that they faced. These experiences influenced the views of key US officials about how to provide this type of economic assistance. Some of these officials worked on the design of the IMF and the IBRD.[53]

The third attempt to promote more effective global governance was the failed attempt in the Americas to create an Inter-American Bank.[54] The bank failed because of opposition from the banking community and the Congress in the United States. It would have funded both development projects and macro-economic policy financing in its member states. Many of the officials both in the US government and in other South American countries that participated in the discussions about the Inter-American Bank were also participants in the Bretton Woods conference.

[50] See P Clavin and J-W Wessel, 'Transnationalism and the League of Nations: Understanding the Work of Its Economic and Financial Organisation' (2005) 14 Contemporary European History 465–492. See also J Martin, *The Meddlers: Sovereignty, Empire and the Birth of Global Economic Governance* (Harvard University Press 2022).

[51] See P Clavin, 'Men and Markets' in G Sluga and P Clavin (eds), *Internationalisms: A Twentieth-Century History* (CUP 2016). See also J Martin, ibid.

[52] ibid 108, 109.

[53] See E Helleiner, *Forgotten Foundations of Bretton Woods: International Development and the Making of the Postwar Order* (Cornell University Press 2014) 18–24, 136. See also, generally, JM Boughton, *Harry White and the American Creed: How a Federal Bureaucrat created the Modern Global Economy (and failed to get the Credit)* (Yale University Press 2021).

[54] Helleiner, ibid 91, 123. Boughton, ibid.

Environmental and social impacts

Over time, possibly the most controversial aspect of the operations of the multilateral financial institutions like the World Bank has been their approach to the environmental and social impacts of their operations. This will be discussed in more detail in later chapters.[55] However, it is useful to note that in the inter-war period only limited attention was paid to these issues. Unless particular activities or transactions had cross-border impacts, their social and environmental impacts were seen as domestic issues. As a result, they fell within the exclusive jurisdiction of each sovereign state. This meant that both other states and international organizations should refrain from commenting on these issues.[56]

Nevertheless, these issues did receive some attention during the inter-war period. In regard to the environment, the most significant case is the Trail Smelter arbitration involving a dispute between Canada and the United States.[57] This case, which involved polluting activities in Canada having adverse environmental impacts in the United States, resulted in Canada paying damages to the injured US parties . It also helped establish the 'polluter pays' principle as part of international law.[58]

Another relevant development regarding social impacts was the creation of the International Labour Organization (ILO) in 1919. This meant that there was an international organization focused on the conditions of labour in its member countries.[59] However, neither the organization nor its standards appear to have had any direct involvement in international financial transactions in the inter-war years. This could be because labour issues were not seen as having any cross-border impacts that would justify the ILO or any other international actor commenting on them.[60]

[55] See Chapters 4, 5, and 8.

[56] See R Jennings and A Watts (n 22) at 109. See also *Trail Smelter Arbitration United States v Canada* [1938/1941] 3 RIAA 1905.

[57] *Trail Smelter Arbitration*, ibid.

[58] ibid at section 1 point 3 at 1966. See also P Sands, *Principles of International Environmental Law* (CUP 2003) 279–281.

[59] See 'Constitution of the International Labour Organisation (ILO) 1919', Art 1 with annex, <https://www.ilo.org/dyn/normlex/en/f?p=1000:62:0::NO:62:P62_LIST_ENTRIE_ID:2453907:NO> (accessed 14 March 2023).

[60] See G Rodgers, E Lee, L Swepston, and J van Daele, *The International Labour Organization and the quest for Social* Justice *1919–2009* (Cornell University Press 2009) 1, 37–45. See also DR Maul, 'The International Labour Organization and the Struggle against Forced Labour from 1919 to the Present' (2007) 48(4) Labor History 477–490.

Conclusion

The chapter makes three key points. First, it argues that prior to Bretton Woods, international financial transactions were governed by municipal law. Both sovereigns and corporations that needed to raise foreign exchange had to do so in domestic financial markets. They could either borrow funds from banks or they would issue bonds that would be bought by private banks and investors. Thus, these transactions would be based on contracts which would usually be subject to the law of the state in which the creditor bank or bond market was located. Moreover, the operation of the international monetary system, which was based on the gold standard, meant that that there were minimal institutional arrangements for the governance of international financial and monetary affairs. As a result, the leading roles in global financial affairs were played by private bankers and investors. States only became involved in these matters if they were requested to do so by these private parties and they agreed to the request or in the rare case of debts owed by one sovereign to another, as in the case of war reparations.

Second, the creation of the Bretton Woods institutions was informed by the lessons learned from the economic crises of the inter-war period and the ultimately unsuccessful attempts to respond to them. In particular, an important motivating force behind the establishment of the IMF and IBRD was the determination of their creators to avoid the economic problems that had characterized the inter-was period and were believed to have been contributing causes of the Great Depression and the Second World War.

Third, environmental and social issues played a relatively insignificant role during this period. As a result, they were not directly addressed in the drafting of the Articles of Agreement for the IBRD and the IMF.

Each of these three propositions would ultimately be challenged in the course of the operations undertaken by the institutions established at the Bretton Woods Conference. The purpose of this book is to describe these developments and explain their international legal significance. The next chapter will discuss the Bretton Woods Conference and the institutions that it produced. Thereafter the book will systematically discuss various aspects of the operations of these institutions and their international legal significance.

2
Bretton Woods and the Creation of the International Monetary Fund and the World Bank

By the time the Second World War began, it was clear that the pre-war international economic order was unsustainable and that the international community would have to develop new international financial and monetary arrangements for the post-war era. While a full discussion of the causes of this crisis is beyond the scope of this book,[1] it is necessary to highlight three contributing factors that are relevant to the construction of the new international financial order that would emerge after the war.

The first development, as discussed in Chapter 1, was the end of international monetary arrangements based on the gold standard.[2] The consequences of the collapse of the gold standard highlighted the importance of a stable currency regime and the severe human costs that can be caused by a lack of policy coordination and cooperation between states regarding their economic policies. It can lead states to adopt mercantilist monetary and trade policies that are designed to promote their exports and limit their imports. This in turn can have consequences that can be mutually harmful for all countries. They all may experience declines in both imports and exports, leading to lost jobs, income, and social dislocations. They may also experience problems accessing finance as funds flow to those countries with the strongest economies.

The second development was political. The tragic impacts of the First World War had changed the politics in many countries. As a result of the

[1] There is an extensive literature on this topic. See eg RN Gardner, *Sterling-Dollar Diplomacy in Current Perspective: The Origins and the Prospects of our International Economic Order* (McGraw-Hill 1969) for a more detailed discussion of the causes of this crisis.

[2] See L Ahamed, *Lords of Finance: 1929, The Great Depression, and The Bankers Who Broke the World* (Penguin Press 2009) 10–28, 570–609; and B Eichengreen, *Golden Fetters: The Gold Standard and The Great Depression, 1919–1939* (OUP 1992) 70–83.

large number of deaths and the suffering caused by the war, there was a loss of trust in the pre-war elites and a rise in political forces demanding that more attention be paid to social welfare and to improving working conditions. This also manifested itself in growing support for both communism and fascism in many states.[3] These developments made it unlikely that after the Second World War there could be a return to international monetary and financial arrangements that relied on automatic adjustment mechanisms, such as the gold standard, in order to maintain stable international monetary relations. The reason was that such an approach depended on wages and employment being adjustable downwards, so that the fixed currency value could be maintained. This in turn could mean that the adjustment costs would be primarily imposed, without consultation, on workers and the poor. The changing political conditions made it unlikely that it would be possible to impose these costs on them after the Second World War.

The third development was the acceptance both by the United States itself and its allies that the US was the pre-eminent economic power in the world. It could, therefore, be expected to play the leading role after the war. While the rise of the United States to a leading position in the global economy pre-dated the First World War, the country had been reluctant to assume new global economic governance responsibilities after the First World War or as part of the efforts to deal with the economic crises experienced during the inter-war period.[4] The one notable exception was that it played an active role in the discussions on how to deal with German war reparations and in the efforts to oversee German payments of these obligations.[5] This was, no doubt, because of the implications that this issue had for the ability of the other former combatants to pay their war debts to the

[3] See B Eichengreen and T Hatton, 'Interwar Unemployment in International Perspective' (1988) IRLE Working Paper, 40–48 for a more detailed discussion of the inter-war year politics. See further I Kershaw, *Popular Opinion and Political Dissent in the Third Reich* (OUP 1983) 83.

[4] See S Edwards, 'The London Monetary and Economic Conference of 1933 and the End of the Great Depression: A "Change of Regime" Analysis' (2017) NBER Working Paper No 23204 2–5.

[5] See A Ritschl, 'Reparation Transfers, the Borchardt Hypothesis and the Great Depression in Germany, 1929-32: A Guided Tour for Hard-Headed Keynesians' (1998) 2 European Review of Economic History 49–72 for details on both the Young Plan and Dawes Plan. For more of Ritschl's work on the Young Plan and Dawes Plan, see A Ritschl, 'The German Transfer Problem, 1920–1933: A Sovereign Debt Perspective' (2012) 19(6) European Review of Economic History 1–25.

United States and because of the substantial exposure that US banks had to German borrowers during the inter-war years.

In short, therefore, it was clear by the outbreak of the Second World War that the old global economic order could not be restored. The post-war economy would require new monetary and financial governance arrangements if it were to be stable and to function in a way that allowed the participating states and their citizens to prosper. It was also clear that the United States would be the leading power in these new arrangements.

In fact, the United States had learned from its failure to fully engage with global economic governance after the First World War. It was determined to play the leading role in this regard after the Second World War. Consequently, in late 1941, the US Secretary of the Treasury instructed Harry Dexter White, a senior official in the Treasury, to begin planning for the governance of the post-war economy. In response, White drafted plans for an international stabilization fund and an international bank.[6] These plans were not developed from whole cloth. White based his ideas for the stabilization fund on his experiences with the operations of the US Exchange Stabilization Fund, which had been established in 1934[7] and was intended to stabilize the value of the dollar after the United States left the gold standard. He also relied on the 1936 Tripartite Agreement with France and the United Kingdom, later joined by Belgium, the Netherlands, and Switzerland, that sought to stabilize relations between their respective currencies.[8] As indicated in Chapter 1, he may also have been influenced by his own experiences helping South American countries and the experience of the League of Nations assisting countries such as Austria to deal with their macro-economic imbalances.[9] In addition, he based his ideas for the international bank on the proposal for an Inter-American Bank that he had played a role in preparing and that President Franklin Roosevelt had submitted, unsuccessfully, to US Congress in 1940.[10]

[6] See R Mikesell, *The Bretton Woods Debates: A Memoir (Essays in International Finance: No 192)* (Princeton University Press 1994). See also JM Boughton, *Harry White and the American Creed: How a Federal Bureaucrat Created the Modern Global Economy (and Failed to Get the Credit)* (Yale University Press 2021) 1–42.

[7] Gold Reserve Act of 1934; currently 31 USC § 5117; and see MD Bordo and AJ Schwartz, 'From the Exchange Stabilization Fund to the International Monetary Fund' (2001) NBER Working Paper No 8100.

[8] SVO Clarke, 'The Influence of Economists on the Tripartite Agreement of September 1936' (1977) European Economic Review 10(3) 375–389.

[9] See P Clavin, 'Men and Markets' in G Sluga and P Clavin (eds), *Internationalisms: A Twentieth-Century History* (CUP 2016).

[10] ibid. See also Boughton (n 6); and Mikesell (n 6), 5–10.

White's idea was to establish an international stabilization fund that would help countries facing temporary balance of payments problems obtain the financing needed to deal with these problems. These countries would use the financing to stabilize the value of their currency and avoid adopting measures that would be destructive of domestic or international prosperity. He proposed that the United States and other participating countries would contribute stipulated amounts of their own currency to the fund and that the fund could then provide financing to countries in need of particular currencies to address their balance of payments problems. Given that the United States was expected to be the predominant economy after the war and that, as a result, there would be a strong international demand for US dollars, White's plan effectively replaced the pre-war gold standard with an international monetary system that was based on the US dollar. The second institution was an international bank that, either directly through loans or indirectly through providing guarantees, would help fund the reconstruction of Europe.

Around the same time, John Maynard Keynes began to develop his plans for an International Clearing Union. He was stimulated to do this by a proposal from the German Minister of Finance for a German-dominated post-war international financial regime.[11] Keynes envisaged that his Clearing Union would have the authority to create its own currency, Bancor, that states could use to make international payments and to support the value of their domestic currency. In this way the Union would support countries facing current account deficits. It would enable them to avoid adopting measure that would be destructive of either domestic or international prosperity. Given the expected dominance of the United States over the global economy, the Union would be heavily dependent on the US providing the bulk of the resources for it to function effectively.[12]

Thus, by 1942, planning for the post-world war global financial system was under way. There were informal discussions among the allies during 1943. While these discussions were dominated by the White and Keynes proposals and by interactions between the United States and the United Kingdom, other countries were consulted. Some of them, such as France

[11] ibid.

[12] R Skidelsky, *John Maynard Keynes, 1883–1946: Economist, Philosopher, Statesman* (Penguin 2005) 682–690, 700–707. Skidelsky provides a compelling account of the life and influences of a Keynes, giving an invaluable insight into the economic philosophy of Keynes. See also Mikesell (n 6) 14–15 on the US rejection of the ICU; and Zachary D Carter, *The Price of Peace: Money, Democracy, and the Life of John Maynard Keynes* (Random House 2021) 1–27.

and Canada, made their own proposals regarding the structuring of the envisaged post-war institutions. At this time, attention was focused on the future monetary arrangements and the exchange stabilization institution.[13] Relatively little attention was given to the proposal for an international bank. These discussions resulted in enough agreement between the US and the UK that in April 1944 they released a Joint Statement of Experts on the Establishment of the International Monetary Fund (IMF).[14]

The negotiations were shaped by the fact that the United States would be the richest and most powerful actor in the global economy and would be providing the largest portion of the resources for any new institutional arrangements. Consequently, the structure, size, and governance arrangements for the new institution that were described in the Joint Statement were much closer to the United States than the UK plan.

The US invited a small group of countries to meet from 15–30 June 1944 in Atlantic City for preliminary discussions about the joint plan.[15] The idea was to use this meeting to get other countries to buy into the principles for the new institutions agreed by the US and the UK. They would then present their proposal to a larger group of countries at a subsequent conference. In the event, many of the key issues regarding the international bank were resolved with little disagreement at this meeting. In addition, there was enough agreement on the principles governing the monetary fund that the larger meeting could focus on drafting the treaty that implemented the already agreed principles and organizational details.[16]

The larger meeting, officially known as the International Monetary and Financial Conference of the United and Associated Nations and unofficially as the Bretton Woods Conference, took place from 1–22 July 1944 at the Mount Washington Hotel in Bretton Woods, New Hampshire.[17]

There were forty-four participating countries, of which eighteen came from South America, twelve from Europe, five from Asia, four from Africa, three from North America, and two from the Middle East.[18] In addition,

[13] Mikesell (n 6) 2. See also Gardner (n 1).

[14] 'Joint Statement of Experts on the establishment of the International Monetary Fund, April 21 1944' <https://fraser.stlouisfed.org/files/docs/historical/eccles/034_11_0002.pdf> (accessed 18 September 2020).

[15] Mikesell (n 6) 24–30; see also Boughton (n 6); Skidelsky (n 12); and Carter (n 12).

[16] Boughton (n 6); Skidelsky (n 12); and Carter (n 12).

[17] K Schuler and A Rosenberg, *The Bretton Woods Transcripts* (Centre for Financial Stability 2013).

[18] The following is the full list of participating countries: Australia, Belgium, Bolivia, Brazil, Canada, Chile, China, Colombia, Costa Rica, Cuba, Czechoslovakia, Dominican Republic, Ecuador, Egypt, El Salvador, Ethiopia, France, Greece, Guatemala, Haiti, Honduras, Iceland,

there were four international bodies and one European country present as observers. One of the reasons that the conference was held in Bretton Woods was that the Mount Washington resort was one of the few that was both big enough and willing to accept such a diverse group of delegates, which included Jews and people of colour.[19]

It is important to note that there were significant limitations on the conference participants' ability to influence the structure and function of the institutions agreed by the United States and United Kingdom. This was the case even though these institutions were intended to manage the post-war international financial system in the interests of all present and future participants in the system.

The first limitation was that, given the political and economic realities of the time, it was inevitable that the institutions would be designed to serve the interests of the United States.[20] These interests included establishing the monetary and financial basis for international free trade, ending the preferential trading arrangements enjoyed by the colonial powers with their colonies, and situating the dollar as the foundational currency in the international monetary system. In addition, since it would be providing the largest share of funds for the institutions, the United States was also interested in securing a powerful voice in the functioning of the two institutions. This meant that it wished to ensure that, at least on the most critical issues, it had a veto. It was, however, willing to share power on most issues with some other key states, such as its close ally, the United Kingdom. The US was helped in achieving its objectives by the fact that many issues had been resolved between it and the UK and accepted by the participants in the Atlantic City meetings. This constrained the scope for discussion at Bretton Woods.

The second handicap was that large parts of Africa, Asia, and the Middle East were still colonized. As a result, with only a few exceptions, such as

India, Iran, Iraq, Liberia, Luxembourg, Mexico, Netherlands, New Zealand, Nicaragua, Norway, Panama, Paraguay, Peru, Philippines, Poland, South Africa, USSR, UK, USA, Uruguay, Venezuela, Yugoslavia. There were also observers from Denmark, the League of Nations, International Labour Organization (ILO), United Nations Interim Commission on Food and Agriculture, and United Nations Relief and Rehabilitation Administration; see K Schuler and M Bernkopf, 'Who Was at Bretton Woods?' (2014) Center for Financial Stability, available at <http://www.centerforfinancialstability.org/bw/Who_Was_at_Bretton_Woods.pdf> (accessed 20 September 2020).

[19] Mikesell (n 6) 34, 35–42; see Helleiner, *Forgotten Foundations of Bretton Woods: International Development and the Making of the Postwar Order* 18–24; and Schuler and Rosenberg (n 17).

[20] Mikesell (n 6) 58–62.

India and South Africa, the colonized regions in these geographic areas were not able to participate in the Bretton Woods negotiations. This meant that the concerns and interests of the people in these colonies received minimal consideration at Bretton Woods. Moreover, when these colonies ultimately gained their independence, they joined institutions that were already established and fully operational. These states were therefore forced to accept the existing governance arrangements and operating practices and procedures of the institutions. They have never really succeeded in substantially altering these arrangements.

Third, many of the European countries were represented by governments in exile who were unable to communicate freely with their own populations or bureaucracies. They also could not be sure that after the war ended, they would be accepted as the legitimate representatives of their states.

Nevertheless, it would be a mistake to assume that the countries present at the Bretton Woods Conference were mere passive participants in the process.[21] As indicated above, some states, such as Canada, presented their own plans for the arrangements for global economic governance. Others, such as some of the Latin American countries and India, advocated for these arrangements to include a focus on financing of development, in addition to the focus on the financing of reconstruction and stable exchange rates. They also warned about the risk that the new international organizations would pay inadequate attention to the concerns of developing countries. For example, one of the Indian delegates, in unsuccessfully proposing that the draft purposes of the future International Monetary Fund should include paying 'due regard' to the needs of developing countries, stated that he was moved to make this amendment because:

> of the experience which we have had in the past of the working of various international organizations during the last twenty years and more. It has been our sad experience that in the working of these organizations, the approach to every problem has been from the point of view of economically advanced countries, and it is our answer, sir, that in the new organizations that we are setting up, the needs of the less advanced countries must be prominently kept in view.[22]

[21] See generally Schuler and Rosenberg (n 17).

[22] ibid 5.

The conference was divided into three commissions.[23] The first commission, chaired by Harry Dexter White, focused on the institution that would become the International Monetary Fund. The second, chaired by John Maynard Keynes, focused on the institution that would become the International Bank for Reconstruction and Development (IBRD). The third commission, chaired by Eduardo Suárez of Mexico, considered other means of promoting international financial cooperation.

The records of the conference seem to suggest that most of the attention at the conference was paid to the International Monetary Fund. This is not surprising given that most countries, including the US and the UK, were concerned with avoiding the trade and monetary policies that had contributed to causing the depression of the 1930s and with establishing a new basis for the international monetary system. Their view was that among the most important causes of the depression were the protectionist policies followed by many states and the beggar-thy-neighbour approaches they took to the value of their currency after the collapse of the gold standard. Consequently, they were particularly concerned with ensuring that the new financial arrangements would help countries maintain reasonably stable exchange rates and would not impose any unreasonable constraints on the payments for current transactions, such as imports and exports.[24] They also wanted to establish new arrangements that would help them obtain the necessary liquidity to meet these objectives. Given that the US was expected to provide most of these funds, it was particularly interested in limiting the size of the resources that it would have to contribute and in ensuring that it obtained adequate safeguards, both in the governance of the new institutions and in their operating principles, to protect its interests.[25]

It is important to stress that the notion of establishing an international organization to oversee these monetary arrangements was novel. Relatively few of the participating delegations had any real experience with such an organization or with delegating to an entity outside their own jurisdiction

[23] ibid.

[24] The participants in the Bretton Woods Conference contemplated that the trade implications of these balance of payments issues would be addressed in the drafting of the agreement establishing the anticipated International Trade Organization (ITO). Subsequently only a part of the planned ITO, the General Agreement on Tariffs and Trade (GATT), became operational. However, it provides in Article XII that states, subject to some constraints, can impose some temporary trade restrictions to deal with balance of payments problems. See GATT Article XII, available at <https://www.wto.org/english/docs_e/legal_e/gatt47_01_e.htm#articleXII>.

[25] See generally Gardner (n 1). For other histories, see Schuler and Rosenberg (n 17).

oversight over their exchange rate policy. This seemed to imply ceding some of each state's sovereignty to an outside and potentially independent actor.

On the other hand, all the delegations had experience borrowing from banks to fund their development projects. Consequently, while the IBRD was an innovative approach to the funding of development and reconstruction, it was a more familiar concept to the delegates. Thus, it was easier for them to reach agreement on its arrangements.

The alleged efficiency of this conference as compared to international conferences today is often commented on.[26] It is argued that, unlike the many inconclusive international conferences that take place today, the three commissions at Bretton Woods managed to establish two entirely new institutions during a three-week international meeting. However, as the above description intimates, this is not an accurate depiction of the process leading to the creation of the IMF and the IBRD. In fact, Bretton Woods was the culmination of a three-year process, part of which only involved one dominant country, part of which involved negotiations between two countries and those that they chose to consult informally and only the last part of which took place at the multi-state Bretton Woods Conference.

In addition, while Bretton Woods ended with enough agreement for the texts of the agreements establishing these two institutions to be submitted for ratification by the signatory states, there were still important issues that were left unresolved. These included the roles of the executive directors, the nature of the conditions—if any—that should be attached to IMF financing, and the location of the headquarters of the two institutions.[27]

A brief description of what was created at the Bretton Woods Conference

The Bretton Woods Conference ended with the participants signing two new treaties, one of which established the IMF,[28] and the other the IBRD.[29]

[26] See eg GM Meier, 'The Bretton Woods Agreement - Twenty-Five Years After' (1971) 23(1) Stanford Law Review 235–275.

[27] See Mikesell (n 6) 52–55, 60–62.

[28] For the treaty for establishing the IMF, see Articles of Agreement of the International Monetary Fund (22 July 1944) entered into force 27 December 1944 <https://www.imf.org/external/pubs/ft/aa/pdf/aa.pdf> (accessed 14 March 2023).

[29] HJ Bittermann, 'Negotiation of the Articles of Agreement of the International Bank for Reconstruction and Developments' (1971) 5(1) The International Lawyer 59–88. For the Treaty of establishing the IBRD, see International Bank for Reconstruction and Development Articles

The terms of these agreements, their international legal significance, and how they have been applied in the operations of the two institutions over time, will be discussed in detail in Chapters 5 and 6.

The purpose of this section is merely to give readers a brief overview of what the delegates at Bretton Woods created.

The IMF

The first institution that the delegates created was the IMF.[30] It was established as a fund to which each member state would contribute resources and from which each member state was entitled to temporarily withdraw resources to deal with its balance of payments problems, provided it was complying with the obligations specified in the IMF's Articles of Agreement. and the amount that it could withdraw from the fund [31] The size of each state's quota, in fact, was determined politically and agreed at Bretton Woods, but was formally based on a formula that purported to determine each country's quota based on the size of the country's economy and its role within the global economy.[32] The member state contributed a portion of its quota in gold and the rest in its own currency.

The quota played, and still plays, a central role in the functioning of the IMF.[33] It determines the size of each member state's contribution to the IMF, the amount of financing it can obtain from the IMF and the state's share of the total vote in the IMF. Since each state has a different quota, it follows that they would have different size votes in the IMF. The bigger and richer states have more votes than the smaller and poorer states. Since the Articles provided for majority voting, the IMF was established as an organization in which states could be obliged to accept that the organization could do certain things, such as adopt operational policies and procedures, with which

of Agreement (22 July 1944) entered into force 27 December 1944, available at (accessed 15 May 2023).

[30] See Mikesell (n 6) 24.

[31] ibid 25–27.

[32] ibid.

[33] P Ramlogan and B Fritz-Krockow, 'IMF Fund Handbook: Its Functions, policies and Operations' (2007) *IMF Handbook* <https://www.elibrary.imf.org/view/IMF069/03766-9781589066250/03766-9781589066250/C1.xml?language=en&redirect=true#relatedDocsWidget> (accessed 20 September 2020). See also IMF Factsheet, 'Quotas' <https://www.imf.org/en/About/Factsheets/Sheets/2016/07/14/12/21/IMF-Quotas> (accessed 20 September 2020).

they disagree. In other words the IMF, in effect, required its member states to surrender some of their sovereign decision-making prerogatives to the organization when they joined it.

The establishment of the IMF produced an international monetary organization with the purpose of supporting a stable means of payments for current transactions.[34] It was thus intended to replace the gold standard, according to which the participating countries set the value of their currency in terms of gold and were then expected to conduct their economic policies in such a way that they maintained this value for their currency, with only limited scope for fluctuations in this value.

The new Bretton Woods system required countries to set the par value of their currency in terms of the US dollar, which in turn was fixed in terms of a set amount of gold.[35] The values of each of the currencies was allowed to fluctuate within a limited band around the par value for the currency.[36] If a particular country's economy changed so much that restoring equilibrium required changing the value of the currency by more than the permissible degree of fluctuation around its par value, the state was required to consult with and obtain the prior approval of the IMF.

In order to encourage countries to adopt and maintain a stated par value for their currency, the IMF agreement offered countries two carrots. The first was that member states, upon joining the IMF, could delay adopting a par value until their economies were stable enough that they could realistically determine their currencies' par value and maintain that value.[37] Thus, they were allowed to choose a transition period of indefinite duration before accepting the obligations of the par value system. Second, the IMF agreement provided that the IMF would offer financial support to countries that were experiencing balance of payment problems and therefore difficulty supporting the par value of their currency.[38] The amount of the support that the IMF would offer would be based on the member state's

34 Gardner (n 1).

35 See International Monetary Fund Articles of Agreements 1944, Art I (iii). See also MD Bordo and H James, 'The International Monetary Fund: Its Present Role in Historical Perspective' (National Bureau of Economic Research 2000) 7724 NBER Working Paper No 7724. On the limited band around the par value for each G10 country currency, see MD Bordo, 'The Bretton Woods International Monetary System: A Historical Overview' in (eds) MD Bordo and B Eichengreen, A Retrospective on the Bretton Woods System: Lessons for International Monetary Reform (Chicago University Press 1993) 23–25.

36 Currencies could fluctuate within a range of 1 per cent above and 1 per cent below the par value.

37 IMF Articles, Art XIV.

38 ibid Art I (v).

quota in the IMF. An important issue left unresolved at Bretton Woods was whether or not there would be conditions attached to this funding.[39] However, the IMF decided, early in its operations, that it would need to attach conditions designed to increase confidence that the state would be able to repay the IMF in a timely manner.

There are two other important points about the IMF. First, member states agreed that they would allow the IMF to conduct regular surveillance over their monetary policies in order to ensure that the country was following policies consistent with maintaining its currency's par value.[40] The IMF would offer the country advice during these surveillance missions which the country was free to use as it saw fit.

Second, the monetary commitments that each member state made by signing and ratifying the IMF Articles was focused on its current transactions.[41] Thus it was obliged to allow free payments for all current transactions and to adopt policies designed to support this obligation. This meant that payments should be unrestricted for all international trade transactions and other payments falling due within the current period, usually determined to be a year.[42] However, each state retained the right to impose whatever restrictions it deemed appropriate on capital transactions.[43] This refers primarily to productive investments with a duration longer than the current period. It should be noted that the Articles do not contain a formal definition of either current or capital transactions.

The IBRD

The IBRD was established to be a bank that would help finance the reconstruction of Europe after the Second World War and the development of its poorer member states.[44] Each participating state would buy shares in the

[39] Keynes expressed his misgivings about a new IMF attaching conditions to its financing, arguing that it was akin to exercising 'grandmotherly' influence and control; see S Dell, 'On Being Grandmotherly: The Evolution of IMF Conditionality', 1 (*Essays in International Finance* No 144, Princeton University 1981).

[40] IMF Articles, Art IV.

[41] ibid, Art VIII(ii).

[42] This arrangement for current transactions was consistent with the expected free-trade regime that was expected to be part of the International Trade Organization and eventually became an essential characteristic of the GATT.

[43] IMF Articles, Art VI.

[44] International Bank for Reconstruction and Development, Articles of Agreement, Art I(i), available at <https://www.worldbank.org/en/about/articles-of-agreement/ibrd-articles-of-agreement> (accessed on 14 March 2023).

bank. The number of shares would be determined by a formula that was analogous to that used to determine IMF quotas. Each share would have an equal vote in the affairs of the IBRD but, since member states would have different numbers of shares, they would have different sized votes in the affairs of the IBRD.[45]

The IBRD was authorized to make loans and provide guarantees on financing for projects that contributed to raising the productivity of labour and the standard of living of the people of those member states in which it operated.[46] Thus, unlike the IMF, which provided general financing to the budget of its member states, the IBRD was restricted, except in special circumstances, to funding particular projects.[47] This meant it was expected to fund the procurement of the goods and services needed to construct specific projects, such as infrastructure projects. Furthermore, the IBRD Articles indicated that the IBRD should only provide loans or guarantees in situations in which the member state was unlikely to obtain financing from any other sources.[48] Thus, the IBRD would act as a type of lender of last resort for these projects and was not expected to compete with other sources of finance.

Post-Bretton Woods Conference developments

The two instruments agreed at Bretton Woods required ratification by twenty-nine of the participating states to enter into force. It was agreed that this should take place by 27 December 1945.[49] The two most important countries in this regard were the United States and the United Kingdom. In both cases, ratification came close to the deadline and only after extensive legislative debate.

In the case of the United States, Congress held extensive hearings at which a range of witnesses, including Harry Dexter White and representatives of the banking community, testified.[50] It is important to note that the

45 IBRD Articles, Art V(3).
46 , Art III.
47 ibid, Art III(1).
48 ibid.
49 See Schuler and Rosenberg (n 17).
50 Bretton Woods Agreements Act Hearings Before the Committee on Banking and Currency United States Senate Seventy-Ninth Congress First Session 1945 on HR 3314, 57, 140–142, <https://fraser.stlouisfed.org/title/bretton-woods-agreements-act-767>.

most significant opposition to the agreements came from the US financial community and their supporters in the Congress. Their opposition was focused primarily on the IMF. They had two primary concerns about the IMF. First, they were concerned that because of the US's economic strength, it would have to bear the primary burden of financing the new institution. In addition, if there was a shortage of dollars, there was a risk that other countries would respond to their increasing need for US dollars by taking actions to restrict imports and payments for other current transactions in order to limit dollar outflows from their home states.[51] Second, they were concerned that, given the fact that the new monetary system would not have an independent anchor such as was the case with the gold standard, countries would be able to respond to balance of payments problems by devaluing their currencies against the dollar, which could harm US trade.[52]

The US financial institutions were less opposed to the IBRD and, in fact, some witnesses expressed support for ratification of the IBRD agreement.[53] There were three reasons for this position. The first was that the IBRD was expected to act primarily as a guarantor of loans rather than as a direct lender itself. Thus, it was a potential supporter of the lending transactions entered into by financial institutions, particularly in areas which they viewed as risky. Second, the IBRD was expected to primarily fund projects that would not otherwise be funded. This seemed to suggest that it would not be competing with the financial institutions for business. Finally, the financial community was used to working with a government-sponsored bank, the US Export–Import Bank, which it viewed as a useful support to their own activities. The fact that the IBRD's lending transactions would be modelled on those of the US Export–Import Bank contributed to their confidence in the institution.[54]

There was also debate about the agreements in the UK, including in the House of Lords of which Keynes was a member.[55] In this case, the opponents, understanding that the UK was likely to be a recipient of funds from

[51] ibid 105, 140–142.

[52] ibid 103–104 per Mr Brown, Chair of Chicago Bank.

[53] ibid 57. Mr White stated that the Bretton Woods proposals were necessary to promote stable and orderly exchange arrangements under which international trade and investment would flourish and to encourage international investment for productive purposes so that countries could again produce, trade, and prosper.

[54] See D Kapur and A Raychaudhuri, 'Rethinking the Financial Design of the World Bank' (2004) CGD Working Paper No 352. Center for Global Development <http://www.cgdev.org/publication/rethinking-financial-design-world-bank-workingpaper-352> (accessed 21 September 2020).

[55] See Hansard on the International Monetary Fund 1944, HL vol 131 cc834–83, p 6.

the institutions rather than a provider of funds, were concerned about the impact of the operation of these institutions on UK sovereignty. They were concerned that the institutions might attached conditions to their funding that could limit the government's policy space. In addition, some were concerned that the end of the gold standard would undermine the credibility of the British pound and its role as a reserve currency, thereby complicating the future management of the British economy. A third source of opposition was the emphasis on free trade. Many of the opponents were concerned that this would undermine the system of Imperial Preference that protected the privileged trading position of the UK in its colonies. It would also create new problems for the UK in regard to the sterling balances that some colonies had built up during the war and which they now wished to use to support their own development.[56] In particular, some of these colonies wanted to have the option of using their funds to buy goods and services from the United States. In the end, the opposition in the House of Lords was overcome with the help of a large loan from the US to the UK.[57]

Following the agreements entering into force, the IMF and the IBRD held their inaugural meetings in Savannah, Georgia from 8 to 18 March 1946.[58] At this meeting, the issues left unresolved at Bretton Woods were decided. It is important to note that the Articles of the IMF and the IBRD stipulate that the headquarters should be in the member state with the largest vote in the organization. This meant that the headquarters had to be in the United States and the only issue to be decided in Savannah was the specific location. Many delegates, including Keynes, were anticipating that the headquarters would be in New York, which was the US's leading financial centreowever, the US Treasury, which was suspicious of the financial institutions, wanted to locate the two institutions away from New York and so favoured Washington.[59] Given the political realities of the time, the US Treasury, unsurprisingly, got its wish. In addition, it was agreed that executive directors would be full-time officials of the institutions and would be based at the headquarters of the institutions.

56 Gardner (n 1).
57 ibid.
58 Mikesell (n 6) 52.
59 ibid.

Following the Savannah meeting, the member states selected the heads and boards of directors for both institutions and in 1947 they opened for business.[60]

Assessment

As indicated above, there were some significant shortcomings associated with the Bretton Woods Conference. While these deficiencies would create problems that would haunt the two institutions throughout their history, the achievements at Bretton Woods were substantial. The institutions they created have exerted a strong influence in shaping the world we live in today. There were three important international legal achievements.

First, the agreements reached at Bretton Woods laid the foundation for a new monetary order that would be based on an agreed set of rules.[61] As indicated above, it is important to note that the rules were only applicable to current transactions. Pursuant to these rules, each country would determine the value of its particular currency in terms of the US dollar, whose value was fixed at $35 per ounce of gold. The rules, however, allowed member states to decide to change the par value of their currency on their own initiative, provided the change was less than the stipulated limits around their par values. Any change larger than the stipulated limits required the consent of the IMF. The new system therefore afforded most countries more discretion than the gold standard but bound them to follow the agreed rules. Failure to do so could amount to a breach of an international agreement. This was an unprecedented development in international monetary law.

Second, the IMF and the IBRD were the first international financial institutions in history authorized to sit in judgement of specific economic policies or activities of their member states and to impose consequences if they determined that the activities did not comply with their treaty-based obligations.[62] This meant, for example, that the IMF was authorized in certain

[60] Over seventy years later, the IMF and IBRD are still in operation. Information on both institutions is available on their respective websites: <https://www.imf.org/external/index.htm> and <https://www.worldbank.org/> ccessed 22 September 2020).

[61] See M Gautian, 'Rules or Discretion in Monetary Policy: National and International Perspectives' in C Cottarelli and T Baliño (eds), *IMF Frameworks for Monetary Stability Policy Issues and Country Experiences* (IMF 1994) 19–42.

[62] Gardner (n 1). These institutions were the first to have this generalized authority. It should be noted, however, that there were some isolated precedents of an international organization imposing policy conditions on countries in exchange for certain economic benefits.

circumstances to deny their member states permission to change the value of their currencies by more than a specified amount. Thus, the agreements reached at Bretton Woods implied that countries would cede a part of their monetary sovereignty to the new institutions. Moreover, the IMF could exercise surveillance over their monetary policy and, in principle advise them that they were failing to meet their commitments to the IMF. It could also decide to deny the requests of their member states for financial support.

Similarly, the IBRD was the first international financial organization authorized to lend money and guarantee loans to sovereign borrowers. It would therefore be in a position to determine if its sovereign borrowers had complied with the terms of their agreements and thus should be granted access to the financing for which they had contracted. The IBRD would be able to deny access to the agreed funds to non-compliant member states. This new approach to financing reconstruction and development raised important concerns about what sorts of conditions the IBRD could attach to its financial transactions. As we will see in later chapters, some of these issues were addressed in the institution's Articles of Agreement. Both the application and interpretation of these Articles and the member states' response to them evolved over time and through practice.

Third, both institutions were explicitly built on the basis of weighted voting.[63] This meant that sovereign states would not have equal voices in the two institutions. In addition, they could be forced to accept and comply with decisions in regard to monetary and financial matters with which they did not agree.

It was perhaps to be expected that two such novel institutions, created during war time but expected to operate during peacetime, would not function as expected. This was certainly the case with both the IBRD and the IMF.

First, in both cases, not all the participants in the Bretton Woods Conference ultimately joined the institutions. Most importantly, the Soviet Union and its allies decided either not to join or withdrew within a short period.[64] The result was that the two institutions were caught up in the

This happened, for example, in the case of the Dawes and Young Plans dealing with German reparations after the First World War and League of Nations support for countries like Austria, Greece, and China during the inter-war years. See J Martin, The Meddlers: Sovereignty, Empire and the Birth of Global Economic Governance (Harvard University Press 2022).

[63] See WN Gianaris, 'Weighted Voting in the International Monetary Fund and the World Bank' (1990) 14(4) Fordham International Law Journal 910.

[64] Gardner (n 1).

dynamics of the Cold War. This ultimately influenced how they did business and with whom. One important manifestation of this was that soon after their creation, the United States established the Marshall Plan to aid the reconstruction of Western Europe.[65] This meant that the recipient countries, which were expected to be the primary users of the services and resources of both the IMF and the IBRD, obtained their necessary foreign exchange through the Marshall Plan and not from these institutions. The result was that a number of European countries were in less need of IMF support than originally anticipated and so could afford to delay assuming all the obligations of IMF membership until the late 1950s. In addition, it meant that these states had relatively limited need for IBRD financing, although states such as France and the Netherlands did borrow significant amounts from the IBRD.[66] It also meant that within a few years, the IBRD was concentrating on the development part of its mandate and was providing funding to developing countries rather than to European states seeking to fund their post-war reconstruction.[67] These developments therefore meant that many of the original states did not operate subject to the discipline of the IMF until a number of years after its establishment.

Second, the participants at Bretton Woods did not anticipate the wave of decolonization that took place from the mid-1950s onwards. As the former colonies won their independence, they joined the institutions and began to make use of their services. The resultant increase in the number of member states and the differences in their needs from the original member states, have over time had important implications for the governance and the operations of the two institutions. These changes and their implications will be explored in Chapters 5 and 6.

Third, the par value system ultimately proved to be unsustainable. This issue will be explored in further detail in hapter 6. However, for current purposes it is sufficient to note that when the United States broke the link between the US dollar and gold in August 1971, it effectively ended the par value system, which in turn meant the end of the IMF's original function in the Bretton Woods system. This left the IMF without a clearly defined role.

[65] C Tarnoff, 'The Marshall Plan: Design, Accomplishments, and Significance' (2018) *Congressional Research Service Report* 1–10. See also B Steil, *The Marshall Plan: Dawn of the Cold War* (Simon & Schuster 2018) 1–100.

[66] See E Toussaint, 'World Bank and IMF support to dictatorships: Series: 1944-2020, 76 years of interference from the World Bank and the IMF (Part 10)' (2020) CATDM Paper, available at http://www.cadtm.org/World-Bank-and-IMF-support-to-dictatorships (accessed on 18 July 2023).

[67] Kapur and Raychaudhuri (n 54).

It therefore began to assume new functions after 1971.[68] These new functions and their international legal implications are discussed in hapter 6.

Fourth, the creation of the IMF was expected to lead to the demise of the Bank for International Settlements.[69] The BIS had been created primarily to deal with German First World War reparation payments but had rapidly come to play a role as an actor in international financial affairs particularly in regard to central banks. It had also incurred the anger of many allied countries because it had continued to provide financial services to the German central bank during the Second World War. The BIS was therefore potentially a rival to the IMF, and it was agreed at Bretton Woods that it should be closed. this happened, it would have been an unusual instance of an international organization being closed. However, remained open and today it is still an important actor in international financial and monetary affairs. It operates as a bank for central banks, as a convener of regular meetings of central banks, and as a host to important financial regulatory bodies. It is also an important source of information banking and financial systems.[70]

[68] See D Bradlow, 'Stuffing New Wine into Old Bottles: The Troubling Case of the IMF' (2001) 3 Journal of International Banking Regulation 9–36.

[69] Gardner (n 1).

[70] See the Bank of International Settlement website at <https://www.bis.org/> (accessed 25 September 2020).

3

The Articles of Agreement of the International Financial Institutions

This chapter provides an overview of the treaties that created the International Monetary Fund (IMF)[1] and the International Bank for Reconstruction and Development (IBRD).[2] The organizations' Articles of Agreement (Articles) set out the mandates, functions, and governance arrangements for each organization and the rights and responsibilities of their member states. They are also an expression of the vision of the Bretton Woods Conference delegates for the governance of the post-Second World War international monetary and financial system and the role that the IMF and the IBRD should play in it. Understanding the way in which this vision is articulated in the treaties will be helpful in assessing how the two organizations have interpreted and applied the Articles in their operations, how this has evolved over time, and how it is contributing to the challenges that they are currently facing. These latter topics will be discussed in Chapters 5 and 6.

This chapter is divided into four sections. The first section discusses some general international legal issues that are relevant to these two treaties. The next section focuses on the IMF's Articles. The third section describes the IBRD's founding treaty. The sections on IMF and IBRD are further divided into the following six subsections: the purpose of the institution, membership issues, governance, financial resources, functions, and general issues. The final section is a conclusion.

[1] 'International Monetary Fund Articles of Agreement 1944' <https://www.imf.org/external/pubs/ft/aa/index.htm> (accessed 26 January 2021).

[2] 'The International Bank for Reconstruction and Development (IBRD) Articles of Agreement 1944' <https://www.worldbank.org/en/about/articles-of-agreement/ibrd-articles-of-agreement> (accessed 26 January 2021).

General international law issues

The Articles of Agreement that create the IMF and the IBRD were signed by the forty-four states that participated in the Bretton Woods conference. They entered into force at the end of 1945, by which time twenty-nine states had ratified the Articles.[3] By the time the institutions began operations in 1947, an additional ten signatory states had ratified the Articles. Since that time, the membership of both institutions has grown substantially so that today the IMF has 190 member states[4] and the IBRD, has189 member states..[5]

These two treaties entered into force before the Vienna Convention on the Law of Treaties[6] was drafted. However, to the extent that the Vienna Convention codifies the customary international law of treaties, it expresses the international legal standards applicable to the interpretation of the Articles of Agreement of the IMF and the IBRD.[7] The two most pertinent provisions of the Vienna Convention relating to the interpretation of treaties, Articles 31 and 32, are usually viewed as incorporating the applicable customary international law prior to the Vienna Convention entering into force.[8] Consequently, they should be viewed as being applicable to the IMF and IBRD Articles.

Pursuant to Article 31, a treaty should be interpreted in 'good faith in accordance with the ordinary meaning to be given to the terms of the treaty in their context and in the light of its object and purpose'.[9] The Article goes on to explain that other factors that may be relevant to interpreting a treaty are subsequent agreements between the parties regarding the particular treaty,

[3] See International Monetary Fund Articles of Agreement (n 1) 125 <https://www.imf.org/external/pubs/ft/aa/index.htm>). See also E Umeonyirioha, 'The Bretton Woods International Financial Institutions: Perspective of the Underdeveloped States' (2020) 6 World Journal of Social Sciences and Humanities 15–27.

[4] See <https://www.imf.org/en/About#:~:text=The%20IMF%20works%20to%20achieve,of%20its%20190%20member%20countries> (accessed 9 November 2022).

[5] See <https://www.worldbank.org/en/who-we-are/ibrd> (accessed 9 November 2022).

[6] Vienna Convention on the Law of Treaties, May 23, 1969 1155 UNTS 331; 8 ILM 679 (1969) <https://legal.un.org/ilc/texts/instruments/english/conventions/1_1_1969.pdf> (accessed 26 January 2021).

[7] EW Vierdag, 'The Law Governing Treaty Relations between Parties to the Vienna Convention on the Law of Treaties and States Not Party to the Convention' (1982) 76(4) The American Journal of International Law 779–801; and PV McDade, 'The Effect of Article 4 of the Vienna Convention on the Law of Treaties 1969' (1986) 35(3) The International and Comparative Law Quarterly 499–511.

[8] ibid. See also A Aust, 'Vienna Convention on the Law of Treaties (1969)' in *Max Planck Encyclopedia of Public International Law* (2006) 1–8.

[9] Vienna Convention on the Law of Treaties, Art 31.

subsequent practice by the parties relating to the application of the treaty, and any rules of international law that may be relevant to the relationship between the parties to the treaty. Article 32 states that if the application of Article 31 leads to ambiguity in the interpretation of the treaty or to outcomes that are 'manifestly absurd or unreasonable', the parties can resort to supplementary means of interpretation including the preparatory work for the treaty and the circumstances in which it was concluded.[10]

These provisions mean that in order to understand the IMF and IBRD Articles, we need to start with the ordinary meaning of the text of the Articles. In this regard it should be noted that the Articles of Agreement are models of creative and effective legal drafting. In both cases, the Articles provide clear guidance on how the organizations are to be structured and governed. This allowed the original member states to be confident that they understood what role they would play in its governance and the scope of their rights and responsibilities as members of the organizations. At the same, the Articles provided the management and executive directors of these organizations with the operational flexibility they would need to adapt and adjust their mandates as conditions evolved over time. The treaty drafters provided this flexibility by leaving key terms in the statement of the purposes of the organizations and in the provisions dealing with constraints on their operations undefined. For example, even though a primary purpose of the IBRD is to promote 'development',[11] its Articles do not define the term 'development'. Another stated IBRD purpose that the Articles leave undefined is 'encouraging' investments in member states and thereby 'assisting' member states 'in raising productivity, the standard of living and conditions of labor'.[12] Similarly, an important purpose for the IMF is to give members confidence by making the resources of the IMF 'temporarily available' to them 'under adequate safeguards'[13] so that they can correct their balance of payments problems without resorting to measures that are 'destructive of national or international prosperity'.[14] The Articles do not define any of these terms.

The drafters of these Articles further enhanced the adaptive capacity of these organizations by stipulating that the authority to interpret the Articles resides in the first place with their Boards of Executive Directors (EDs).[15]

[10] Vienna Convention on the Law of Treaties, Art 32.
[11] IBRD Articles, Art 1(i).
[12] IBRD Articles, Art 1.
[13] IMF Articles, Art 1(v).
[14] IMF Articles, Art 1(vi).
[15] IMF Articles, Art XXIX(a). See also IBRD Articles, Art IX(a).

A dissatisfied member state can appeal the Board of Executive Directors' decision to the organization's Board of Governors, its highest decision-making body. The decision of the latter is final. It is important to note that this arrangement has two significant consequences. First, it protects the independence of the organizations. This follows from the fact that their Articles do not provide for any outside party, such as the International Court of Justice, to play a decisive role in the interpretation of the Articles. Second, since the management of the entities work closely with their boards, it means that the management are able to exercise considerable influence over how their founding documents are interpreted and implemented.

In this regard it should also be noted that the general counsels of both institutions have opined, and their EDs and Board of Governors have, at least implicitly, agreed that their Articles should be interpreted teleologically.[16] This means that they should be interpreted in a way that promotes the organizations' stipulated purposes. Given the ambiguity with which these purposes have been drafted, this approach gives their management considerable latitude in deciding how to interpret the Articles. It also suggests that the founders expected the management to take a pragmatic approach to the functioning of the two institutions.

A second general point to note about these two entities is that, even though they were created before the United Nations (UN), they are formally designated as specialized agencies of the UN.[17] Like all specialized agencies, their relationship with the UN is governed by a specific relationship agreement.[18] In most respects, their relationship agreements are similar to those of other UN specialized agencies. The institutions and the UN agree to share information and cooperate with each other and with the various other organs of the UN system. However, unlike most specialized

[16] IF Shihata, 'The Creative Role of the Lawyer – Example: The Office of the World Bank's General Counsel' (1999) 48 Catholic University Law Review 1048–1049 available at <https://scholarship.law.edu/lawreview/vol48/iss4/4> (accessed 27 January 2021). See J Gold, 'The Relationship between the International Monetary Fund and the World Bank' (1981) 15 Creighton Law Review 499, 522.

[17] UN Charter 24 October 1945, 1 UNTS XVI available at <https://www.un.org/en/about-us/un-charter> (accessed on 14 March 2023).

[18] UN Charter, Arts 57 and 63. Agreement Between the United Nations and the International Monetary Fund, 17 September 1947, entered into force 15 November 1947 in 'IMF, Selected Documents Relating to the Fund, the United Nations, and other International Organizations' in IMF, *Selected Decisions and Selected Documents of the International Monetary Fund* (IMF 1998) 695–701 <https://www.elibrary.imf.org/view/book/9781451971149/sc03.xml> (accessed 29 June 2022) The text of the agreement between the UN and the IBRD is available at: https://thedocs.worldbank.org/en/doc/877831508427688702-0290022017/render/AgreeementbetweentheUnitedNationsandIBRD1947.pdf (accessed on 20 June 2023)

agencies, the agreements with the IMF and IBRD stipulate, in Article 1(2) of each relationship agreement, that the relevant institution '[b]y reason of the nature of its international responsibilities and the terms of its Articles of Agreement is, and is required to function as, an independent international organization'. The parties also agree, in Article IV, to consult with each other and exchange views on matters of mutual interest but stipulate that they will not make any formal recommendations to the other organization without prior consultations. Moreover, they confirm, in Article 1(3), that 'nothing in this agreement shall be construed to require either of them to furnish any information the furnishing of which would, in its judgment, constitute a violation of the confidence of any of its members or anyone from whom it shall have received such information, or which would otherwise interfere with the orderly conduct of its operations'. In other words, both the IMF and the IBRD, while retaining the formal status of a UN specialized agency, are given substantive independence.

International Monetary Fund

Purposes

According to Article I of its Articles of Agreement, the purposes of the IMF include:[19]

[19] IMF Articles, Art I. The full text of Art I is as follows:

'i) To promote international monetary cooperation through a permanent institution which provides the machinery for consultation and collaboration on international monetary problems.
(ii) To facilitate the expansion and balanced growth of international trade, and to contribute thereby to the promotion and maintenance of high levels of employment and real income and to the development of the productive resources of all members as primary objectives of economic policy.
(iii) To promote exchange stability, to maintain orderly exchange arrangements among members, and to avoid competitive exchange depreciation.
(iv) To assist in the establishment of a multilateral system of payments in respect of current transactions between members and in the elimination of foreign exchange restrictions which hamper the growth of world trade.
(v) To give confidence to members by making the general resources of the Fund temporarily available to them under adequate safeguards, thus providing them with opportunity to correct maladjustments in their balance of payments without resorting to measures destructive of national or international prosperity.
(vi) In accordance with the above, to shorten the duration and lessen the degree of disequilibrium in the international balances of payments of members.'

- to promote international monetary cooperation through consultation and collaboration;
- to promote orderly and stable exchange arrangements among members;
- to assist in the establishment of a multilateral system of payments for international trade;
- to give members confidence by making the resources of the IMF 'temporarily available' to them 'under adequate safeguards' for the purpose of correcting their balance-of-payments problems 'without resorting to measures destructive of national or international prosperity'; and
- 'in accordance with' these other purposes, to 'shorten the duration and lessen the degree of disequilibrium in the balance-of-payments of members'.

The expectation of the drafters of these Articles was that the IMF would achieve these purposes through overseeing and supporting the efforts of its member states to implement and maintain a system of stable par values for their respective currencies. This meant that each member state would commit to maintain a specified value for its currencies, expressed in terms of the US dollar, which in turn would be linked in a fixed relationship to gold.[20] In return for maintaining the expressed par value for its currencies, each member state would benefit from the predictability of a system of relatively fixed exchange rates. In addition, they would gain access to IMF financial support in the event that they were experiencing problems in maintaining the par value of their currency.

This arrangement also offered member states two other sources of support to facilitate their compliance with the par value system. First, they were allowed a certain flexibility in maintaining their currency's par value. They could let the value of their currency fluctuate within certain defined limits around its par value.[21] This meant that each member state had some policy space that it could utilize before it would be required to adopt policies designed to correct the source of its currency's deviation from its par

[20] See R Mikesell, *The Bretton Woods Debates: A Memoir (Essays in International Finance: No 192)* (PUDE 1994).

[21] Initially, the currencies could fluctuate by up to 1 per cent around their par values before member states were required to take action. See HG Johnson, 'The Case for Flexible Exchange Rates, 1969' (1969) 24 Federal Reserve Bank of St. Louis Review 12–24. See also J Gold, 'The Legal Structure of the Par Value System' (1973) 5 Law and Policy in International Business 155–167 and DD Driscoll, *What is the International Monetary Fund?* (1997) 10–11 <https://www.elibrary.imf.org/downloadpdf/book/9781557754080/9781557754080.pdf>.

value. In addition, in the case of a 'fundamental disequilibrium' a member state could, with IMF permission, change the par value of its currency. The Articles do not define 'fundamental disequilibrium' but it was generally understood to mean that the currency was deviating by more than 10 per cent from its par value.[22]

Second, while they would be expected to allow unrestricted payments for current transactions,[23] states could impose restrictions on capital transactions.[24] This would help it maintain some control over its international financial relations and its monetary policy. The Articles also provided that, with IMF permission, member states facing particularly difficult situations could place some restrictions on current payments. In this case, they could count on other states to respect and help enforce these restrictions on 'exchange contracts'.[25]

It is important to note that the par value system ended in 1971 when the United States broke the link between the US dollar and gold.[26] This ultimately led to the second amendment to the IMF Articles that replaced the par value system with a system of fiat money. This meant that each member state is free to decide for itself how the value of its currency should be determined. The only restriction is that states cannot set the values of their currencies in terms of gold. This development and its implications are discussed in Chapter 6.

Membership

The IMF was established as an international monetary institution to which all sovereign states could belong.[27] This means, in practice, that any state that is a member of the UN is eligible to join the IMF. However, before it can join, a state's application for membership in the IMF must be submitted to the IMF's Board of Directors. After reviewing the application, the Board

22 Gold (n 21), 161–162.

23 IMF Articles, Art VI.II (2)(a). See also, IMF, The International Monetary Fund and Current Account Convertibility (2004) 1, 4–33 <https://www.imf.org/external/np/leg/sem/2004/cdmfl/eng/elizal.pdf> (accessed 25 June 2022).

24 IMF Articles, Art VI.

25 IMF Articles, Art VIII (8)(2)(b).

26 See, eg, MD Bordo, 'The Bretton Woods International Monetary System: A Historical Overview' in MD Bordo and B Eichengreen (eds), *A Retrospective on the Bretton Woods System: Lessons for International Monetary Reform* (University of Chicago Press 1993) 3.

27 IMF Articles, Art II.

makes a recommendation to the Board of Governors on whether to admit the applicant and on what terms.[28] The Board of Governor's decision is final.

Upon joining the IMF, each member state is assigned a quota.[29] The calculation of the original member states' quotas was one of the more contentious issues at Bretton Woods. They were calculated by an official at the US Treasury who used a formula designed to produce the desired allocation of quotas among the states that were expected to join the IMF.[30] The formula, which has been adjusted over time, seeks to take account of the size of the country's economy and its contribution to the global economy.[31]

A member state's quota is relevant to three aspects of membership in the IMF. First, it determines the size of a member state's vote in the IMF.[32] This means that the IMF is based on a system of weighted voting so that different states have different-sized votes. According to this system, each member state's vote consists of two portions. The first portion, known as the basic vote, is based on the principle that all member states are co-equal sovereign states. Originally, each member state was assigned 250 votes as their 'basic vote' and the total basic votes accounted for about 11 per cent of the total votes in the IMF. Over time, as the quotas grew, these basic votes became a smaller share of the total votes. Eventually, in 2010, the member states agreed to increase the share of basic votes in the total votes. They agreed that the total basic vote would always be equal to 5.502 per cent of the total votes. Consequently, today each member state receives an equal share of the 5.502 per cent of the total IMF vote that is allocated to the basic vote.[33]

The second portion is determined by the size of each Member state's quota. Each member state receives one vote for each 100,000 Special Drawing Rights (SDRs) of its quota.[34] The net effect of this voting system is that the bigger and richer member states have a larger voice in the IMF than the smaller and poorer member states.

[28] Section 21 IMF By-laws: Rules and Regulations of the International Monetary Fund 1944 <https://www.imf.org/external/pubs/ft/bl/pdf/by-laws.pdf> (accessed 29 January 2021).

[29] See International Monetary Fund quotas <https:\\www.imf.org/external/np/exr/facts/quotas.htm> (accessed 28 January 2021).

[30] Mikesell (n 20).

[31] IMF Factsheet, 'Quotas' 24 October 2022 https://www.imf.org/en/About/Factsheets/Sheets/2022/IMF-Quotas> (accessed 20 June 2023).

[32] See IMF Articles, Art XII, Section 5(a).

[33] IMF Articles. This amendment to the Articles was adopted in 2010 to increase the share of the basic votes in the total vote in order to increase the vote of the smallest and poorest member states in the IMF.

[34] IMF Articles, Art III.

Quotas are also relevant to the IMF's finances.[35] Each member state is expected to make a contribution, known as a subscription, to the resources of the IMF. The size of the subscription is based on its quota. The subscription is contributed in two parts: originally 25 per cent was paid in gold and 75 per cent in the member state's local currency. The gold portion, known as the reserve tranche, is relatively easily available to the member state. It can access this reserve tranche merely by informing the IMF that it needs the funds to deal with a balance of payments problem. Each member state can treat its reserve tranche as part of its foreign reserves. Today, both the size of the quota and the contribution for the reserve tranche are calculated in terms of SDRs, the IMF's specific reserve asset, and unit of account.[36] Members are required to contribute their reserve tranche either in SDRs or in convertible currencies, which practically means in the primary currencies in the global economy—US dollars, euros, pounds, yen, renmimbi, and Swiss francs. The total value of these subscriptions is allocated to the IMF's general resource account. They are used to fund the IMF's financial support to member states.

Finally, quotas influence each member state's access to IMF financing. The amount of funding that the member state can receive from any of the IMF's financing facilities is expressed in terms of a percentage of its quota. This was intended to ensure that all member states receive access to IMF resources on a reasonably uniform basis, relative to their quotas.

Governance

The highest authority in the IMF is its Board of Governors.[37] Each member state is entitled to appoint one Governor to this Board. Most states appoint either their Minister of Finance or the governor of their central bank to this position. The Board of Governors meets formally once a year at the IMF's annual meeting. It can delegate—and in fact has delegated—most of its powers to the IMF'S Board of Executive Directors. However, there are some

[35] M Guitián, *Fund Conditionality: Evolution of Principles and Practices*, IMF Pamphlet (1981).

[36] See IMF Finance Dept, '4. Special Drawing Rights' in IMF Financial Operations 2018 <https://www.elibrary.imf.org/view/IMF071/24764-9781484330876/24764-9781484330876/ch04.xml?language=en> (accessed 28 January 2021) for more discussion of the Special Drawing Rights. See also Driscoll (n 21).

[37] IMF Articles, Art XII.

non-delegable powers, such as decisions on admitting new members to the IMF, making quota adjustments, and amending the Articles of Agreement. While most decisions in the IMF can be made by simple majorities; these non-delegable decisions require a super majority. For example, decisions relating to changes in quotas or allocations of Special Drawing Rights require an 85 per cent majority, which means that the United States, which holds 17.43 per cent of the total vote, has a veto over these decisions.[38]

The Articles stipulate that the Board of Executive Directors is responsible for conducting the business of the IMF.[39] Originally, the IMF had a twelve-member Board of Executive Directors. The Articles specified that the five member states with the largest quotas would each appoint one Executive Director. The remaining seven Executive Directors would be elected to represent constituencies of the other member states. It was initially agreed that two of the seven would be from South America.[40] As the membership of the IMF has grown, the size of the Board has also increased. Pursuant to Article XII, Section 3, the Board shall consist of twenty EDs but the Board of Governors, by an 85 per cent majority vote, can increase or decrease the size of the Board. To date it has determined that there should be twenty-four EDs representing the 190 countries that belong to the IMF.[41]

Since the IMF's establishment, the way in which the Executive Directors are selected has not changed substantially. Initially, the five member states with the largest quotas appointing their own EDs, and the others were elected by constituencies of member states. Today, all EDs are elected. However, seven states—China, France, Germany, Japan, Saudi Arabia, the United Kingdom, and the United States—belong to single country constituencies which elect their own ED. Another ED represents a constituency of two states with the ED always coming from the larger state, Russia. The remaining sixteen EDs represent constituencies of the remaining 182 countries. These constituencies are formed by voluntary groupings of member states, which in general are arranged on the basis of geography.

[38] ibid. As of the most recent (2016) quota review, the US has a quota equal to SDR82,994,200, which is equal to 17.43 per cent of the total IMF quotas <https://www.imf.org/en/About/executive-board/members-quotas> (accessed 6 February 2023). It should be noted that other groups of states, for example the member states of the European Union, may collectively have enough votes to veto decisions that require an 85 per cent majority vote.

[39] IM Articles, Art XII, Section 3.

[40] IMF, Annual Report of the Executive Directors, September 1946, 2–3 <https://www.imf.org/external/pubs/ft/ar/archive/pdf/ar1946.pdf> (accessed 25 June 2022).

[41] See <https://www.imf.org/en/About/executive-board/eds-voting-power> accessed 6 February 2023.

However, there are some significant exceptions to this general rule. For example, Spain is a member of a seven-country constituency that includes six Central and South American states. The constituencies also differ significantly in size. They range from the single-country constituencies discussed above to the two Sub-Saharan African constituencies which each have over twenty members.[42]

The votes of the EDs differ. They each are authorized to exercise a vote equal to the sum of the votes of the members of their constituency.[43] Thus, the two Sub-Saharan African constituencies each have under 3 per cent of the total vote while the constituency in which Spain participates has about 4.5 per cent of the total vote and the constituency in which the United States is the only member has over 17 per cent of the total vote.[44] The ED for a multi-state constituency cannot split his/her vote even if the states in the constituency disagree about how they wish the ED to vote on a particular issue.[45]

It is important to note that the impact of this weighted voting is mitigated by the fact that normally, the IMF Board operates by consensus.[46] This means that, in fact, an ED who is highly respected by the other EDs can have significant influence in the Board, despite having a small share of the vote.

The Articles of Agreement do not discuss in great detail how the Board of Executive Directors should perform its responsibilities. One reason for this is that the leading delegations at the Bretton Woods Conference disagreed about how the Board should function. Some advocated for a Board that is full time and based at the IMF. Others argued for a part-time board with the members only coming to the IMF for meetings. At the 1946 inaugural meeting of the Board of Governors in Savannah, Georgia, it was decided that the Executive Directors would be based full-time at the IMF headquarters in Washington, DC and that they would be delegated all derogable powers of the Board of Governors.[47]

The Articles also now provide that each ED should be supported by one or two Alternate Executive Director, depending on the size of the

[42] See IMF Factsheet, 'Executive Directors and voting powers' March 2023 <https://www.imf.org/external/np/sec/memdir/eds.aspx> (accessed 29 January 2021).

[43] IMF Articles, Art XII, Section 3.

[44] See IMF Factsheet, 'Executive Directors and voting powers' (n 42).

[45] IMF Articles, Art XII, Section 5.

[46] L van Houtven, 'Governance of the IMF Decision Making, Institutional Oversight, Transparency, and Accountability' (2002) 53 IMF Pamphlet series 20, 23–29.

[47] Mikesell (n 20), 52.

constituency.[48] In addition, they each have a small staff of advisors and support staff. They function as both officials of the IMF and representatives of their constituencies.[49]

As indicated above, the Board is responsible for overseeing the operations of the IMF. Thus, its responsibilities include approving all IMF financing operations, reviewing all IMF country and thematic reports, and all IMF policies and internal organizational matters. The Board's operating rules and principles are set out in its Bylaws.[50]

The work of the IMF is done by its management and staff, which is headed by the IMF Managing Director.[51] In a formal sense, the staff and management are accountable to the Board. This means that the Board, in addition to its responsibilities in regard to the finances, human resources, and operational policies of the IMF, must also oversee the work of the management and staff. The Managing Director is also the chair of the Board of Executive Directors.

Financial resources

The IMF receives most of its resources from the subscriptions of its member states. As indicated above, these funds are contributed to the IMF's general resources from where they can be used in the IMF's operations. It is important to note that this arrangement means that a substantial portion of the IMF's resources are in the local currency of its member states and so may be effectively unusable by the IMF. It should be noted that the total value of the quotas in 2022 was about $675 billion.[52] This was less than 1 per cent of global GDP in 2017. By comparison, in 1947, quotas were equal to about 3 per cent of global GDP.[53]

48 IMF Articles, Art XII, Section 3(e).

49 IMF Articles, Art XII, Section 3.

50 IMF By-laws: Rules and Regulations (n 28).

51 IMF Articles, Art XII, Section 4(a).

52 IMF Factsheet, 'Quotas'<https://www.imf.org/en/About/executive-board/members-quotas> (accessed 14 March 2023).

53 Global GDP in 2021 was about $96.5 trillion <https://databankfiles.worldbank.org/public/ddpext_download/GDP.pdf> (accessed on 14 March 2023). In 1946, World GDP was $0.228 trillion and $ 0.250 trillion in 1947. See <https://www.thebalance.com/us-gdp-by-year-3305543> (accessed 3 February 2021). The total value of IMF quotas was $7,721.5 million in 1947. See IMF Annual Report of the Executive Directors September 1947 at p 20, 42. The report is available at: <https://www.imf.org/external/pubs/ft/ar/archive/pdf/ar1947.pdf> (accessed 20 June 2023) The current value of the IMF quotas is $675 billion. See IMF Factsheet 'IMF Quotas' (n 52).

Pursuant to its Articles, the IMF membership review the quotas every five years and can decide to either change the amount of the quotas of all or a sub-group of member states or to change the formula used to determine the quotas.[54] However, agreement on these changes requires approval by 85 per cent of the total votes of the member states. This requirement makes substantial changes in the allocations of quotas difficult. As a result, over time the quotas have become less aligned with the reality of power in the global economy. For example, Luxembourg, which in 2019 had a population of about 614,000 and a GDP of about US$71 billion had a quota of SDR1321.8 million, while Thailand, with a population that year of about 69 million and a GDP of about $509 billion had a quota of SDR1081.9 million.[55]

The IMF's second source of funds is borrowing from its member states. Currently, it borrows through an arrangement known as the New Agreement to Borrow.[56] Pursuant to this arrangement, a group of states, primarily the G20 states, have agreed to lend the IMF specified amounts of funds in the event that the IMF needs them.[57] These resources will be used to support IMF financial arrangements with countries in difficulty. Earlier in its history the IMF had a comparable arrangement with a smaller group of countries known as the General Agreement to Borrow.[58]

The IMF is also the trustee for a number of trust funds that have been established by specific groups of its member states for specific purposes.[59] It is important to note that these trust funds are managed outside the normal operations of the IMF and so can be subject to different rules. Consequently, they do not have to conform to the usual principles of uniformity and universality that govern IMF operations.[60] They can distinguish between different

[54] IMF Articles, Art III, Section 2.

[55] IMF Factsheet, 'IMF Members' Quotas and Voting Power, and IMF Board of Governors' <https://www.imf.org/external/np/sec/memdir/members.aspx> (accessed 29 January 2021).

[56] IMF Factsheet, 'IMF Standing Borrowing Arrangements' <https://www.imf.org/~/media/Files/Factsheets/English/Standingborrowingarrangement.ashx> (accessed 29 January 2021).

[57] ibid. The states agreed to double the size of the NAB in 2020 from SDR182 billion to SDR365 billion.

[58] ibid.

[59] IMF, '15 Trust Funds in International Law: The Contribution of the International Monetary Fund to a Code of Principles' (1984) 2 Legal and Institutional Aspects of the International Monetary *System*.

[60] IMF Pamphlet 46, *The Unique Nature of the Responsibilities of the IMF: Areas of Risk for the Code of Conduct* <https://www.imf.org/external/pubs/ft/pam/pam46/pam4605.htm> (accessed 29 January 2021). Uniformity requires the IMF to ensure that similarly situated members have access to financial support from its general resources on a non-discriminatory (ie

categories of IMF member states. For example, the Poverty Reduction and Growth Trust Fund[61] is used exclusively for the benefit of low-income countries. In 2022, the IMF created the Resilience and Sustainability Trust Fund to help qualifying low- and middle-income countries address pandemics and climate related emergencies. This Trust Fund supplements the resources that these countries receive through regular IMF financing arrangements.[62]

Finally, the IMF has the authority to issue its own reserve currency, the Special Drawing Right (SDR).[63] Pursuant to its Articles, upon a vote of 85 per cent of the total votes by members, it can make allocations of SDRs. The value of the SDR is based on a basket of currencies, consisting of specified portions of the US dollar, the euro, the Japanese yen, the UK pound sterling, and the Chinese renminbi. The allocations are distributed among members according to their quotas. The member states can use their SDR allocations for specifically designated purposes. These include meeting their obligations to some of the international financial institutions and certain other prescribed holders of SDRs and for transactions between themselves.[64]

Functions

The IMF was designed to provide supervisory and financial services to its member states. It was expected to exercise oversight of the system of par values by conducting, pursuant to Article IV of its Articles, surveillance of each of its member states. Originally, these Article IV operations were to determine that they were following monetary policies that were consistent with the maintenance of the par value of its currency.[65] The original Articles

uniform) basis. Universality means that all IMF member states can access its financial and other services. These concepts are discussed in more detail in Chapter 6.

[61] IMF Factsheet, 'IMF Support for Low-income Countries' <https://www.imf.org/en/About/Factsheets/IMF-Support-for-Low-Income-Countries> (accessed 29 January 2021).

[62] See <https://www.imf.org/en/Topics/Resilience-and-Sustainability-Trust> accessed 9 November 2022 for more information on this trust.

[63] IMF Articles, Art XV. See also IMF Factsheet, 'Special Drawing Rights (SDRs)' <https://www.imf.org/en/About/Factsheets/Sheets/2016/08/01/14/51/Special-Drawing-Right-SDR> (accessed 29 January 2021).

[64] The SDRs are discussed in more detail in Chapter 6.

[65] IMF Articles, Art IV(3)(a). See IMF, 'IMF Executive Board Adopts New Decision on Bilateral Surveillance over Members' Policies', Public Information Notice No. 07/69 (21 June 2007): <www.imf.org/external/np/sec/pn/2007/pn0769.htm> (accessed 29 January 2021). For an overview of criticisms of IMF surveillance, see JW Head, 'Seven Deadly Sins: An Assessment of Criticisms Directed at the International Monetary Fund' (2004) Kansas Law Review 52 521.

did not specify how these surveillance missions were to be done. These details were left to the IMF leadership to decide. It determined that the IMF staff would undertake regular missions, usually every year, to their member states where they would collect information and consult about those aspects of their monetary and payments policies that were relevant to the maintenance of the par value of the country's currency.[66] The IMF staff would report on these missions to the Board and would use the information learned from these missions in preparing the various IMF studies and reports on the international monetary system and the global economy. The IMF could also use this information in determining the conditions that it would attach to any financial support that it may provide to any of its member states.[67]

It is important to note that the reports from these country surveillance missions are only intended to be advisory. Thus, each member state can decide for itself how to respond to the IMF's reports from these missions. However, any member state that is contemplating seeking IMF financial support would know that the IMF could base the conditions attached to this financing in part on the conclusions it draws from the surveillance missions to the country.

It is also important to note that when the par value system ended, the IMF had to rethink the purpose and scope of its surveillance missions. The reason was that the missions could no longer focus on establishing if member states were following policies designed to maintain the par value of their currencies. Now, the missions needed to focus on whether the member states were following policies designed to support sustainable balance of payments positions and to contribute to a stable international monetary system.[68] The implications of this shift are discussed in Chapter 6.

The IMF's other important function is to provide financial support to those member states that seek its support in dealing with their balance-of-payments problems.[69] The amount of financing that the IMF can offer any member state is dependent on the state's quota and the total size of the IMF's resources. The delegates at Bretton Woods provided some general guidance to the IMF in regard to the financial support it provides to member states. For example, they specified that the IMF would swap the

[66] MG de Vries, *The IMF in a Changing World 1945–85* (IMF 1986).

[67] RM Lastra, 'The Role of the IMF as a Global Financial Authority' (2011) European Yearbook of International Economic Law vol 2 8–9.

[68] IMF Articles, Art IV.

[69] For more information on IMF financial operations, see IMF, 'About the IMF: Lending by the IMF', <https://www.imf.org/external/about/lending.htm> (accessed 29 January 2021).

foreign exchange with the member state seeking financing in exchange for its local currency. They also specified that the member state must be facing a payments problem in regard to current transactions and that it cannot use IMF resources for capital transactions.[70] However, they did not specify what actions, if any, the IMF expects the member state to undertake to correct the monetary and economic problems that caused it to seek IMF financing. The IMF Articles do, however, stipulate that it should provide financing to Member states subject to 'adequate safeguards' and in order to 'correct maladjustments in their balance of payments without resorting to measures destructive of national or international prosperity'.[71]

The member states, acting through their EDs, decided that the IMF should make its support conditional on the recipient adopting certain policy reforms. The purpose of this conditionality[72] is to ensure that IMF resources are used by member states to resolve their balance-of-payments problems consistent with their obligations under the IMF's Articles. In an effort to promote compliance with these conditions, the IMF disburses its funds in a series of tranches (rather than in a single lump sum). In order to access each tranche, the member state must satisfy the IMF that it has complied with the applicable IMF conditionalities.

It is important to note that the way in which member states access IMF financing facilities that are supported by the IMF's General Resources is *sui generis*.[73] It involves the member state submitting a Letter of Intent to the IMF and a decision by the Board of Executive Directors. The Letter of Intent is usually signed by the minister of finance and central bank governor of the member state. It states that the member is facing a balance of payments problem, that it intends to adopt a number of specified policies that are designed to correct the problem and that it is seeking IMF financial support from a specified IMF financing facility to help it implement these policies. The Letter will also include information on the schedule for implementation of the policies and their expected outcomes. Based on this Letter, the

[70] IMF Articles, Art XIX.

[71] IMF Articles, Art I(v). See A Dreher, 'IMF Conditionality: Theory and Evidence' (2009) 141 Public Choice 233–267.

[72] IMF, 'Guidelines on Conditionality' <https://www.imf.org/External/np/pdr/cond/2002/eng/guid/092302.pdf> (accessed 29 January 2021). Clause 11 of the Guidelines on Conditionality provides that the IMF will monitor the borrowing country's performance under agreements entered into with the IMF on the basis of prior actions, performance criteria, programmes and other reviews, and other variables and measures established as structural benchmarks or indicative targets.

[73] J Gold, *The Stand-By Arrangements of the International Monetary Fund: A Commentary on their Formal, Legal, and Financial Aspects* (IMF 1970) XII 295.

IMF Board takes a decision, referred to as a 'Standby Decision', in which it states that it supports the member state's proposed policies and has decided to make a specified amount of financing, determined on the basis of the member state's quota and the terms of the specific financing facility, available to the member state. Its decision will also set out the phased way in which the financing will be provided. This means that it will initially provide the member state with a portion of the total financing and promise that if the member state meets the enumerated performance criteria or identified actions by the specified times, it will make further tranches of the funding available. The IMF staff will conduct periodic reviews of the situation in the member state to determine if it is satisfying the specified criteria or has taken the stipulated actions. It is important to note that the member state and the IMF carefully—and sometimes contentiously—negotiate the terms of both the Letter of Intent and the Standby Decision before they are submitted to the Board.

Once the arrangement is in place, the member state accesses the first tranche of the IMF financing by swapping foreign exchange from the IMF in exchange for its local currency. At a future date, as agreed, the member state will reverse the transaction. It will swap its foreign exchange for the IMF's holding of local currency. The source of this obligation is the Articles of Agreement and not the specific documents setting out the transaction between the member state and the IMF.[74]

For many years the IMF has maintained that the member state's promises in the Letter of Intent and the IMF's promises in the Standby Decision are parallel rather than reciprocal promises. In addition, it maintains that, because the authorizations for the two swap transactions arise from different sources they are independent of each other. The IMF maintains that the implication of these two characteristics of the IMF transaction is that the Standby Arrangement does not create a binding and enforceable contract between the two parties. Consequently, unlike in the case of the IBRD, there is no need to register the arrangement with the UN and there is no legal liability in the event the member state fails to adopt or implement the policies it set out in its Letter of Intent.[75]

Over time the IMF has developed a number of different facilities, each of which is designed to address a different payments problem faced by its

[74] IMF Articles, Art V, Section 7.
[75] Gold, The Stand-By Arrangements of the IMF (n 73).

member states.[76] Each of these facilities offer member states different levels of support. They also differ in their terms and associated conditionalities. However, all the IMF facilities that are funded through its general resources and its borrowed resources are subject to the IMF's principles of universality and of uniformity.[77] This means that the facilities are available to all similarly situated member states that meet the requirements for access to the facility on the same proportionate basis. These principles do not preclude the IMF from designing its facilities so that they are likely to be more suitable for some member states than others. For example, its Compensatory and Contingency Financing Facility[78] is designed, in part, to support countries facing difficulties because of sudden drops in their commodity export earnings. While in principle any state can qualify for support from this facility, it is more likely to be of use to countries that are heavily dependent on export earnings from one particular commodity or a small number of commodities.

The resources that the IMF has available to support member states have been supplemented by some trust funds. These funds are provided by richer IMF member states to be managed by the IMF as trustee for the benefit of a specified group of IMF member states. For example, the IMF has received donations from some member states to create a Catastrophe Containment and Relief Trust.[79] This particular Trust provides grants to qualifying low-income countries to meet their obligations to the IMF. Consequently, it allows the member states to save the payments it was expecting to have to make to the IMF but without any cost to the IMF. It is important to note that the IMF is only acting as the trustee for this Trust and is not using its general resources in its operations. It therefore can agree that the donors can attach conditions to this financing that are not consistent with the principles of uniformity and universality.

[76] IMF Factsheet, 'IMF at a glance' <https://www.imf.org/en/About/Factsheets/IMF-at-a-Glance#:~:text=Resources%3A%20Member%20quotas%20are%20the,conducts%20general%20reviews%20of%20quotas.&text=The%20Board%20of%20Governors%20meets,IMF%E2%80%93World%20Bank%20Annual%20Meetings%20> (accessed 29 January 2021).

[77] IMF, 'The unique nature of the responsibilities of the IMF: areas of risk for the code of conduct'. Also see Gold, The Stand-By Arrangements of the IMF (n 73).

[78] See IMF External Relations Dept, 'The IMF's Compensatory and Contingency Financing Facility: Helping adjusting countries weather adverse external shocks', Finance & Development (IMF 1988).

[79] IMF Factsheet, 'Catastrophe Containment and Relief Trust', <https://www.imf.org/en/About/Factsheets/Sheets/2016/08/01/16/49/Catastrophe-Containment-and-Relief-Trust> (accessed 29 January 2021).

The IMF's third function is to provide technical assistance to its member states.[80] This assistance is provided in a number of different forms. The most obvious is that the IMF will provide technical advice to member states on request regarding specific technical challenges that the member state is facing. The IMF also offers general technical training for the officials of its member states. In addition, it will provide advice informally to member states during their Article IV surveillance missions and the missions involved in its Financial Sector Assessment Program.[81] Finally, the IMF provides more general technical support to its members through its various publications.

Disputes and amendments

The IMF Articles do provide for amendments to the Articles.[82] In fact, the IMF has amended its Articles seven times since 1944.[83] Some of these amendments were primarily intended as updates of the Articles but some were designed to make substantial changes in the functioning of the institutions. An example of the first category is the amendment to change the way the basic votes are calculated. Examples of the second category are the amendments to create a new international currency, the Special Drawing Right, and to deal with the end of the par value system. The latter amendment established a new basis for the international monetary system. Instead of the system being based on currencies with par values linked to a gold-based US dollar, it created a system of fiat money in which member states were free to let their currencies float freely and to have its value set in foreign exchange markets. One consequence of this amendment, as indicated above and as will be discussed in more detail in a later chapter,[84] was to change the scope and focus of IMF surveillance missions. They are no longer focused on the maintenance of a par value for the member state's currency. They are now concerned with assessing whether a member state is following policies designed to maintain a stable macro-economy and thereby to contribute to

[80] IMF Factsheet, 'Technical Assistance' <https://www.imf.org/external/about/techasst.htm> (accessed 1 February 2021).

[81] IMF Factsheet, 'Financial Sector Assessment Program' <https://www.imf.org/en/About/Factsheets/Sheets/2016/08/01/16/14/Financial-Sector-Assessment-Program> (accessed 1 February 2021).

[82] IMF Articles, Art XXVIII.

[83] IMF Articles, Art XVII.

[84] See also Mikesell (n 20).

a stable international monetary system. The number of issues that are relevant to such an assessment are considerably greater than was the case with the prior focus of IMF surveillance during the period in which the par value system functioned.

The IMF Articles also provide for the resolution and management of dispute between the IMF and member states. As indicated above, the final decision in this regard rests with the Board of Governors.

The World Bank

Purposes

Pursuant to Article I of its Articles of Agreement,[85] the objectives of the IBRD are to:

- assist in the reconstruction and development of the territories of member states by supporting the investment of capital for productive

[85] IBRD Articles, Art 1, available at <https://www.worldbank.org/en/about/articles-of-agreement/ibrd-articles-of-agreement> (accessed 15 March 2023). The full text of the Article is as follows:

'The purposes of the Bank are:

(i) To assist in the reconstruction and development of territories of members by facilitating the investment of capital for productive purposes, including the restoration of economies destroyed or disrupted by war, the reconversion of productive facilities to peacetime needs and the encouragement of the development of productive facilities and resources in less developed countries.

(ii) To promote private foreign investment by means of guarantees or participations in loans and other investments made by private investors; and when private capital is not available on reasonable terms, to supplement private investment by providing, on suitable conditions, finance for productive purposes out of its own capital, funds raised by it and its other resources.

(iii) To promote the long-range balanced growth of international trade and the maintenance of equilibrium in balances of payments by encouraging international investment for the development of the productive resources of members, thereby assisting in raising productivity, the standard of living and conditions of labor in their territories.

(iv) To arrange the loans made or guaranteed by it in relation to international loans through other channels so that the more useful and urgent projects, large and small alike, will be dealt with first.

(v) To conduct its operations with due regard to the effect of international investment on business conditions in the territories of members and, in the immediate postwar years, to assist in bringing about a smooth transition from a wartime to a peacetime economy.'

purposes, including 'the encouragement of the development of productive facilities and resources in less developed countries';
- promote private foreign investment by means of guarantees or participations in loans and other investments made by private investors;
- promote the long-range balanced growth of international trade and the maintenance of equilibrium in balances of payments by encouraging international investment for the 'development of the productive resources of members, thereby assisting in raising productivity, the standard of living and conditions of labor in their territories';
- arrange loans made or guaranteed by it for the more useful and urgent projects; and
- conduct its operations with due regard to the effect of international investment on business conditions in the territories of member states.

Based on these purposes, it is clear that the IBRD's purposes are focused on the 'reconstruction' and 'development' of its member states. It is expected to achieve this purpose primarily by funding development 'projects'.[86] Only in 'special circumstance'[87] should the IBRD provide funding for non-project related purposes. As indicated, IBRD's Articles of Agreement do not define such key terms as 'development', 'project', or the 'special circumstances' that justify non-project lending. This means, in principle, that the IBRD management and staff are free to decide for themselves how to define these terms.

It is also important to note that the IBRD's funding is not provided on concessional terms. It is merely funding provided on more favourable terms than the terms its borrowers, acting on their own, can obtain from commercial sources.[88]

Membership

Any state that is a member of the IMF can join the IBRD.[89] Members of the IBRD are also eligible for membership in the other organizations that were

[86] IBRD Articles, Art III(4)(vii).

[87] IBRD Articles, Art III.

[88] JD Ciorciari, 'The Lawful Scope of Human Rights Criteria in World Bank Credit Decisions: An Interpretive Analysis of the IBRD and IDA Articles of Agreement' (2002) 33(2) Cornell International Law Journal <http://scholarship.law.cornell.edu/cilj/vol33/iss2/2> (accessed 1 February 2021).

[89] IBRD Articles, Art 2, Section 1(a).

created later by the members of the IBRD and constitute the entities in the World Bank Group. The other organizations in the World Bank Group are:

- *International Development Association (IDA).* This institution was established in 1960 to provide financing for low-income countries, which are defined as countries having a gross national income (GNI) per capita below a specified amount.[90] It extends financing to them for longer periods than IBRD loans and at no interest. IDA does charge a small administration fee, expressed as a percentage of the principal amount of the IDA credit. Given these generous terms, IDA's capital needs to be replenished every three years. Since these replenishments must be made by each contributing state from their national budgets, the IDA funding process is a politicized process that has implications for the operations of the whole Bank group.[91]
- *International Finance Corporation (IFC).*[92] The IFC was established in 1956 to finance the development of the private sector in IBRD Part 2 countries, that is countries that are eligible to borrow from the IBRD. It contributes both debt and equity financing to clients investing in eligible countries. The IFC has its own capital and raises funding on its creditworthiness.[93]
- *Multilateral Investment Guarantee Agency (MIGA).*[94] MIGA provides political risk insurance for investments in IBRD Part 2 countries. These investments are primarily those being made by foreign investors.[95]

[90] International Development Association (IDA) Articles of Agreement available at <https://thedocs.worldbank.org/en/doc/2a209939e876fdcd0d957036daebff6e-0410011960/original/IDA-Articles-of-Agreement-English.pdf> (accessed 15 March 2023). In FY 2023, IDA funding is available to countries with a GNI per capita below $1255 per annum <https://ida.worldbank.org/en/financing> (accessed 20 June 2023).

[91] International Development Association, 'What is IDA?' <http://ida.worldbank.org/about/what-is-ida#:~:text=The%20International%20Development%20Association%20(IDA,helps%20the%20world's%20poorest%20countries.&text = IDA%20complements%20the%20World%20Bank's,Reconstruction%20and%20Development%20(IBRD)> (accessed 3 February 2021).

[92] International Finance Corporation (IFC), 'Articles of Agreement' available at <https://www.ifc.org/wps/wcm/connect/corp_ext_content/ifc_external_corporate_site/about+ifc_new/ifc+governance/articles> (accessed 15 March 2023).

[93] IFC, 'About IFC' <https://www.ifc.org/wps/wcm/connect/corp_ext_content/ifc_external_corporate_site/about+ifc_new> (accessed 3 February 2021).

[94] 'Multilateral Investment Guarantee Agency (MIGA) Convention' available at <https://www.miga.org/sites/default/files/archive/Documents/MIGA%20Convention%20(April%202018).pdf> (accessed 15 March 2023).

[95] MIGA, 'About MIGA', <https://www.miga.org/about-us> (accessed 3 February 2021).

- *International Centre for Settlement of Investment Disputes (ICSID).*[96] ICSID is an arbitral institution. It offers arbitral services in cases involving disputes between foreign investors and host states that have signed the ICSID Convention.[97]

Each of these institutions has its own founding treaty and international legal personality. They each have a specialized developmental mandate and governance arrangements that are analogous to those of the IBRD. Each institution has its own Board of Executive Directors and Board of Governors. They are discussed in more detail in Chapter 5. For the purposes of this chapter, 'the Bank' refers only to the IBRD and IDA.

Governance

The governance arrangements in the World Bank Group are similar to those in the IMF. This means that the highest decision-making body is the Board of Governors, with each member state appointing one Governor.[98] The Governors are usually ministers in the member state government, such as the minister of finance or the minister of development. The Governors have delegated almost all their authority to the Board of Executive Directors.[99] The World Bank Group currently has a board of twenty-five Executive Directors.[100] The five largest shareholders are each represented by one Executive Director and the remaining twenty Executive Directors represent constituencies of member states.

Like in the IMF, the member states have weighted votes in the governance of the IBRD and most of the other institutions in the World Bank Group.[101] Each member state's vote is determined by the number of shares they are allocated when they join the IBRD.[102] Its allocation of shares is

[96] 'International Centre for Settlement of Investment Dispute Convention', available at <https://icsid.worldbank.org/sites/default/files/ICSID%20Convention%20English.pdf> (accessed 15 March 2023).

[97] World Bank Group, 'About ICSID', > (accessed 3 February 2021).

[98] IBRD Articles, Art V.

[99] IBRD Articles, Art V, Section 4.

[100] World Bank Group Board of Directors <https://www.worldbank.org/en/about/leadership/directors> (accessed 1 February 2021).

[101] The one exception is ICSID. Each member state has one representative on the ICSID Administrative Council and each representative has one vote. ICSID, 'About ICSID: Administrative Council', available at <https://icsid.worldbank.org/about/member-states/administrative-council> (accessed on 15 March 2023).

[102] IBRD Articles, Art V, Section 3(a).

based on a formula that is analogous to the formula used to calculate IMF quotas. These shares determine the state's contribution to the IBRD and its vote in the organization but not the amount it can borrow from it.[103]

As is the case in the IMF, the votes in the IBRD that each member receives consists of two parts. The first part, known as the basic votes, consists of its share of an equal distribution among all members of 5.5 per cent of the total shares and votes in the IBRD.[104] The second part consists of one vote for each additional share that the member state owns in the IBRD.[105] Given that each member has a different share allocation, the total vote of the member states will vary according to their allocation of shares in the Bank.

The day-to-day operations of the Bank are conducted by the President, who also chairs the Board of Executive Directors, and the management and staff of the Bank.[106] The management of the Bank is expected to propose policies and activities to the Board, who must then decide whether or not to approve the proposals. In addition, the management present all Bank loan agreements to the Board for their approval. The Articles stipulate that the officers of the Bank owe their loyalty to the Bank and the member states commit to respect the international character of the Bank.[107]

One interesting aspect of these governance arrangements is that the Board, usually working with Bank staff, has the capacity to prepare the drafts of treaties to create new institutions.[108] It can then recommend to the Board of Governors and the member states that they should approve and sign the treaties. This is, for example, the process that was followed in developing the treaties creating the other members of the World Bank Group besides the IBRD.

[103] IMF Factsheet, 'Quota' 4 March 2021, <https://www.imf.org/en/About/Factsheets/Sheets/2016/07/14/12/21/IMF-Quotas> (accessed 25 June 2021). See also D Lachman, 'How Should IMF Resources Be Expanded' in EM Truman, *Reforming the IMF for the 21st Century* (Peterson Instittute for International Economics 2006) 471.

[104] IBRD Articles, Art V, Section 3(a)(i).

[105] IBRD Articles, Art V, Section 3(a)(ii).

[106] IBRD Articles, Art V, Section 5(a) & (b).

[107] IBRD Articles, Art V, Section 5(c)

[108] Commentary on the Convention establishing the Multilateral Investment Guarantee Agency October 11 1985, <https://www.miga.org/documents/commentary_convention_november_2010.pdf> (accessed 2 February 2021). See also W Liang, 'The World Bank and the Creation of the International Center for Settlement of Investment Disputes: Legality and Legitimacy' in *International Organizations and the Promotion of Effective Dispute Resolution* (Brill 2019).

Capital structure

The capital of the IBRD consists of the payments that member states make to purchase their shares in the IBRD. This purchase price consists of three parts.[109] First the member pays a small portion, approximately 2 per cent of the price, in foreign exchange. Originally this portion was paid in gold but it is now paid in convertible currencies. Second, it pays approximately 18 per cent in its own local currency. These two portions together make up the paid-in portion of the share price. It is important to note that this arrangement means that a substantial amount of the IBRD's paid-in capital is in the form of the local currency of its member states. Consequently, a substantial portion of the Bank's paid-in capital is unusable in international transactions.

The third portion, accounting for the remaining 80 per cent of the purchase price, is referred to as callable capital.[110] This means, in effect, that the member state provides the Bank with an IOU acknowledging that it owes the Bank this portion of the purchase price. It will only be obliged to pay this portion when called by the IBRD to do so. To date, the IBRD has never needed to demand that its member states contribute their share of the callable portion of its capital.

The Bank relies on this callable capital, and its implication that the Bank is supported by the full faith and credit of all its member states, to raise funds on favourable terms on international financial markets.[111] The IBRD, in part because of its callable capital, is currently rated as an AAA borrower.[112] The investors in its bonds include both public and private entities.

The Bank's funding model highlights that it is functioning as a financial intermediary. It is a more creditworthy borrower than those member states that are eligible to borrow from it and so can raise funds in financial markets at a more favourable rate than they can. Consequently, it can also lend these funds to its qualifying member states at better rates than they can get on their own. One implication of this arrangement is that the IBRD is relying on the repayments from its borrowers to meet its own obligations to

[109] IBRD Articles, Art II, Sections 2 and 7.

[110] IBRD Articles, Art II, Section 5(ii).

[111] World Bank Group 2020, 'Annual Report Content-Supporting Countries' Development Through Capital Markets' <https://www.worldbank.org/en/about/annual-report/supporting-countries> (accessed 1 February 2021).

[112] Fitch Rating Action Commentary, 'Fitch Affirms IBRD at "AAA"; Stable Outlook' January 28 2021, <https://www.fitchratings.com/research/sovereigns/fitch-affirms-ibrd-at-aaa-stable-outlook-28-01-2021> (accessed 2 February 2021).

its creditors. This necessarily constrains the terms and conditions on which it lends to its member states. It also limits the flexibility with which it can treat any member state facing financial challenges. This follows from the fact that, in effect, the cost of any flexibility that it shows any one borrower is shared with the Bank's other borrowing member states.[113]

Given that it raises its capital through sale of shares, the IBRD has some features in common with any joint stock company. However, it is important to note that unlike most companies, the IBRD, although profitable, does not pay dividends to its shareholders. Moreover, its shareholders cannot sell their shares and cannot pledge them in order to raise funds from other sources.

Functions

The IBRD was initially expected to carry out its purposes primarily through providing guarantees. However, it rapidly became clear that its members needed more direct support and it began to lend money to qualifying member states.[114] The Bank makes these loans to support 'projects' in its member states.[115] In special circumstances, its loans are used to finance policy-based activities in its member states.[116]

Unlike the IMF, the Bank distinguishes between its member countries based on their level of wealth and development. It divides its members into two parts, based on their GNI per capita. Only Part 2 countries, which are defined as those countries with a GNI per capita below a specified level, are eligible to borrow from it.[117]

The fact that Part 1 countries are not eligible to borrow from the IBRD, do not earn dividends on their shares, and are unable to sell or use their shares in any way raises a question as to what benefits these countries get from membership in the IBRD. The answer lies in the uses that borrowers make of their IBRD loans. They use these funds to purchase the goods and

[113] D Bradlow and D Hunter, *International Financial Institutions and International Law* (Kluwer Law International 2010).

[114] The Bank also renders important non-financial services to its members. See the World Bank, 'About Us: Operations', <http://go.worldbank.org/1YXPMBNDO0>; and the World Bank, 'About Us: Challenge', <http://go.worldbank.org/DM4A38OWJ0> (accessed 2 February 2021).

[115] IBRD Articles, Art III, Section 1.

[116] IBRD Articles, Art III, Section 4(vii). See also Ciorciari (n 88) 349–350.

[117] World Bank Group, *A Guide to the World Bank* (WBG Washington 2003) 73–78.

services that they need to construct the projects or to implement the policies that the loans are helping to finance. The Bank requires that the provider of these goods and services be selected through a process using its international competitive bidding rules.[118] These rules stipulate that companies in all IBRD member states are eligible to bid for these contracts. Inevitably many of these contracts go to companies in Part 1 countries. Thus, these countries benefit from the profits and jobs generated from the contracts that their companies win to supply Bank-funded projects.

The Bank's lending operations are subject to some constraints. Pursuant to its Articles it may only loan money either to a member state or to a public or private entity within the territory of a member. When the borrower is not the member state itself, the loan must be guaranteed by the member state in whose territory the project to be financed is located.[119] Consequently, every lending operation of the Bank leads to either a loan or guarantee agreement with a sovereign state.

These agreements between the Bank and the borrowing or guaranteeing state, therefore, are contracts between an international organization and a sovereign state which means that they qualify as international agreements. Consequently, pursuant, to Article 103 of the UN Charter,[120] the Bank registers all its loan agreements with the UN.[121] Thus, they are all public documents.

The loan agreement consists of two parts. The first part is a document designated as the 'General Conditions' which are incorporated by reference into all loans made by the IBRD.[122] The second part is an agreement that is specific to each particular transaction. This second agreement specifies that in the event of conflict between it and the General Conditions, the specific agreement prevails.[123] Consequently, it is possible, in principle, for the

[118] World Bank Group, 'Procurement Framework and Regulations for Projects after July 1, 2016' <https://www.worldbank.org/en/projects-operations/products-and-services/brief/procurement-new-framework> (accessed 2 February 2021).

[119] IBRD Articles, Art III, Section 4(v).

[120] UN Charter.

[121] A Broches, *International Legal Aspects of the Operations of the World Bank* (Hague Academy 1959).

[122] World Bank Group Document General conditions applicable to loan and guarantee agreements (EnglishGeneral Conditions), <https://documents.worldbank.org/en/publication/documents-reports/documentdetail/858201468152713438/general-conditions-applicable-to-loan-and-guarantee-agreements> (accessed 2 February 2021). IDA credits have a similar structure to IBRD loans.

[123] General Conditions (n 122), Art I, Section (1.02).

terms of the General Conditions to be amended through the specific loan agreement to meet the needs of specific transactions.

It is important to note that the Bank's loan agreements are similar to standard unsecured commercial bank loan agreements. Consequently, most of the clauses of the General Conditions are drafted in similar language to the clauses in standard commercial bank loan agreements. It is outside the scope of this book to provide a detailed description of each of these clauses.[124] However, there are two provisions in the agreement that are of interest for current purposes. First, there is no specific governing law stipulated in the IBRD General Conditions. Instead, they specify that the agreement is 'valid and enforceable in accordance with their terms notwithstanding the law of any state or political subdivision thereof to the contrary'.[125] This means that no municipal law can be relied on to determine how the contract should be interpreted. In addition, it means that any gaps in the way in which the parties understand the terms of the contract should be filled by public international law. This is particularly interesting because the public international law applicable to international agreements is the Vienna Convention on the Law of Treaties[126]—and it does not necessarily address the many possible issues that can arise in the course of the implementation of an international loan to a complicated development project.

The second provision is the choice of forum for resolving disputes. The forum chosen is arbitration.[127] Given the international legal status of the parties, it is understandable that they wish to avoid domestic courts and domestic arbitral institutions. It is also unlikely that the borrower state would wish its dispute with the IBRD to be overseen by ICSID. Consequently, it is understandable that the IBRD has designed its own arbitral process. This means that the governing forum in IBRD loan agreements is an *ad hoc* arbitral procedure.

It should however be noted that to date, despite the thousands of loan agreements that the IBRD has signed over the course of its more than

[124] For a general discussion of the clauses of a standard loan agreement, see JW Head, 'Evolution of the Governing Law for Loan Agreements of the World Bank and other Multilateral Development Banks' (1996) 90 American Journal of International Law 214.

[125] See IBRD Articles, Art III, Section 4; General Conditions (n 122), Art I. See also Head, ibid.

[126] UN Vienna Convention on the Law of Treaties (23 May 1969) UNTS 1155 (331) entered into force 27 January 1980, available at <https://legal.un.org/ilc/texts/instruments/english/conventions/1_1_1969.pdf> (accessed 15 March 2023). There is a treaty on agreements between states and international organizations, but it has not entered into force.

[127] General Conditions (n 122), Art VIII.

70 years of operation, the arbitration clause has never actually been invoked and so has never been tested.[128] It is hard to know with certainty why this is the case. However, it is unlikely that dissatisfied borrowers would find the prospect of suing one of their major creditors appealing, given that the cost of winning the case could include being cut off from future IBRD financing. In addition, there is a risk that a public dispute with the IBRD could have adverse impacts on the borrower's credit rating, and access to both official and commercial sources of finance. This suggests that, in fact, disputes between the IBRD and its borrowers are resolved through negotiation rather than legal action.

The Articles of the Bank expressly stipulate that the IBRD must take a non-political approach to its financial operations. Section IV(10) of its Articles, prohibits it from taking political considerations, including the political character of its borrowers, into account in its lending decisions. In addition, the Articles instruct the Bank to only take 'economic considerations' into account in its lending decisions.[129] These considerations include assessing the likelihood of the loan being repaid. The Articles do not define any of the indicated terms making it difficult for both IBRD staff and outside observers, including borrowers, to know what the Bank will treat as political considerations and what as economic. This political prohibition has been a source of controversy for the Bank—an issue that we will discussed in more detail in Chapter 5.

Disputes and amendments

The IBRD Articles do provide for amendments to the Articles.[130] In fact, the Articles of the IBRD have been amended three times, largely for technical reasons. Article III Section 6 was added in 1965 to allow the IBRD to make loans to the IFC. In 1989, Article VIII, dealing with amendments to the Articles was changed from requiring a vote of three-fifths of the members and four-fifths of the total vote to requiring three-fifths of the members and 85 per cent of the total votes. This had the effect of making amendments more difficult. Article V Section 3 was amended in 2012 to change

[128] AR Sureda, 'Informality and Effectiveness in the Operation of the International Bank for Reconstruction and Development' (2003) 6 Journal of International Economic Law 565, 588–591.

[129] IBRD Articles, Art IV (10). The IDA Articles contain a similar political prohibition.

[130] IBRD Articles, Art VIII.

the way in which basic votes were allocated among members so that they would always constitute a specified percentage of the total votes.

The IBRD Articles also provide for situations of dispute between it and its member states.[131] As indicated above, the final decision in this regard rests with the Board of Governors.

Conclusion

The Articles of Agreement of the IMF and IBRD create two specialized international organizations. Their terms and conditions were drafted with consummate skill. As a result, they have been able to adapt to the changing circumstances in which these institutions have had to function over time. However, since language can never be infinitely elastic, there is always a risk that, as the conditions in which they operate change, the elasticity in their terms could be exhausted and their suitability to the conditions in which they have to operate could begin to decline. This possibility and its implications will be explored in greater detail in later chapters that focus on the evolution of these two organizations.

[131] IBRD Articles, Art V, Section 2(b).

4 The Status of International Financial Institutions under International Law

This chapter focuses on the international legal status of the International Monetary Fund (IMF) and the institutions in the World Bank Group (WBG). For the purposes of this chapter, the most relevant members of the WBG are the three institutions that finance development projects in their member states, namely the International Bank for Reconstruction and Development (IBRD), the International Development Association (IDA), and the International Finance Corporation (IFC). In this chapter they are collectively referred to as the WBG.

The chapter is divided into two sections. The first section discusses the IMF and the WBG (collectively the international financial institutions (IFIs)) as subjects of international law. The second section focuses on the privileges and immunities of the IFIs as actors under international law. It is important to note that this chapter provides a general overview of how the applicable principles of international law apply to the IFIs as international organizations. The following two chapters will focus on how the operations of the WBG and the IMF have evolved over time and the impact of this evolution on the applicable international legal principles for each institution.

The IMF and WBG as subjects of international law

As discussed in Chapter 3, the IFIs were each created by international treaties, signed and ratified by each of their member states. They are therefore creatures of international law and their powers, rights, and obligations arise from the applicable international law. In this context, international law, pursuant to Article 38 of the Statute of the International Court of Justice,[1] can be understood to consist of any treaties to which the organizations are signatories, the principles of customary international law, and general principles of law.

The International Court of Justice held in the *Reparations* case[2] that inter-state organizations created by treaty are subjects of international law. This means, first, that they have their own legal personality and, in formal legal terms, have an existence that is independent of their member states. Second, it means that their powers, rights, and responsibilities are determined firstly by the terms of their founding treaties. In this regard, it is important to note that their founding treaties are *lex specialis* and so take precedence over any general international law instruments and principles that may be inconsistent with them.[3] However, to the extent that they are not inconsistent, the IMF and the WBG are bound by other applicable international agreements; principles of customary international law and general principles of law.[4]

The legal personality of these institutions is recognized in each of their articles. For example, Article VII Section 2 of the IBRD Articles[5] states that:

> The Bank shall possess full juridical personality, and, in particular, the capacity:
> (i) to contract;
> (ii) to acquire and dispose of immovable and movable property;
> (iii) to institute legal proceedings.

The Articles of the other members of the WBG and the IMF have similar provisions.[6]

This means that the entities in the WBG have the capacity to enter into loan contracts, to decide to whom to make loans and to raise funds on

[1] Art 38 UN, *Statute of the International Court of Justice*, 18 April 1946 available at <https://legal.un.org/avl/pdf/ha/sicj/icj_statute_e.pdf> (accessed 15 March 2023).

[2] Reparation for injuries suffered in the service of the Nations, Advisory Opinion, [1949] ICJ Rep 174, ICGJ 232 (ICJ 1949), 11 April 1949.

[3] J Crawford, *Brownlie's Principles of Public International Law* (OUP 2012) 22, 90. See also J Klabbers, *International Law* (1st edn, CUP 2013) 48–50, 54–55.

[4] Art 38, Statute of the International Court of Justice.

[5] IBRD Articles.

[6] IDA Articles, Art VIII Section 2; IFC Articles, Art VI Section 2; IMF Articles, Art IX Section 2.

financial markets. Similarly, the IMF has the capacity to enter into financial agreements or arrangements with its member states. In principle, the institutions can also sue and, subject to their privileges and immunities, be sued in disputes arising from these financial contracts.

The member states, however, have not given the IFIs unconstrainted independence. For example, in the Articles they have specified the factors that should guide the institutions in exercising their powers. A key concern of the member states in this regard is to ensure that the IFIs respect the sovereignty of their member states in their operations. Thus, for example, the member states have limited the ability of the IFIs to interfere in the domestic affairs of their member states.

In the case of the WBG, each institution's Articles includes an explicit prohibition against basing its decisions to provide financing or other services to its member states on political grounds. For example, Article IV(10) of the IBRD Articles stipulates:[7]

> The Bank and its officers shall not interfere in the political affairs of any member; nor shall they be influenced in their decisions by the political character of the member or members concerned. Only economic considerations shall be relevant to their decisions, and these considerations shall be weighed impartially in order to achieve the purposes stated in Article I.

The member states have bolstered their concerns about potential interference by the institutions in the WBG in their member's sovereign prerogatives by specifying that the entities in the WBG must only take economic and efficiency considerations into account in their lending decisions. For example, Article 3 Section 5(b) of the IBRD Articles states:[8]

> The Bank shall make arrangements to ensure that the proceeds of any loan are used only for the purposes for which the loan was granted, with due attention to considerations of economy and efficiency and without regard to political or other non-economic influences or considerations.

It is important to note that, despite the ostensibly clear injunctions that the institutions in the WBG are precluded from taking political issues into

[7] IDA Articles, Art V Section 6; IFC Articles, Art III Section 9.
[8] IDA Articles, Art V Section 1(g); IFC Articles, Art III Sections 1, 3, and 6.

account in their decisions and that they should base their decisions only on economic considerations, the Articles do not define the terms 'political affairs', 'political character', or 'economic considerations'. This means that the management and staff of the Bank have substantial latitude to interpret these terms, provided they can justify their interpretation in terms of the object and purpose of the Bank.

The member states also tried to limit each institution's interactions with its member states by requiring that each state designate one government actor as the contact point for all interactions between the institution and the member state.[9] In the case of the WBG, the designated contact point is usually the Ministry of Finance. This designation does not preclude the WBG from interacting with other actors in the member state's government or society. However, it is expected that they arrange these interactions through the designated contact point.

The separation between the institutions and the member states is further strengthened by the requirement that their member states respect the international character of the organizations and refrain from unduly interfering in their operations. For example, Article V Section 5(c) of the IBRD Articles states:[10]

> The President, officers and staff of the Bank, in the discharge of their offices, owe their duty entirely to the Bank and to no other authority. Each member of the Bank shall respect the international character of this duty and shall refrain from all attempts to influence any of them in the discharge of their duties.

It should be noted that the officers of the Bank include its Executive Directors. The application of the above provision to the Executive Directors of the WBG, however, is complicated.[11] On the one hand they have a duty of loyalty to the organization and, as a result, are expected to only take decisions that promote its mandate and to act in the best interests of the WBG. On the other hand, it is understood that they are appointed by the relevant constituency of member states and are expected to represent those member

[9] IBRD Articles, Art III Section 2; IDA Articles, Art V Section 1(d); IFC Articles, Art IV Section 2.

[10] IDA Articles, Art VI Section 5(c); IFC Articles, Art IV Section 5(c) IFC Articles of Agreement 1956.

[11] World Bank Group Facts, 'Boards of Directors' <https://www.worldbank.org/en/about/leadership/directors> (accessed 10 April 2021).

states on the board of the WBG. This suggests that they have a responsibility to consult with these member states and to promote their interests to the board. The Articles do not provide guidance on how Executive Directors should balance these two sets of responsibilities.

The Executive Directors' dilemma does not, however, alter the requirement that the Bank should act independently of its member states and should make decisions on economic and not political grounds.

The IMF is in a similar but not identical situation to the WBG. Its Articles of Agreement do not contain an explicit political prohibition. Instead, the Articles stipulate that the IMF in its surveillance of its member states should, pursuant to Article IV(3)(b) of its Articles of Agreement:

> respect the domestic social and political policies of members, and in applying these principles the Fund shall pay due regard to the circumstances of members.

The IMF has historically interpreted this provision as being more or less equivalent to a political prohibition.[12] It is important to note that, because of the macro-economic focus of the IMF's work it is hard for it to totally exclude political considerations from its decision-making. However, in order to limit its attention to political factors, the IMF has interpreted Article IV(3)(b) broadly. It has tended to interpret the stipulation that it 'respect' the domestic and social policies of members and that it 'pay due regard' to their circumstances to mean that it should defer to its members' decisions on these matters.[13]

On the other hand, the Articles also push the IMF to pay some attention to the policy-making capacities and decisions of those member states seeking its financial support. The IMF Articles specify, in Article V Section 3, that in its financing decisions, the IMF must ensure that the way in which it provides the financing 'will assist members to solve their balance of payments problems in a manner consistent with the provisions of this

[12] J Gold, 'Political Considerations Are Prohibited by Articles of Agreement When the Fund Considers Requests for Use of Resources', IMF Survey, 23 May 1983, 146. See also SC Thacker, 'The High Politics of IMF Lending' (1999) 52(1) World Politics 38–75 <www.jstor.org/stable/25054100> (accessed 15 April 2021).

[13] As will be discussed in Chapters 6 and 8, this does not mean that the IMF does not, when it deems it necessary, take a more active stance in regard to these matters. Indeed, the IMF's decisions and actions in this regard have historically been a source of controversy. See, for example, D Bradlow, 'The World Bank, the IMF, and Human Rights' (1996) 6 Transnational Law & Contemporary Problems 47.

Agreement' and that it 'will establish adequate safeguards for the temporary use of the general resources of the Fund'.

This suggests that the IMF must form a judgement about whether or not the policies that any particular member state proposes to adopt for dealing with its balance of payments problems are likely to lead to a resolution of the problem and to enable the member state to return the financing to the IMF at the agreed time. In making this assessment, the IMF, at least in the days of the par value system, would focus only on the macro-economic and financial implications of the member state's policies.[14] In this sense, Article IV Section 3 can be seen as roughly equivalent to the stipulation that the WBG should only take economic considerations into account in their financing decisions.

The IMF's Articles contain other provisions that seek to constrain the ability of the IMF to interfere in the internal affairs of its member states. As in the case of the IBRD, its Articles of Agreement limit who it can engage with in the member state governments. Thus, Article V Section 1 stipulates that:

> Each member shall deal with the Fund only through its Treasury, central bank, stabilization fund, or other similar fiscal agency, and the Fund shall deal only with or through the same agencies.

The IMF's Articles, like those of the institutions of the WBG, seeks to bolster the independence of the IMF by stating, in Article XII Section 4(c), in almost identical words to those used in the Articles of the IBRD that the Managing Director and staff owe their loyalty only to the IMF and that the member states are obliged to respect the international character of the IMF. It is noteworthy that the provision does not refer specifically to officers of the IMF. This would seem to suggest that this provision does not apply to the Executive Directors.

As indicated above, these provisions on the independence and powers of the IFIs are open to interpretation. International law and international relations tend to adopt a functional approach in interpreting the powers, rights, and responsibilities of international organizations.[15] Pursuant to

[14] JM Boughton, The IMF and the Force of History: Ten Events and Ten Ideas that have Shaped the Institution (2004) 04(75) IMF Working Paper 1–25.
[15] D Mitrany, 'The Functional Approach to World Organization' (1948) 24(3) International Affairs (Royal Institute of International Affairs: 1944) 350–363.

this approach, their powers and capacities should be interpreted in light of their object and purpose as expressed in their founding treaties.[16] This means that, in addition to their express powers, the IFIs are presumed to have those additional implied powers needed for them to perform their assigned functions.

This functional view of the powers of international organizations was given judicial imprimatur by the International Court of Justice (ICJ) in its advisory opinion interpreting the agreement between the World Health Organization (WHO) and Egypt.[17] In this case, the Court opined that international organizations have both the express powers stipulated in their founding treaties and any additional implied powers that are necessary to perform their mandates. In this regard, it is also important to note that this approach is supported by Article 31(1) of the Vienna Convention[18] which stipulates that treaties should be interpreted in light of their object and purpose, that is, teleologically.

The privileges and immunities of the IFIs

One challenge that international organizations face is that, because they do not control territory and must undertake all their operations on the territory of one or more of their member states, they are vulnerable to interference from their member states. Consequently, and consistent with the functional approach to international organizations, they have been given at least enough immunity to ensure that they are able to conduct their operations in the territories of their member states with sufficient freedom to implement their mandates.[19] In this regard, it was recognized that they would need immunity from both the member state's prescriptive jurisdiction and from being sued in the courts of its member states. In addition, they require that the member states respect the inviolability of their premises, records, mail, and their immunity from taxation, and that their personnel should

[16] J Gold, 'The Interpretation by the International Monetary Fund of Its Articles of Agreement (1954) 8 International & Comparative Law Quarterly 257; IFI Shihata, 'Human Rights, Development, and International Financial Institutions' (1992) 8 American University of International Law & Policy.

[17] Interpretation of the Agreement of 25 March 1951 between the WHO and Egypt, Advisory Opinion, [1980] ICJ Rep 73, ICGJ 212 (ICJ 1980), 20 December 1980.

[18] UN, Vienna Convention on the Law of Treaties.

[19] See Klabbers (n 3). V Engström, *Constructing the Powers of International Institutions* (Martinus Nijhoff 2012).

have immunity at least when acting within the scope of their responsibilities. This immunity has been incorporated into their founding treaties so that each international organization's Articles of Agreement contains an article discussing in detail its privileges and immunity. For example, Article VII Section 1 of the IBRD Articles of Agreement, stipulates that '[t]o enable the Bank to fulfil the functions with which it is entrusted, the status, immunities and privileges set forth in this Article shall be accorded to the Bank in the territories of each member'. The remainder of the Article spells out in more detail the scope and nature of the IBRD's immunity.[20] It addresses the various issues indicated above.

The immunity of the organization is also usually expressly discussed in the bilateral treaty between the IFI and the host state of its headquarters or representative offices.[21] In addition, since the IMF and WBG are UN specialized agencies, their immunity is recognized in the specific convention on the topic that is applicable to UN specialized agencies.[22] In this regard, it is important to note that the United States, the host state for the IMF and the WBG, has not ratified the Convention on the Privileges and Immunities of the Specialized Agencies.[23] Instead it has a statute—the Immunity of International Organizations Act[24]—that addresses the issue.

An example of the functional approach to the powers and capacities of international organizations is that there are differences in the immunity of the IMF and the IBRD because of the different ways in which they finance their operations. The IMF is expected to obtain all its resources from its member states, either through their subscriptions or through borrowing arrangements between the IMF and the member states. As a result, it was not envisaged that the IMF would need to raise funds on private financial

[20] Also see IDA Articles, Art VIII Section 1; IFC Articles, Art VI Section 1; IMF Articles, Art IX Section 1.

[21] See, eg, Host Country Agreement Between the Bank for International Settlements and the United Mexican States Relating to the Establishment and Status of a Representative Office of the Bank for International Settlements in Mexico 5 November 2001 <https://www.bis.org/about/hostctrymx.pdf> (accessed 12 April 2021).

[22] Convention on the Privileges and Immunities of the Specialized Agencies New York, 33 UNTS 33 261 21 November 1947.

[23] ibid.

[24] International Organizations Immunities Act of 1945 22 USC 28 is a United States federal law enacted in 1945. The US Supreme Court has interpreted this statute as providing the same immunity as states have as set out in the Foreign Sovereign Immunities Act of 1976 28 USC 97. See *Jam v International Finance Corporation*, 17-1011, 139 US S. Ct. 759: 203 L. Ed. 2d 53. 27 February 2019.

markets. Consequently, its Articles stipulate that it has absolute immunity unless it expressly waives its immunity.[25]

On the other hand, the IBRD was expected to raise most of its funds from commercial financial markets. In order to attract investors, it would therefore need to be as amendable to suit as any other issuer of bonds. Consequently, its Articles stipulate that it will waive its immunity for this purpose and that it will appoint an agent for service of process in its member states.[26]

The IMF and WBG as international legal actors

Having established that the IFIs are international legal subjects, this section focuses on the rights and responsibilities of the IFIs as international legal actors. It does so by considering how each of the primary sources of international law applies to them.

International treaties

The first point to note is that the IMF and the three organizations in the WBG, as subjects of international law, can voluntarily assume international legal obligations and responsibilities through signing international agreements.

In fact, they have all signed treaties. Since they are all specialized agencies of the United Nations, as indicated above, they each have entered into a relationship agreement with the UN.[27] This treaty spells out the relationship between the UN and each organization. As discussed in Chapter 3, the relationship agreements of the IFIs almost amount to a declaration of

[25] IMF Articles, Art IX Section 3.

[26] IBRD Articles, Art VII Section 2; . IFC Articles, Art VI Section 3 contains a similar limitation on IFC immunity for the same reason. See also IDA Articles, Art VIII Section 3. It has a similar limitation on IDA immunity. .

[27] See UN Charter, Arts 57 and 63. See also Agreement Between the UN and the International Bank for Reconstruction and Development 1948: available at: <https://thedocs.worldbank.org/en/doc/877831508427688702-0290022017/render/AgreeementbetweentheUnitedNationsandIBRD1947.pdf> (accessed 20 June 2023) (UN and IBRD) See L Perinbam, IMF External Relations Dept, 'The World Bank and the United Nations' (1966) Finance & Development 292 and Agreement Between the United Nations and the International Monetary Fund, 15 November 1947, reprinted in Selected Decisions and Selected Documents of the International Monetary Fund 543 (20th issue, 1995). (UN and IMF).

independence. The agreement specifies that both the UN and the relevant IFI acknowledge the specialized and sensitive nature of the mandates of the IMF and the WBG and that this constrains the scope for their collaboration and sharing of information with the UN. For example, Article I Section 2 of the agreement between the UN and the IMF states:[28]

> By reason of the nature of its international responsibilities and the terms of its Articles of Agreement, the Fund is, and is required to function as, an independent international organization.

The agreement further elaborates in Article I Section 3:[29]

> The United Nations and the Fund are subject to certain necessary limitations for the safeguarding of confidential material furnished to them by their members or others, and nothing in this agreement shall be construed to require either of them to furnish any information the furnishing of which would, in its judgment, constitute a violation of the confidence of any of its members or anyone from whom it shall have received such information, or which would otherwise interfere with the orderly conduct of its operations.

The agreement also requires each organization to consult with the other before making formal recommendations to it.[30] In addition, in Article VI, the IMF promises to pay 'due regard' to decisions of the UN Security Council taken pursuant to Articles 41 and 42 of the UN Charter.[31] The IMF is entitled to participate, when appropriate, in the meetings of UN organs. The agreements between the UN and the WBG contain similar provisions.[32]

In fact, the relationships between the UN, its other specialized agencies, and the IFIs are generally cooperative. For example, the IFIs have collaborated with other UN specialized agencies and UN programmes in various projects and programmes in particular countries, and they have participated in UN sponsored international meetings. They have also provided copies of their reports to the UN and have met on a regular basis with the

[28] Similar provisions exist in the agreement between the UN and IBRD, Art 1(3).

[29] ibid.

[30] UN and IBRD, Art IV; UN and IMF, Art IV.

[31] Similar provisions exist between UN and the members of the WBG. See, for example, UN and IBRD, Art VI

[32] UN and IBRD, Art X; UN and IMF, Art X.

UN Economic and Social Council. In addition, the IFIs have acknowledged that, despite the relatively flexible language cited above, they must defer to UN Security Council resolutions, adopted pursuant to Chapter VII of the UN Charter.[33] Even absent this requirement, the IFIs would, de facto, have to comply with the resolution. This follows from the fact that each member of their Board of Executive Directors would be bound by their home state's obligation to comply with the relevant resolution when voting on the applicable IFI board.

In return, the UN has generally been restrained in its engagements with the IFIs. It seeks to consult with the IFIs on issues of mutual interest. For the most part, it has engaged discretely with the IFIs on particular issues where they have concerns. Nevertheless, as is discussed in the following chapters, there have been occasions where the relationship between the UN and the IFIs has been more controversial.[34]

Besides these relationship agreements, the IFIs can enter into bilateral agreements with individual states. Thus, the IFIs have concluded agreements that establish the arrangements that are applicable to the functioning of their headquarters or their representative offices in the relevant member state.[35] These agreements will delineate such issues as the scope of the organization's privileges and immunities and the obligation of the host state to allow officials from its member states to enter its territory and participate in the affairs of the IFI, regardless of the relationship between the host state and the other member states.

Another example of the capacity of IFIs to conclude international agreements is the loan agreements of the IBRD. Its Articles stipulate that it can only lend to its member states or with the guarantee of its member states.[36] Consequently, every IBRD loan transaction involves an agreement between a sovereign state and an international organization and so includes either a loan agreement or a guarantee agreement that is a treaty.[37] This means, pursuant to the UN Charter, that these agreements must be registered with the UN and are publicly available.[38] It also means that they will need to

[33] Shihata (n 16).

[34] See Chapter 5 for discussion of the case of the World Bank loans to South Africa and Portugal in the 1960s.

[35] As indicated above, the host state for the IFIs is the United States.

[36] IBRD Articles, Art 3 Section 1.

[37] A Broches, 'International Legal Aspects of the Operations of the World Bank (Volume 98)', in *Collected Courses of the Hague Academy of International Law* (1959). <http://dx.doi.org/10.1163/1875-8096_pplrdc_A9789028613522_02> (accessed 21 June 2023).

[38] UN Charter, Article 102 UN Charter.

go through the process of ratification required for similar types of international agreements in its member states. The same situation will apply to all IDA agreements with its member states or guaranteed by these member states. However, this principle will not apply to the IFC since its mandate is to lend to the private sector in its member states.

Interestingly the situation is different in the case of the IMF. It maintains that its standby arrangements are not contractual in nature and so do not qualify as international agreements.[39] Consequently, they do not have to be registered with the UN and are not required to be made publicly available—although states always have the option of doing so on their own initiative. Similar considerations are applicable to the other IMF financing facilities that use the organization's general resources. IMF financing that is not sourced from its general resources may be in a contractual form. For example, the concessional financing that the IMF offers qualifying member states from the Poverty Reduction and Growth Trust are provided in the form of a loan.[40] Consequently, the agreement between the Trust and the member state qualifies as an international agreement between a sovereign and an international organization and so arguably should be registered with the UN.

Customary international law

Given that they are subjects of international law, customary international law, as applicable, is binding on international organizations. However, given that each IFI has a specialized function, it may not be clear precisely which customary international law principles are applicable to any particular IFI. This is partially because there is a general lack of clarity about the contents of customary international law. In addition, because a *lex specialis* will trump a *lex generalis*, it is in principle possible for the specific provisions of the international organization's founding treaty to override potentially applicable customary international law principles.[41] The one exception to this general statement is that all principles that have the status of *jus cogens* will be binding on the IFIs.[42]

[39] Gold, 'The Interpretation by the IMF' (n 16) 289.

[40] IMF Factsheet, 'IMF Support for Low-income Countries' <https://www.imf.org/en/About/Factsheets/IMF-Support-for-Low-Income-Countries> (accessed 13 April 2021).

[41] See Crawford (n 3) 654.

[42] ibid 24–26.

Given the above, the starting point for identifying the customary international law principles applicable to the IFIs is to determine if there are any customary international law principles that are specifically applicable to international financial and monetary affairs. In fact, there are not customary principles that are directly and explicitly applicable to international monetary and financial affairs. However, the general principles of good faith and *pacta sunt servanda* and its limiting provision of *clausula rebus sic stantibus* are applicable to the operations of the IFIs.[43] In addition, they, like all subjects of international law, must respect state sovereignty. The extent to which respect for state sovereignty constrains the IFIs' operations in their member states is a matter of considerable debate.[44]

It is important to note in this regard that the IFIs, as subjects of international law, in principle, can be creators of customary international law as well as being bound by it.[45] Any customary international law principles that they create would have to demonstrate that they are supported by both practice and *opinio juris*.[46] It is important to note that these principles can be limited to specialized organizations or can be of more general application.

There are two issues that are of interest concerning the applicability of customary international law to the IFIs. One relates to the social and environmental impacts of their operation. The other deals with the issue of their accountability. Each of these issues is discussed below.

Customary international law and environmental and social impacts

The entities in the WBG have environmental and social safeguard policies that are applicable to the impact assessments that the WBG undertakes as part of the due diligence associated with its operations.[47] These policies specify, based on their nature, size, and impact, the scope of the *ex ante*

[43] For *pacta sunt servanda*, see Klabbers (n 3) 41. For *clausula rebus sic stantibus*, see J Kulaga, 'A Renaissance of the Doctrine of *Rebus Sic Stantibus*?' (2020) 69(2) International and Comparative Law Quarterly 477–497.

[44] This issue is discussed in more detail in Chapters 5 and 6.

[45] JE Alvarez, *International Organizations as Law-Makers* (1st edn, OUP 2005).

[46] A Boyle and C Chinkin, *The Making of International Law* (OUP 2007).

[47] See World Bank, 'Environmental and Social Framework' <https://www.worldbank.org/en/projects-operations/environmental-and-social-framework>. See also IFC, Sustainability Framework <https://www.ifc.org/wps/wcm/connect/topics_ext_content/ifc_external_corporate_site/sustainability-at-ifc/policies-standards/sustainability+framework> (accessed 13 April 2021).

environmental and social impact assessments that are required for each of the projects and programmes that it finances. The policies will also usually be used by their borrowers to guide them in their preparation of project proposals. They also have an influence on the terms of WBG financing for the project and on the implementation and monitoring of the project. These policies have also influenced the approach taken to environmental and social issues by other multilateral development banks.[48] In fact it has become standard practice among the multilateral development financing institutions to conduct such environmental and social impact studies. Indeed, the practice has been so widespread and long-lasting that it may be concluded that these development banks view the practice as being obligatory. Consequently, it could be concluded that the requirement to do *ex ante* environmental and social impact assessments is a customary international law principle applicable, amongst others, to multilateral development banks.[49]

It is important to note that to date there has been one international financial institution that does not, as a standard operating practice, conduct such impact assessments. The IMF does not currently have a practice of doing such impact assessments. It does not object to the principle so much as maintain that it is not applicable to it because it is not a project lender. However, it must be noted that the IMF has begun to talk more openly about its need to address environmental issues such as climate change and social issues such as gender and inequality more systematically in its operations.[50] It would not be surprising if this development leads ultimately to it adopting a practice of doing some form of environmental and social impact

[48] See, eg, African Development Bank Group's, Policy on the Environment 2004; Asian Development Bank, Focus on Environment <https://www.adb.org/what-we-do/themes/environment/main>; and Inter-American Development Bank, Sustainability and Safeguards <https://www.iadb.org/en/about-us/sustainability-and-safeguards> and European Bank for Reconstruction and Development, Environmental and Social Policy <https://www.ebrd.com/environmental-and-social-policy.html> (all accessed 13 April 2021).

[49] The principles of due diligence and impact assessment are generally established customary law in the international environmental law area. See Owen McIntyre, 'The Role of Customary Rules and Principles of International Environmental Law in the Protection of Shared International Freshwater Resources' (2006) 46(1) Natural Resources Journal 157–210.

[50] K Georgieva and R Weeks-Brown, 'The IMF's Evolving Role within a Constant Mandate' (2023) 26(1) Journal of International Economic Law 17–29 <https://doi.org/10.1093/jiel/jgac064>; New Priorities for the Global Economy Speech by Kristalina Georgieva, IMF Managing Director, 5 February 2020 in Workshop on New Forms of Solidarity, Vatican City <https://www.imf.org/en/News/Articles> (accessed 14 April 2021).

assessments in at least some of its operations.[51] This aspect of IMF operations will be discussed in more detail in Chapter 6 of this book.

Human rights

One particularly contentious issue in regard to the applicability of customary international law to the IFIs is human rights. It is clear that the IFIs are not signatories to any human rights treaties. However, they are subjects of international law and specialized agencies of the UN. Consequently, it is reasonable ask if this leads to them having any human rights responsibilities or human rights obligations pursuant to applicable customary international law principles.

The first point to note is that as specialized UN agencies they are bound by .the principles of the UN Charter which state that one of the purposes of the UN is promoting respect for human rights.[52] This means that the IFIs have an obligation, at a minimum, to respect human rights in their operations and to ensure that they do not do anything to undermine the ability of their member states to respect human rights.[53] They are also required to comply with the Universal Declaration of Human Rights (UDHR)[54] which states that every 'organ of society' should encourage respect for human rights.[55] The IFIs are clearly identifiable as 'organs of society'.

It is important to note that the UDHR is formally a declaration and not a treaty which means that it does not directly impose any obligations on any subject of international law. However, since it was adopted in 1948, its status has grown dramatically. It is recognized and supported by all states and all international organizations. In addition, many corporations refer to it in their human rights, labour and social responsibility policies.[56] In fact,

[51] See, eg, 'IMF Strategy Toward Mainstreaming Gender' available at <https://www.imf.org/en/Publications/Policy-Papers/Issues/2022/07/28/IMF-Strategy-Toward-Mainstreaming-Gender-521344> (accessed 10 November 2022).

[52] UN Charter, Preamble and Art 1.

[53] UN Charter, Art 2.

[54] The United Nations Universal Declaration of Human Rights 1948 (UDHR), available at <https://www.un.org/en/about-us/universal-declaration-of-human-rights>.

[55] UDHR, Preamble.

[56] eg, 'Barclays Bank Statement on Human Rights November 2016' <https://home.barclays/content/dam/home-barclays/documents/citizenship/our-reporting-and-policy-positions/policy-positions/Barclays-Statement-on-Human-Rights-2016.pdf> (accessed 20 June 2023) ; and 'Microsoft Global Human Rights Statement' <http://download.microsoft.com/download/7/4/C/74C9403C-12BC-4037-B4DF-17750C617871/Microsoft%20Global%20Human%20Rights%20Statement%20English%20Sept%202013.pdf> (accessed 21 June 2023).

its status is such that some commentators contend that its contents have achieved the status of customary international law.[57] Many others contend that this does not mean that all its provisions should be construed as having this status. Instead, they maintain each right claimed in the document must be assessed separately to see if it meets the two-part test required of all customary international law principles. They would further contend that not all thirty provisions of the UDHR satisfy this test.[58]

This is not the place to undertake a comprehensive analysis of which provisions in the UDHR have acquired customary international law status. However, it is clear that one of the principles that has acquired this status is the right of access to an effective remedy in cases of harm.[59]

IFIs and an effective remedy

As the case law indicates there are a variety of ways in which the IFIs can comply with this standard of law.[60] The key requirement is that it should offer all those parties who claim they have been harmed by the IFIs an effective remedy of some sort.

However, at this point it is useful to assess to whom the IFIs do offer an effective remedy. In this regard, it is helpful to consider each of their various categories of stakeholders separately and to consider what sort of remedy the IFIs offer each of them. It is important to note that an effective remedy, at a minimum, means that the stakeholder has an opportunity to have their claims that they have been wronged addressed. Ideally the remedy will involve a hearing in some form on their claim. In addition, it should result in the complainant obtaining, if appropriate, some form of relief—this could include having the offending conduct stopped, the harm that the

See also some industry standards, for example, Principles on Responsible Investing: https://www.unpri.org/sustainability-issues/environmental-social-and-governance-issues/social-issues/human-rights (accessed on 21 June 2023); <https://www.unpri.org/>, Equator Principles (EPs) <https://equator-principles.com/about-the-equator-principles/ /> (accessed on 21 June 2023).

[57] H Hannum, 'The Status of the Universal Declaration of Human Rights in National and International Law' (1995) 25 Georgia Journal of International and Comparative Law 314–340.

[58] Bradlow, 'The World Bank, the IMF and Human Rights' (n 13).

[59] ibid. See, eg, D Bradlow, 'Using a Shield as a Sword: Are International Organizations abusing their Immunity?' (2016) 31(1) Temple International & Comparative Law Journal 45–68.

[60] See, for example, *Waite and Kennedy v Germany*, Merits, App No 26083/94, ECHR 1999-I.

complainant has suffered and the role that the perpetrator played in causing it acknowledged, the perpetrators held accountable, the awarding of compensation, or some combination of these individual forms of relief.[61]

The IFIs stakeholders to be considered in this section are their member states, their staff and management, their contractors, their investors, and those individuals and communities that are affected by their operations. The remedy offered to each of them is discussed below.

Member states

The member states have a number of channels through which they can seek to hold an IFI accountable. As members of the IFI, they are entitled to direct representation on its Board of Governors. In addition, they are represented on its Board of Executive Directors either directly or through membership in a Board constituency.[62] This means that they have channels through which they can raise their concerns about the organization and its operations and have them addressed at the highest levels in the organization. They also have rights pursuant to the Articles of Agreement of the organization. These rights would include the right to withdraw from the organization in the case of serious disputes.[63]

In the case of the WBG, the member states would have contractual rights in any loan or credit transaction they conclude with the WBG. In most loan agreements or credit agreements there is an arbitration clause that they could invoke in a dispute with the WBG regarding the particular transaction.[64]

This is not the case with the IMF which maintains that it does not have a contractual arrangement with the member states in the case of its standard

[61] ibid. See also A Reinisch and UA Weber, 'In the Shadow of Waite and Kennedy: The Jurisdictional Immunity of International Organizations, the Individuals Right of Access to the Courts and Administrative Tribunals as Alternative Means of Dispute Settlement' (2004) 1 International Organizations Law Review 59–110.

[62] IBRD Articles, Art V Section 4; IDA Articles, Art VI Section 4; IFC Articles, Art IV Section 4; IMF Articles, Art XII Section 3.

[63] IBRD Articles, Art VI Section 1; IDA Articles, Art VII Section 1; IFC Articles, Art V Section 1; IMF Articles, Art XXVI.

[64] See, eg, Art IX Loan Agreement International Bank for Reconstruction and Development and Nacional Financiera, S.A. and Comision Federal De Electricidad (Mexico) dated 6 January 1949 available at <https://documents1.worldbank.org/curated/en/247811468045868546/pdf/multi0page.pdf> (accessed 9 February 2023).

financial arrangements which are financed from its general resources.[65] In these arrangements, the member state, if it feels it has not been treated appropriately, can decline the financing being offered by the IMF. It should also be noted that the IMF can decline to provide the member state with the financing if it does not satisfy the conditionalities associated with the financing. Unlike in the case of a loan agreement, this will have no legal consequences.

Staff and management

The staff and management are employees of the IFIs. Given the immunity of the IFIs, their employees, unlike most employees, cannot take their employer to court in any state. In addition, since they are not subjects of international law, they cannot bring an action against it in any international court. To avoid depriving their employees of their basic right of redress, the IMF and the WBG like many other international organizations, have established their own administrative tribunals to hear cases involving disputes with their employees. These administrative tribunals are given an independent status within the organization.[66] The Executive Directors appoints the judges to these tribunals. They are appointed for fixed terms and cannot be removed except for cause. These judges are usually retired judges from the member states. They have the power to hear and decide claims based on the organization's own employment policies and any applicable legal principles. Their decisions are final and are made publicly available. This means that over time, a body of precedent has been developed that can be used by employees and the IFIs to shape their employment contracts and relationships. The tribunals also have the authority, where appropriate, to award damages. The IFIs must respect and execute these awards.

[65] J Gold, 'The Relationship between the International Monetary Fund and the World Bank' (1981) 15 Creighton Legal Review 499, 522.

[66] CF Amerasinghe, 'The Future of International Administrative Law' (1996) 45(4) The International and Comparative Law Quarterly 773–795. See WBG Administrative Tribunal Rules 1980 and IMF Rules of Procedure of the Administrative Tribunal of the International Monetary Fund 2004.

Contractors and investors

The IFIs have multiple contractual arrangements. They enter into contracts to procure the goods and services they need in order to function. Since the IFIs are immune from suit, contractors are unlikely to enter into arrangements with the IFIs unless they are offered an alternate forum for resolving disputes. The IFIs provide this by including arbitration clauses in their agreements.[67] In most cases, however, the parties are likely to resolve their disputes through negotiation rather than arbitration.

The situation is somewhat different in the case of WBG bondholders. It was always envisaged that the WBG would finance its operations through issuing bonds on financial markets. It was understood that in order to do this, the WBG would need to provide the holders of these bonds with some means to hold the WBG accountable for non-performance of their contractual obligations. As a result, the Articles provide that each entity in the WBG can waive its immunity so that these investors can sue to enforce their contractual rights For example, Article X Section 3 of the IBRD's Articles states that:

> Actions may be brought against the Bank only in a court of competent jurisdiction in the territories of a member in which the Bank has an office, has appointed an agent for the purpose of accepting service or notice of process, or has issued or guaranteed securities.

This means, in effect, that when the entities in the WBG enter the financial market place they will be treated like any other debtor.[68]

Individuals and communities

In order to understand how the IFIs deal with their accountability to this category of stakeholder, it is helpful to discuss the IMF and WBG separately.

The projects financed by the WBG have the potential to adversely affect individuals and communities, sometimes with devastating effects. For

[67] See, eg, Section 3 World Bank Group Procurement Regulations for IPF Borrowers, available at <https://www.worldbank.org/en/projects-operations/products-and-services/brief/procurement-policies-and-guidance> (accessed 9 February 2023).

[68] See, eg, *World Bank Group v Wallace* [2016] 1 SCR 207.

example, large infrastructure projects can result in involuntary resettlements of communities, harm to indigenous communities, loss of the livelihoods of individuals and communities, loss of access to health services, education services, and serious environmental damage.[69] It is important to recognize that in these cases the WBG has only provided financing for the project. The ultimate responsibility for implementing and operating the project lies with the borrower and the project sponsor. However, each of the entities in the WBG, as indicated above, has detailed environmental and social policies in which it explains to the world how it deals with these aspects of its operations and what they can expect from it in this regard.[70] Thus, it is not unreasonable for communities and individuals to rely on these policies and to expect the WBG to comply with them. Consequently, they expect that they should be able to hold the WBG accountable when it fails to comply with these policies and this non-compliance causes them harm.[71] This expectation is independent of whatever responsibilities and obligations the borrower and the project sponsor have to the affected individuals and communities.

The challenge for these individuals and communities who feel that they have been harmed by the WBG's failure to comply with its own policies and procedures is identifying a forum in which they can seek to hold the WBG accountable for this non-compliance. They do not have a contractual relationship with the WBG and so do not have access to an arbitral forum as would be the case with aggrieved contractors and investors. In addition, because of the immunity of the WBG, they cannot seek redress in their domestic courts. In principle they could ask their government to raise their concerns through the channels available to member states seeking to hold the WBG accountable. However, given the requirement that the WBG only lend to member states or with the guarantee of their member state, it is likely that the member state is a supporter of the project. Consequently, it is

[69] See, eg, the description of the harm suffered by complainants in such cases investigated by the World Bank Inspection PaneLas *Kazakhstan: South-West Roads: Western Europe-Western China International Transit Corridor Project* (CAREC 1b & 6B)-P099270 24 December 2020 and IFC's CAO- *Bolivia—Comsur V-01/Bosque Chiquitano* 1 June 2003, available at <https://www.inspectionpanel.org/panel-cases> (accessed 15 March 2023).

[70] World Bank, 'Social and Environmental Framework' available at <https://www.worldbank.org/en/projects-operations/environmental-and-social-framework> (accessed 15 March 2023); IFC Environmental and Social Performance Standards <https://www.ifc.org/wps/wcm/connect/Topics_Ext_Content/IFC_External_Corporate_Site/Sustainability-At-IFC/Policies-Standards/Performance-Standards/> (accessed 21 June 2023).

[71] D Bradlow, 'International Organizations and Private Complainants: The Case of the World Bank Inspection Panel' (1994) 34 Virginia Journal of International Law 553.

extremely unlikely to be willing to raise the concerns of those citizens who have been adversely affected by the project with the WBG.

The WBG has sought to resolve this gap in its accountability by creating independent accountability mechanisms.[72] These mechanisms are authorized to accept and investigate complaints from communities and groups of individuals who claim they have been harmed by the failure of WBG staff and management to comply with the institution's operational policies and procedures. Based on these investigations, the mechanisms submit reports to the Board with their findings on compliance/non-compliance.

The situation with the IMF is more complex. Since it provides general budgetary support rather than project loans and its policy conditionalities are generally at a macro-economic level, it does not have similar detailed operational policies to those of the WBG. As a result, it is harder for communities and individuals to identify the standards of conduct with which it can expect the IMF staff and management to comply. It is also harder for them to demonstrate a causal link between the IMF's financing and the adverse effects that they suffer as a result of the IMF's support to their governments and the conditions attached thereto. This makes it easier for the IMF to avoid being held accountable by communities and individuals for any adverse impacts of their financing.[73] However, the IMF's need for an independent accountability mechanism is growing as it begins to pay more attention to such issues as climate change, gender, and inequality.[74]

The accountability of the IFIs to these individuals and communities is one of the more controversial issues arising from their operations and is explored in more detail in Chapters 5 and 6.

[72] It should be noted that the WBG has one independent accountability mechanism for the IBRD and IDA and a second mechanism for the IFC and MIGA. The World Bank Inspection Panel and the IFC's Compliance Advisor Ombudsman have different governance structures and mandates. These mechanisms are discussed in more detail in Chapter 6.

[73] A similar situation exists even if a visitor to the IMF, with which it has no contractual relationship, is harmed due to alleged IMF negligence. See, for example, *Nyambal v International Monetary Fund*, No 13-7115 (DC Cir 2014) and *Polak v IMF* 08-1416 (DC Cir 2009).

[74] See D Bradlow, 'The IMF needs an Ombudsman with Clout', Financial Times Alphaville, 6 October 2021, available at <https://www.ft.com/content/1c4ce23e-15f2-4461-b9f7-48a198276fe1> (accessed 10 November 2022).

Conclusion

This chapter has shown that the IFIs are subjects of international law. It has set out, in general terms, the international legal implications that follow from this status. Chapters 5 and 6 will build on these general principles. They will explain how they have affected the operations and policies and practices of the IFIs and their relations with their various stakeholders over time.

5

The Evolution of the World Bank

The participants of the Bretton Woods Conference would be very surprised at how their creation, the International Bank for Reconstruction and Development (IBRD), has evolved over time. It is now only one institution in the group of related international organizations known collectively as the World Bank Group (WBG, or Bank). The IBRD currently has almost four times more member states than it had when it opened its doors for business in 1946. In addition, the scope of its operations has expanded beyond providing financial support to infrastructure projects such as roads and dams sponsored by its member states to include funding for social infrastructure, such as primary health and education facilities, funding policy reforms, making debt and equity investments in private corporations in member states, and providing a broad range of advisory services to its member states.

These changes have not affected the status of the IBRD and its related entities as subjects of international law. Nevertheless, the structural and operational changes that have resulted in the formation of the WBG have had international legal consequences. This chapter will focus on these consequences. It is divided into three parts. The first part discusses the structural changes that the World Bank has undergone and their international legal implications. The second section focuses on the operational changes and their international legal implications. The third part is a conclusion.

Structural changes and their international legal implications

There were forty-four states that participated in the Bretton Woods conference, of which twenty-nine had ratified the Articles of Agreement and were members of the IBRD when it opened for business in 1946.[1] Many of these

[1] See ES Mason and RE Asher, *The World Bank since Bretton Woods* (The Brookings Institute Press 1973) 21–34. See D Kapur, P Lewis, and R Webb, *The World Bank: Its First Half Century,*

member states were European states that expected the IBRD to help them recover from the damage that they had suffered during the Second World War. Thus, the first loan that the IBRD made was $250 million (about $3.2 billion in 2022 dollars) to France in 1947 for the rehabilitation of its infrastructure.[2] The first IBRD loan to a developing country was to Chile in 1948.[3]

The IBRD's initial loans to France and other European countries, despite complying with the political prohibition in its Articles of Agreement, highlighted the political sensitivities associated with the IBRD's operations. This follows from the fact that money is fungible. This meant that these initial loans to France and other European borrowers while formally being to fund particular projects, in effect, freed up fiscal space that they could use for other purposes, such as their ultimately unsuccessful efforts to maintain their colonial empires.[4]

The membership of the Bank began to expand rapidly as former European colonies gained their independence and sought to join the leading international organizations, including the IBRD. Its membership underwent another significant increase following the end of the Cold War, when the countries that had been part of the Soviet bloc joined the Bank. Today, 189 states are members of the IBRD.[5]

It is important to note that the mere increase in the number of member states has not changed either the criteria for membership in the IBRD or the rights and obligations of members. It also has not, on its own, affected the Bank's international legal rights and obligations. Nevertheless, the increase in the number of member states has resulted in changes in the governance

vol. 1 & 2 Perspectives (The Brookings Institution Press, 1997) p 57–80. For the list of countries that initially ratified the agreement see The Editors of Encyclopaedia Britannica, *International Bank for Reconstruction and Development. Encyclopedia Britannica* (2011) <https://www.britannica.com/topic/International-Bank-for-Reconstruction-and-Development> (accessed 25 February 2022). See also PY Lipscy, 'Explaining Institutional Change: Policy Areas, Outside Options, and the Bretton Woods Institutions' (2015) 59(2) American Journal of Political Science 341–356.

2 World Bank Archives, 'Digitized Records of the World Bank's First Loan' <https://www.worldbank.org/en/archive/history/exhibits/Digitized-Records-World-Bank-First-Loan> (accessed 16 February 2022).

3 World Bank Archives, '1946-1967 The World Bank as a Builder and Engineer' <https://www.worldbank.org/en/archive/history> (accessed 16 February 2022).

4 B Rich, *Mortgaging the Earth: The World Bank, Environmental Impoverishment, and the Crisis of Development* (Routledge 1994).

5 World Bank, 'Who we are' <https://www.worldbank.org/en/who-we-are#:~:text=With%20189%20member%20countries%2C%20staff,shared%20prosperity%20in%20developing%20countries> (accessed 16 February 2022); and Kapur, Lewis, and Webb (n 1).

of the organization. It has also led to changes in the relationship between the Bank and its individual member states. These developments, in turn, have had international legal implications.

Implications for WBG governance

First, the increased membership made it necessary to increase the size of the Executive Board of the Bank. Initially the Board consisted of twelve Executive Directors(ED) .[6] As discussed in Chapter 3, each of the five largest shareholders in the Bank appointed one of the Executive Directors. The remaining seven Executive Directors each represented a constituency of member states. While there was variation in the size of these constituencies on average, each ED represented about five member states. Today, the Board consists of twenty-five members, representing 189 member states.[7] Seven of the Executive Directors represent single countries. The remaining nineteen EDs each represent a constituency made up of some of the remaining 182 member states. This means on average they each represent constituencies of about ten member states. The size of these constituencies, in fact, varies from two to twenty-three member states.

These Executive Directors perform two functions. First, they are the Board of the Bank and are responsible for the governance of the institution.[8] In this capacity they are required to provide strategic guidance to the institution, approve each of the Bank's loans, and to oversee the management and staff of the institution. In this regard, each Executive Director owes their loyalty to the Bank and the member states are expected to respect their independence and avoid pressuring them to act contrary to their obligations to the Bank.[9]

Second, de facto, each Executive Director is expected by the member states that appoint them to advance the interest of those member states. This expectation is complicated by the fact that each Executive Directors only has one vote in the Board.[10] Consequently, they are unable to fully represent whatever divergent views may exist within their constituency.

[6] World Bank, 'Board of Directors' <https://www.worldbank.org/en/about/leadership/directors> (accessed 16 February 2022). See also IBRD Articles, Art V Section 4(b).

[7] ibid.

[8] IBRD Articles, Art V Section 4(a).

[9] IBRD Articles, Art V Section 4(a) and (e).

[10] IBRD Articles, Art V Section 3 and Section 4(g).

This dual role has two implications. First, it means that those Executive Directors that represent their own countries or represent small constituencies can more easily engage with the member states they represent than those representing large constituencies.[11] Consequently, they can more easily understand their concerns and represent their views at the Board. Conversely, those Executive Directors that represent large constituencies have a more attenuated relationship with the member states in their constituency. This, in turn, suggests that these countries are less likely to know about and fully understand the key policy issues at the Bank, and to be able to convey their views and concerns to the relevant Executive Director and have them raised at the Board. This also makes it harder for them to hold the Bank management and staff accountable for their actions and decisions affecting the country. This is particularly noteworthy because many of the countries in this position are those that are the consumers of the Bank's services. This means that the poorest and weakest member states, who are among the most dependent users of Bank services, have the smallest and softest voice in Bank decision-making and the least ability to hold the Bank accountable for the decisions that it makes. It also means that the relative power of the richer and more powerful member states in the institution has grown commensurably with the increase in membership of the Bank.

The second implication of the expansion in Bank membership is that the services demanded by the Bank membership have changed.[12] The IBRD was initially expected to focus on providing funding for hard infrastructure projects, such as power projects, transportation projects, and water and sanitation projects. However, as its membership grew and the concerns of the new members began to shift towards dealing with the poverty, unemployment, and lack of access to services of their populations, the Bank began to shift its focus from reconstruction and hard infrastructure to poverty alleviation. Thus the Bank, in addition to funding hard infrastructure projects, began to fund agricultural, health, and education projects that were intended to help the borrowing state meet the basic needs of the residents of the state. It also began to provide general purpose development loans, in which the borrower's access to the financing was linked to implementing specific policy reforms. For example, the Bank might provide funding to

[11] D Bradlow, 'International Law and the Operations of the International Financial Institutions' in D Bradlow and D Hunter (eds), *International Financial Institutions and International Law* (Kluwer Law International 2010) 1–30.

[12] Kapur, Lewis, and Webb (n 1) 161. See also J Einhorn, 'The World Bank's Mission Creep' (2001) 80(5) Foreign Affairs 22–35.

reform the structure of the borrower's economy or its management of a particular sector and condition the disbursement of the funds on the borrower implementing particular policy reforms such as changing the labour laws in the country or changing the procedures for hiring and firing teachers.

This expansion in the range of Bank activities initially presented a legal challenge for the Bank. The reason was that the Bank's Articles stipulated that it should finance 'projects'.[13] However, the Articles do not contain a definition of this term. Thus, even though the original understanding was that projects referred to hard infrastructure, the Bank's lawyers opined that projects could include a broader range of activities so long as they were consistent with the purposes of the Bank as expressed in Article 1 of the Bank's Articles. This expansive interpretation allowed the Bank to continue broadening the range of activities that it financed. Today, the Bank defines a project to include any loan that will be used for a particular purpose.[14]

Implications for WBG financing operations

As the IBRD's membership grew both in numbers and the range of differences in their circumstances, it became clear that the IBRD's Articles of Agreement constrained its ability to satisfy all the needs of its growing membership. First, the Articles stipulated that the IBRD should raise the funds for its financing operations in financial markets.[15] Due to its capital structure and prudence as a financial institution, the IBRD came to be seen by investors as a prime borrower. This meant that it was able to raise funds at the cheapest available rates in financial markets. It could then on-lend these funds to its own borrowers at a slight premium over its cost of funds. This meant the IBRD could offer these borrowers more generous terms than they could get on their own from the same investors. However, the fact that it was raising funds at commercial rates and needed to repay its own debts to its investors meant that the IBRD could only offer its member states financing on terms that were too expensive for many of its poorer member states. Consequently, these states were unable to borrow from the IBRD. This in turn meant that they effectively obtained minimal real benefit from being members of the IBRD.

[13] IBRD Articles, Art III Section 1(a).
[14] IFI Shihata, *The World Bank Legal Papers* (Martinus Nijhoff 2000) 157–172.
[15] IBRD Articles, Art IV Section 1.

The IBRD's ability to fully support the development of its member states was also constrained by the fact that the IBRD, pursuant to its Articles, could only lend directly to its member states or to other borrowers if they were supported by the guarantee of a member state.[16] This meant that the IBRD could not easily support the development of the private sector in its member states.

In order to address these constraints, the member states agreed to create new institutions that were affiliated with, but legally independent from the IBRD. Each of these new entities were designed to serve a different developmental need of the IBRD's member states.

The creation of new entities and the formation of the WBG

The first of these institutions was the International Finance Corporation, which was established in 1956.[17] This institution provides debt and equity financing to private sector projects in those member states that are also eligible to borrow from the IBRD. All IBRD member states are eligible to join the IFC although not all have done so. Currently, the IFC has 184 member states. The President of the IBRD is also the president of the IFC. However, the organization's Executive Vice President functions as the chief executive officer of the IFC. It also has its own board, staff, and operational policies and procedures.[18] It is important to note that although technically the IFC has its own board of directors, its membership overlaps to a considerable degree with the Board of the IBRD.

The second institution was the International Development Association (IDA).[19] This institution was established in 1960 with fifteen member states. Today, the IDA has 174 member states.[20] There were two motivations for

[16] ibid.

[17] IFC, *The First Six Decades Leading the Way in Private Sector Development: A History* (2nd edn, 2016 IFC) 12–17 <https://www.ifc.org/wps/wcm/connect/5e70149f-6cad-407a-944e-69d392079b47/IFC-History-Book-Second-Edition.pdf?MOD=AJPERES&CVID=lIwwdJi> (accessed 17 February 2022). See also IFC Articles.

[18] 'IFC Policies and Standards' <https://www.ifc.org/wps/wcm/connect/topics_ext_content/ifc_external_corporate_site/sustainability-at-ifc/policies-standards> (accessed 17 February 2022).

[19] IDA Article 3.

[20] 'What is IDA?' <https://ida.worldbank.org/en/about>. See also, 'How Does the IDA Work?' <https://ida.worldbank.org/en/about/how-does-ida-work> (accessed 17 February 2022).

creating IDA. First, it was intended to respond to the fact that the poorest states could not afford IBRD financing. They needed an entity that could offer them long-term financing on heavily concessional terms. Second, the leading members states in the IBRD were concerned that many newly independent African and Asian member states and their allies in the non-aligned movement were organizing to create a Special United Nations Fund for Economic Development (SUNFED) that would provide concessional financing to the poorest UN member states.[21] These leading states were concerned that the SUNFED, which like all UN created agencies would be based on a one-country one-vote system, would take development financing outside their control. Consequently, as an alternative to a UN-based entity, they proposed to establish a similar entity in the orbit of the IBRD which would operate with the same weighted voting and governance arrangements as the IBRD.

The IDA was created as a legally independent lending window of the IBRD. However, the staff of the IBRD also act as the staff of the IDA. The IDA provides credits with no interest, but with a small administration fee, for long periods of time—initially 35–50 years—to all states that have a GDP per capita below a stipulated amount.[22] In FY2023, the stipulated amount was US$1255.[23] Unlike the IBRD, the IDA is primarily funded by grants from participating countries.[24] Given that it is a long-term concessional funder, IDA is not self-sustaining and has to be replenished approximately every three years. This means that its donors need to make budgetary allocations to IDA at least every three years. These funding arrangements make IDA particularly vulnerable to political pressure from its contributing member states. It is important to note that technically the IDA has its own board of directors but this overlaps to a considerable degree with the Board of the IBRD.

The third institution, established in 1966, was the International Centre for the Settlement of Investment Disputes (ICSID).[25] This is an independent

[21] DJ Shaw, 'Special United Nations Fund for Economic Development (SUNFED)' in DJ Shaw, *Sir Hans Singer: The Life and Work of a Development Economist* (Palgrave 2002) 72–90.

[22] 'What is IDA?' (n 20).

[23] See <https://ida.worldbank.org/en/about/borrowing-countries> (accessed 7 February 2023).

[24] In 2018, IDA began to issue bonds. See, "IDA Makes Historic Capital Market Debut with Inaugural US$1.5 Billion Benchmark Bond: First IDA bond nearly five times oversubscribed", available at: https://treasury.worldbank.org/en/about/unit/treasury/ida/ida-press-releases#:~:text=The%205%2Dyear%20bond%20marks,the%20end%20of%20the%20day. (accessed 21 June 2023)

[25] 'About ICSID' <https://icsid.worldbank.org/About/ICSID> (accessed 17 February 2022). See also ICSID Convention.

arbitral institution. It was established in order to try and encourage foreign direct investment in Bank member states by creating an alternative forum for resolving disputes between host states and their foreign investors. Over time ICSID has become an important, and controversial, forum for investor state dispute settlement.[26]

The fourth institution, which was created in 1988, is the Multilateral Investment Guarantee Agency (MIGA).[27] It also seeks to address perceived barriers to foreign investment. It provides insurance against political risk for foreign investors. Its focus is on providing insurance to foreign investors with the agreement of the host state. MIGA has its own management and staff.[28]

The result is that there are now five legally independent institutions in the World Bank Group. Over time, they have begun to function more as an inter-connected group of entities rather than as a group of siloed entities with common owners. The president of the IBRD also serves as president of each of these organizations, although the IFC and MIGA are both managed on a day-to-day basis by an official who functions as a chief executive officer. In addition, ICSID is headed by a Secretary General who is usually the General Counsel of the IBRD. There is considerable overlap in the constituencies of the different boards and so, for most purposes, the one board of Executive Directors operates as the board for the whole World Bank Group. The one exception to this arrangement is that ICSID is overseen by an Administrative Council, which is chaired by the President of the World Bank.[29]

The World Bank as trustee

The Bank has also sought to address the needs of its expanding membership by assuming the role of trustee for some trust funds established by member states. The Bank recently reformed the operation of its trust programme,

[26] A more detailed discussion of the legal issues relating to ICSID and investor state dispute settlement is outside the scope of this book. See, eg, A Parra, *The History of ICSI*, (2nd edn, OUP 2017).

[27] MIGA, 'About: History' <https://www.miga.org/history> (accessed 17 February 2022). See also MIGA Convention.

[28] A full discussion of MIGA is also outside the scope of this book. For a history of the creation of MIGA, see IFI Shihata, *MIGA and Foreign Investment* (Kluwer Law International 1988).

[29] ICSID Administrative Council <https://icsid.worldbank.org/about/member-states/administrative-council> (accessed 17 February 2022). See ICSID Convention, Art 5.

thereby reducing the number of trusts that it manages from 554 trusts to seventy-one umbrella trusts.[30] The Bank's trust programme allows the Bank and its richer member states to fund operations that may otherwise be precluded by its Articles of Agreement. For example, a single state or a group of states can establish and contribute funding to a trust that is mandated to finance particular types of activities or to provide financing to designated beneficiaries according to the terms and conditions stipulated by the donor states. The Bank acts as the trustee for this trust and is responsible for ensuring that the funds are used in the stipulated manner.[31]

These trusts provide the WBG with some operational flexibility. Some of the member states, for example, created a trust, with the World Bank as trustee, to fund activities in Palestine since Palestine is not a member of the WBG.[32] It has also used the trust mechanism to provide funding for such purposes as research activities and human rights promotion in member states.[33] Another example is that a group of states agreed to fund the Global Environmental Facility on this basis.[34]

Finally, it should be noted that according to the Bank's international competitive bidding rules,[35] companies from all its member states are eligible to bid for contracts financed by Bank loans from its general resources. However, in the case of the trust funds, the donor of the trust can impose any conditions on the use of the funds that the WBG is willing to accept. For example, it can stipulate that only companies from specified countries can bid for such contracts.

[30] World Bank Group Umbrella Newsletter, 'Moving From Design To Delivery' April 2021 <https://thedocs.worldbank.org/en/doc/550096d2ff0971a0a85c91d670ceb02f-0060052021/original/Umbrella-Newsletter-April-2021.pdf> (accessed 18 February 2022).

[31] SE Smyth, 'Collective Action for Development Finance' (2011) 32 University of Pennsylvania Journal of International Law 961 p 1034–1035.

[32] World Bank Featured, 'Palestinian Recovery and Development Plan Multi-Donor Trust Fund' <https://www.worldbank.org/en/programs/palestinian-recovery-and-development-program-trust-fund> (accessed 7 February 2023).

[33] See B Fredriksen, *NETF: The Norwegian Education Trust Fund Supporting Education in Africa 1998-2004* (WBG 2004) 1–6. See also the World Bank Group 2004 Trust Funds Annual Report 10–16.

[34] 'GEF: Who we are' <https://www.thegef.org/who-we-are> (accessed 18 February 2022). See also R Melati, 'The Strategies of United Nations Development Programme (UNDP) With Global Environmental Facility (GEF) To Promote Sustainable Land Management' (2022) 7(1) Jurnal Ilmiah Indonesia 384–395.

[35] <https://www.worldbank.org/en/projects-operations/products-and-services/brief/procurement-new-framework>.(accessed 21 June 2023)

Operational issues

As indicated above, the work of the World Bank Group has changed dramatically. Over time, it has expanded both the range of projects that it funds and the diversity of services that it offers its member states. One unusual example of the range of services that the Bank has offered is that the President of the Bank used his good offices in the 1960s to help India, a founder member of the IBRD, and Pakistan, which joined the Bank in 1950, to negotiate the treaty that resolved their dispute about the management of the Indus River.[36]

More controversially, in the 1980s the World Bank began a programme of policy-based lending, which meant that it provided *general* budget or sectoral financing in return for the borrower satisfying certain policy conditions.[37] These loans were initially known as structural adjustment and sectoral adjustment loans but are now referred to as development policy loans.[38] This was controversial for two reasons. First, pursuant to the articles, the Bank was only expected to provide loans for non-project purposes in 'special circumstances'.[39] However, the Bank has interpreted this term expansively. In fact, an increasing number of the Bank's loans contain policy conditions. For example, in 2005, policy-based lending constituted about 25 per cent of the Bank's lending portfolio for the year. In addition, another approximately 25 per cent of the portfolio contained policy related conditions in project loans.[40] As noted above, the Bank has also accommodated this expansion in its lending operations by adopting an expansive definition of the term 'project'. In effect, any loan that is for a specified purpose can be treated as a project loan.[41]

Second, the policy conditions attached to its operations were in themselves controversial. They were viewed as promoting a particular neoliberal ideology and thus as being used to shape the development trajectory

[36] See Mason and Asher (n 1) 610–620. The text of the 'Indus Water Treaty' (1960) is available at <https://treaties.un.org/doc/Publication/UNTs/Volume%20419/volume-419-I-6032-English.pdf> (accessed 18 June 2022).

[37] Kapur, Lewis, and Webb (n 1) 449–580.

[38] World Bank Development Project Financing <https://www.worldbank.org/en/what-we-do/products-and-services/financing-instruments/development-policy-financing> (accessed 18 February 2022).

[39] IBRD Articles, Art III Section 4(vii).

[40] World Bank, *Review of World Bank Conditionality* (2005) <https://documents.worldbank.org/en/publication/documents-reports/documentdetail/228751468134390047/review-of-world-bank-conditionality> accessed 7 February 2023.

[41] Shihata (n 14).

of the borrower state to suit a particular view of the appropriate relationship between states and markets and of the international economic order. In addition, some of the conditions were viewed as constituting undue interference with the sovereign policy-making prerogatives of the Bank's borrowers and, as such, amounted to affronts to the sovereignty of the member states.[42]

The social and environmental impacts of Bank operations

The Bank's relationship with its member states has also been altered by changing perceptions of the WBG's responsibility for the environmental and social impacts of the activities that they fund or sponsor.[43] The founding parents of the Bank, at least implicitly, incorporated a narrow view of its responsibility in this regard into the Articles of Agreement. This perception was based on the contemporaneous vision of how financial transactions with sovereign borrowers should be negotiated. At the time that the IBRD commenced its operations, the general view was that any entity that was contemplating providing financing to a sovereign borrower would limit its assessment of the borrower's creditworthiness to a range of economic and financial considerations.[44] It would look at the purpose for which the borrower was seeking to raise funds, the borrower's ability to actually achieve the intended purpose, and whether or not the purpose would enable the borrower to generate the revenue stream needed to repay the funds according to the agreed terms.[45] Other issues, such as the social and environmental impacts of these projects, were seen as falling within the sovereign prerogatives of the borrower. Consequently, they should be treated as being outside the scope of the creditor's negotiations with the borrower. The Articles sought to formalize this approach by stipulating that the Bank should only engage with the borrower through a designated authority such as the Ministry of Finance, that it was prohibited from taking political

[42] Kapur, Lewis, and Webb (n 1) 449–580.

[43] R Wade, 'Greening the Bank: The Struggle over the Environment 1970-1995' in Kapur, Lewis, and Webb (n 1) 611–730.

[44] D Bradlow, 'Differing Conceptions of Development and the Content of International Development Law' (2005) 21 South African Journal on Human Rights 47–85.

[45] IBRD Articles, Art III Section 5(b).

considerations into account in its decision-making and that only economic considerations should be relevant to the Bank's decision to lend.[46]

This neat division of areas of responsibility between the Bank and its borrower began to break down for three reasons. The first was that Bank's expanding range of activities pushed Bank officials to pay more attention to the impacts of the projects that it funded on such issues as poverty alleviation and, in at least some projects, on the environmental implications of its projects.[47] Moreover, because these projects were intended to—and did—directly affect the lives and wellbeing of specific communities, they and the civil society groups with which they interacted became more aware of the role that the Bank was playing in their lives. They also became interested in learning more about the role of the Bank. This necessarily meant that the neat division between 'appropriate' topics for Bank discussion and topics deemed outside the scope of Bank concerns began to break down.

Second, the global understanding about the responsibilities of foreign investors, including financial institutions, for the environmental and social impacts of their operations began to change.[48] In particular, it began to be viewed as irresponsible for investors and financial institutions to make decisions about their operations without assessing and accounting for the environmental and social impacts of their operations on the communities and states in which they operate. This changing view of the responsibilities of financial institutions also pushed the Bank to pay more attention to these issues. These environmental and social issues became more salient for the World Bank Group as concerns about the impacts of controversial projects funded by the WBG grew.

Third, growing global concerns about human rights had an impact on the Bank and its operations.[49] In particular, human rights advocates began to question the appropriateness of the Bank lending to states that were accused of serious human rights violations. They argued that the Bank, by lending to these states, was facilitating these violations and, as a result, it could be found to be complicit in these states' breaches of their international human

[46] ibid.

[47] See Kapur, Lewis, and Webb (n 1) 449–580. See also, Rich (n 4) 1–22.

[48] Bradlow (n 44) 47–85.

[49] D Bradlow, 'The World Bank, the IMF, and Human Rights' (1996) 6 Transnational Law & Contemporary Problems 48–89; S Skogly, *Human Rights Obligations of the World Bank and the IMF* (Cavendish 2001) 1–14; M Darrow, *Between Light and Shadow: The World Bank, The International Monetary Fund and International Human Rights Law* (Hart 2006); M Darrow, 'Book Review: Human Rights Accountability of the World Bank and IMF: Possibilities and Limits of Legal Analysis' (2007) 12(1) Social & Legal Studies 12(1) 133–144.

rights treaty obligations. In some cases, these advocates called on the Bank to stop lending to particular states because of the widespread nature of their human rights violations. In other cases, they called for the Bank to pay more attention to the human rights problems, including those caused by the bad governance practices and the corrupt practices of its member states.

The World Bank and human rights

The human rights issue posed a complex legal challenge for the Bank. As discussed in Chapter 4, Article IV(10) of the Bank's Articles of Agreement states that the Bank is precluded from taking political considerations or the political character of the borrowing state into account in its decision-making.[50] This prohibition is strengthened by two other provisions in its Articles. The first states that the bank must only take economic considerations and the borrower's ability to repay the loan into account in its decision-making.[51] The second states that the staff and officers of the Bank owe their loyalty to the Bank and that the member states should refrain from trying to influence them.[52]

The challenge for the Bank and its stakeholders is that the Articles do not define what is mean by either economic or political considerations or the political character of its member states. As a result, the Bank and its various stakeholders have argued about how to interpret these provisions. While the issue has not yet been fully resolved, particularly in regard to human rights, some clarity has been gained through practice.

This issue of how to interpret the political prohibition first became controversial in the 1960s when the IBRD proposed to make loans to apartheid South Africa and to the Portuguese government for a project in Mozambique, which at the time was a Portuguese colony and was experiencing a bitter independence struggle.[53] The UN General Assembly, which viewed the situation in these countries as constituting threats to

[50] IBRD Articles, Art IV(10) states: 'The Bank and its officers shall not interfere in the political affairs of any member; nor shall they be influenced in their decisions by the political character of the member or members concerned. Only economic considerations shall be relevant to their decisions, and these considerations shall be weighed impartially in order to achieve the purposes stated in Article I.'

[51] IBRD Articles, Art III.

[52] IBRD Articles, Art V Section 5(c).

[53] SA Bleicher, 'UN v. IBRD: A Dilemma of Functionalism' (1970) 24(1) International Organization at 31–47.

international peace and security, called for sanctions against their two governments. As part of the resolution, it particularly asked international organizations to refrain from lending to them. The World Bank, relying on its own Articles of Agreement and its Relationship Agreement[54] with the UN, refused to accede to this request. The UN General Assembly responded by calling on the World Bank to explain its refusal to comply. After some hesitation, the World Bank sent its General Counsel to meet with the UN and to explain why, pursuant to its Articles, it believed it should not comply with the request. The General Counsel, referring to the provisions in the IBRD Articles dealing with political affairs, explained that the Bank was precluded by its Articles from taking political considerations or the political character of its member states into account in its lending decisions. Furthermore, the project for which the countries were seeking Bank finance, was, in economic, technical, and financial terms, a creditworthy project. Thus, since the Bank was obliged to comply with its own Articles and to respect the sovereign prerogatives of its member states, it was acting responsibly in funding the project. The General Counsel also argued that pursuant to the Relationship Agreement, the UN was expected to consult with the World Bank before taking any actions that directly affected the Bank and that the UN had not engaged in such consultations.[55]

Many of the delegates to the UN reacted to this argument by contending that the policies followed by these governments were threats to regional peace and security and so were not mere 'political considerations'. Moreover, the project that the Bank was proposing to fund was intended by the borrowers to entrench their power. Consequently, the proposed project involved a sufficiently substantial risk to peace and security in the region that the UN's requests that the Bank should refrain from making the loan should take precedence over the Bank's concerns with avoiding making political loans.

The issue was not resolved and the Bank went ahead and concluded the loan agreements. However, this was the Bank's last loan to Portugal for projects in its colonies and to South Africa until it became a democratic state in

[54] 'Agreement Between the United Nations and the International Bank for Reconstruction and Development (1948)' <https://timeline.worldbank.org/themes/timeline/pdfjs/web/viewer.html?file=%20%20%20%20%20%20%20%20%20%20%20/sites/timeline/files/timeline/archival-pdfs/event12_UNagt_agreement_30151254.pdf> (accessed 22 February 2022).

[55] Art IV (I-3) Agreement Between the United Nations and the International Bank for Reconstruction nd Development 1948.

1994. In addition, since that time the UN General Assembly has not made similar requests to the WBG.

It is important to note that the Bank has always recognized one case in which it is obliged to follow the lead of the UN. This obligation arises when the UN Security Council has imposed sanctions on a state pursuant to resolutions adopted under Chapter VII of the UN Charter. The WBG has recognized that in these cases, where the UN is taking action to deal with a threat to international peace and security, it is obliged to refrain from taking any action that would contravene the UN Security Council resolution. In addition, it has noted that each of its member states, pursuant to such resolutions, are also obliged to oppose any proposed loans to the targets of the sanctions. Consequently, they could not vote to support a Bank loan to the target member state.[56]

The issue of the interpretation of the political prohibition in the WBG Articles has still not been fully resolved. As indicated, initially the WBG viewed all human rights issues as political issues and so outside its mandate. Over time, however, it has changed its position to the extent that it has argued that its development mandate which it now interprets as being focused on poverty alleviation means that it is promoting economic and social rights but that it cannot take responsibility for promoting more political rights.[57] In addition, it has acknowledged that it can deal with a range of governance issues provided they can be shown to have direct economic effects.[58]

It should be noted that the issue of the Bank's capacity to deal with human rights issues has presented a significant legal challenge for the Bank. There have been a number of separate legal opinions on the topic. Different General Counsels have issued formal legal options and have made public statements on the issue.[59] As a result, over time the Bank has expanded the range of issues, generally viewed as human rights issues, that the Bank

[56] Shihata (n 14).

[57] G Sarfaty, *Values in Translation: Human Rights and the Culture of the World Bank* (Stanford 2012) 1–18.

[58] IFI Shihata, 'The World Bank and "Governance" Issues in its Borrowing Members', in IFI Shihata, *The World Bank in a Changing World: Selected Essays* (Martinus Nijhioff 1991) 53–96.

[59] For the opinion of former World Bank General Counsels on the issue, see IFI Shihata, 'The World Bank and Human Rights: An Analysis of the Legal Issues and the Record of Achievements' (1988) 17 Denver Journal of International Law & Policy 39–60; R Danino, 'Legal Opinion on Human Rights and the Work of the World Bank', Senior Vice President and General Counsel (27 January 2006) 1–8 <https://opil.ouplaw.com/view/10.1093/law-oxio/e215.013.1/law-oxio-e215-regGroup-1-law-oxio-e215-source.pdf>; A Palacio, 'The way forward: Human Rights and the World Bank', World Bank Institute, October 2006.

considers to be within its decision-making authority. These issues included the treatment of people being involuntarily resettled in the course of a Bank funded project, the treatment of indigenous people in Bank operations, the procedures for consultation with affected communities, and the impact of Bank operations on the health, education, housing and welfare of the communities affected by its operations.[60] The Bank also pays more attention to the environmental impacts of its projects and these in turn raise concerns about the rights of access of communities to water, clean air, and land. However, in dealing with all these issues, the Bank has usually taken great care to avoid explicitly and formally acknowledging that it is dealing with human rights issues and that it might have any specific responsibilities under international human rights law in regard to these issues.[61] In fact, it is quick to note that it is not a signatory to any human rights treaty and so is not bound by any such treaty.

This view has been challenged by numerous outside stakeholders. These include the UN High Commissioner on Human Rights and the Human Rights Council's special rapporteurs.[62] All of these officials have contended that human rights are a question of international importance. They are a binding obligation on those states that are signatories to international human rights conventions—and all states have signed at least some human rights treaties. Consequently, the WBG has an obligation to respect these states' obligations and to not do anything that could undermine the efforts of states to comply with these obligations. Moreover, some experts have argued that some human rights have achieved the status of customary international law and so are binding on all states and on international organizations like the WBG. Consequently, these experts argue, human rights in general should not be viewed as a political issue but as an international legal requirement that the WBG must respect and seek to promote.[63]

60 These issues are addressed in the Bank's operational policies. See World Bank Environmental and Social Policies <https://www.worldbank.org/en/projects-operations/environmental-and-social-policies> (accessed 22 February 2022).

61 World Bank Environmental and Social Framework <https://www.worldbank.org/en/projects-operations/environmental-and-social-framework> (accessed 23 February 2022). See P Dann and M Riegner, 'The World Bank's Environmental and Social Safeguards and the Evolution of Global Order' (2019) 32 Leiden Journal of International Law 537–559.

62 Report of the Special Rapporteur on extreme poverty and Human rights A/70/274 4 August 2015 1–18. See also P Alston and M Robinson, 'The Challenges of Ensuring the Mutuality of Human Rights and Development Endeavours' in P Alston and M Robinson (eds), *Human Rights and Development Towards Mutual Reinforcement* (Oxford 2005) 3–17.

63 Brief of Amicus Curiae Professor Daniel Bradlow in Support of Plaintiffs-Appellants (*Jam v IFC*) 16 August 2016 1–33 <https://earthrights.org/wp-content/uploads/2016-08-17_amicus_for_appellant_dckt_.pdf> (accessed 23 February 2022). See also D Bradlow, 'Using

It is important to note that many Bank member states do not accept this interpretation. Consequently, the issue remains controversial. Moreover, the Bank's position is likely to continue evolving as the Bank engages more actively with environmental issues such as climate change, and social issues like inequality.

Participation and accountability in Bank operations

It is important to note that, given its financial clout, both the policy conditions that the Bank attaches to its structural and sectoral adjustment loans and the growing number of environmental and social conditions that it incorporates into the terms of its project loans made the Bank, in effect, an influential participant in the domestic policy-making processes of its member states. However, it began playing this role without any accountability to the citizens of those states.[64] This in turn raised concerns that the immunity of the Bank was being used more as a sword to ward off efforts to hold it accountable than as a shield to protect it from interference by its member states.[65]

This situation also contributed to many international civil society organizations becoming more interested in the World Bank. As these organizations began to learn more about the World Bank's operations and their profound social and environmental impacts, they began to oppose some prominent World Bank-funded projects[66]. For example, there were protests against particularly controversial projects funded by the Bank in countries like Brazil, India, and Indonesia.[67] These projects were having clear and incontrovertible adverse impacts on the environment and on large numbers

a Shield as a Sword: Are International Organizations Abusing Their Immunity?' (2017) 1 Temple International and Comparative Law Journal 45–67.

[64] D Bradlow, 'International Organizations and Private Complaints: The Case of the World Bank Inspection Panel' (1993) 34 Virginia Journal of International Law 34 553. <https://ssrn.com/abstract=1710662> (accessed on 21 June 2023).

[65] Bradlow, 'Using a Shield as a Sword' (n 63).

[66] See Rich, *Mortgaging the Earth* (n 4).

[67] ibid. See also N Woods, *The Globalizers: The IMF, the World Bank, and their Borrowers* (Cornell University Press 2006) and R Wade, 'Greening the Bank: The Struggle over the Environment, 1970-1995' in Kapur, Lewis, and Webb (n 1).

of people in the communities in which the projects were located. In short, these communities and civil society organizations argued that the Bank was complicit in projects that had such adverse characteristics as involuntary resettlements of communities, affecting the lives of indigenous communities without seeking their consent, causing damage to the livelihoods of individuals and communities, and reducing access to health and education services and environmental damage. The protesters also demonstrated that these adverse impacts were being imposed on the adversely affected communities without any consultations about the projects or compensation for the harm that they were suffering. In some cases, it was also clear that the Bank had known about the adverse impacts and had not taken any measures to mitigate them.

These protests resulted in reputational damage to the World Bank and in legislative inquiries into their operations. They also resulted in at least the implicit threat that legislatures in some member states would block funding to the World Bank Group, particularly IDA, unless the problems were addressed. In addition, community protests led the Bank to launch an independent investigation into one of its most controversial projects. The Bank's role in funding of the Narmada Dam project in India was investigated by the Morse Commission which found numerous shortcomings in the way in which the Bank had managed its engagement in the project. In addition, it found that the Bank staff and management had not shared all relevant information with the Board of the Bank and that, as a result, the Board was unable to effectively oversee the Bank's operations in India.[68]

These developments also contributed to the WBG's Board ordering an independent investigation, chaired by Willi Wapenhans, to look into the overall development effectiveness of the Bank's operations. The resulting Wapenhans report concluded that there was a loan approval culture in the Bank that led Bank staff to place a higher priority on concluding loan agreements than on ensuring that Bank-funded projects were actually effective in promoting development.[69]

[68] B Morse and TR Berger, *Sardar Sarovar: Report of the Independent Review* (Resource Futures International 1992). Also see, TR Berger, 'The World Bank's Independent Review of India's Sardar Sarovar Projects' (1993) 9(1) American University International Law Review 33–48.

[69] Records of the Portfolio Management Task Force (Wapenhans Report) and follow-up WB IBRD/IDA EXC-12-02-3426S October 1992 <https://archivesholdings.worldbank.org/records-of-portfolio-management-task-force-wapenhans-report-and-follow-up> (accessed 23 February 2022).

Increasing Bank transparency

These developments had two consequences. The first was that it increased demands for the Bank to become more transparent. This was deemed to be important so that outside stakeholders could learn about the Bank's operations and their impacts in a timely manner. This meant that they should learn about the environmental and social impacts of its operations when it was still possible to influence the scope and financing of the project and to mitigate or avoid their adverse impacts. Consequently, civil society organizations began to campaign for the Bank to publicly explain how it conducted its operations and to make the reports underlying its decision-making publicly available at a meaningful time. These campaigns raised the profile of the Bank in all its member states and led to legislatures in these member states becoming more interested in the Bank and in how their country's contributions to the Bank were being used. For example, the US Congress began looking into these issues and demanded that the project reports on which the Board ultimately based its lending decisions be made available to the Board members and their constituents at least 120 days in advance of the Board meeting on the project.[70]

The fact that this information is now made public before the Board takes the final decision to fund a project means that it is possible for interested stakeholders to learn about the project and raise their concerns about its impacts with the Bank management and its Board before the Bank finally commits to the project. This increases the possibility of mitigating the adverse impacts. It also allows civil society to lobby Board members and their own governments to oppose particular projects that they deem particularly harmful. This inevitably has politicized debates about the Bank and Bank-funded projects. For example, it has led the legislatures in rich countries, particularly the United States, to start attaching conditions to their financing for IDA.[71] These conditions can range from demanding that IDA

[70] See Appendix B: Text of the Pelosi Amendment in J Sanford and SR Fletcher, *CRS Report for Congress: Mulilateral Development Banks' Environmental Assessment and Information Policies: Impact of the Pelosi Amendment* (CRS 1998) at 108. See 22 USC 262m-7 (1990) - Assessment of environmental impact of proposed multilateral development bank actions. The 'Pelosi Amendment' requiring all international financial institutions, including the World Bank, to allow public inspection of the environmental impact statements for proposed loans 120 days before final approval and instructs the US representation on the boards of such institutions to vote against any loans that are not subjected to timely public scrutiny.

[71] Rich, *Mortgaging the Earth* (n 4); Kapur, Lewis, and Webb (n 1) 1119–1161.

increase funding for particular types of projects to wanting IDA to become less amenable to funding particular states.

One consequence of these developments was that civil society began demanding that the Bank make publicly available the operational policies[72] through which it informed staff about their responsibilities in their work in any particular lending operation. These policies included the first iterations of the Bank's approach to the environmental and social impacts of its operations. The Bank acceded to the demand to make its operational policies publicly available. It is important to recognize that while the policies, pursuant to internal Bank rules, may be mandatory for Bank staff, they are not binding on the borrower or any other actor unless they are incorporated into particular loan agreements or other agreements between the Bank and its member states. However, they can become implicitly binding on the borrowing state in the sense that unless they comply with those parts of the policies that may be applicable to their project or loan request, they may not secure the approval of the Board for the loan.

Another consequence was that the Bank developed an information disclosure policy.[73] This policy essentially states that all Bank documents are considered disclosable unless specifically determined to be confidential. The confidential category is limited to information that is proprietary, either for the Bank or its clients, or deemed too sensitive to disclose. In order to mitigate the risk of the Bank being unduly expansive in its interpretation of the exceptions to the information disclosure policy, the Bank has established an Information Disclosure Committee and an Information Disclosure Appeals Board.[74] These entities allow any person who believes that they have been unreasonably denied access to any information to complain against the decision and have it reviewed by these two bodies.

Increasing Bank accountability

A third consequence was that the affected communities and the civil society groups that work with them began to advocate for the Bank to become

[72] Available at <https://policies.worldbank.org/en/policies/operational-manual> (last visited 18 June 2022).

[73] 'The World Bank Policy on Access to Information' <https://policies.worldbank.org/en/policies/all/ppfdetail/3693> (accessed 7 February 2023).

[74] 'World Bank Access to Information Appeals Board' <https://www.worldbank.org/en/access-to-information/ai-appealsboard> (accessed 24 February 2022).

more accountable to those who had been harmed or threatened with harm by its projects. This demand faced two challenges. First, the WBG provides financing to a project. It does not implement the project. The ultimate responsibility for the project rests with the borrower and the member state. This suggests that it could be difficult to parse out to what extent the lender, the Bank, is responsible for the harm and to what extent the borrower is responsible. This is particularly complicated when the sovereign is involved in the project either as the borrower or the guarantor of the loan. The reason is that the sovereign borrower is likely to view any external interference in or oversight over its interactions with its own citizens as an affront to its sovereignty.

The second challenge was identifying a forum that was accessible to those groups of individuals or communities seeking to hold the WBG accountable. They cannot seek redress from the Bank in either their domestic courts or any other judicial forum because of the WBG's immunity from jurisdiction in its member states.[75] In addition, they cannot claim access to a comparable arbitral forum as that which is available to aggrieved contractors and holders of WBG bonds.[76] In the case of the latter two groups, their contracts with the WBG give them the right to have any dispute arising from their contract with the Bank heard in an arbitral forum. In principle the affected individuals and communities could ask their government to exercise their rights as member states to hold the WBG accountable. However, given the requirement that the IBRD and IDA only lend to member states or with the guarantee of their member state and that it is unlikely that the IFC or MIGA would support projects that the host member state opposes, it is probable that the member state is a supporter of the project that is the source of the harm. Consequently, the state is unlikely to be willing to take on the concerns of those citizens who claim they have been harmed by the project.[77]

To its credit, the WBG eventually recognized that there was a gap in its accountability structure. It recognized that, because it had publicly

[75] See Chapter 4. Also see, C Xu and G Bin, 'A Critique of Immunity for Multilateral Development Banks in National Courts' (2018) 4(1) The Chinese Journal of Global Governance 49–75; G Thallinger, 'Piercing Jurisdictional Immunity: The Possible Role of Domestic Courts in Enhancing World Bank Accountability' (2008) 2(1) ICL Journal 4–35. Also see, generally, A Reinisch, *International Organisations before National Courts* (Cambridge 2000) 127, 152–168.

[76] World Bank, *Contract Management Practice* (World Bank 2018), 42–46.

[77] D Bradlow (n 64); D Bradlow and S Schlemmer-Schulte, 'The World Bank's New Inspection Panel: A Constructive Step in the Transformation of the International Legal Order' (1994) 34 Zeitschrift fur auslandisches offentliches Recht und Volkerrecht 392–415.

available environmental and social policies in which it explains to the world how it deals with these aspects of its operations, it was, at least implicitly, representing to these stakeholders that they can expect the Bank staff and management to comply with the requirements of these policies in their operations. It was therefore not unreasonable for these external stakeholders to argue that the Bank should expect there to be consequences when it did not comply with these policies and this non-compliance was implicated in causing harm. It therefore began to look for ways to fill the accountability gap.[78]

Three proposals were made about how to make the Bank more accountable.[79] First, four executive directors proposed an internal mechanism that would make it easier for the Bank's Board to initiate investigations and hold the staff and management more accountable to the Board. Second, two civil society activists, David Hunter and Lori Udall, proposed creating an independent panel, comparable to the Morse Commission, that would be able to investigate complaints from affected communities regarding any Bank funded project.[80] The panel would have the authority to investigate any complaints relating to the financing, design, and implementation of the project and to hold the Bank and/or project sponsors accountable for any harm or threat of harm arising from the operation.

Third, Daniel Bradlow proposed that the Bank should create an ombudsman that would be authorized to investigate any complaint from any person who claimed that they had been harmed or threatened with harm by the Bank's failure to comply with its own operational policies and procedures.[81] The ombudsman would not have the authority to investigate the conduct of the borrower. Bradlow maintained that the ombudsman's exclusive focus on the activity of the Bank would avoid the risk of undermining the sovereignty of the borrower state while still allowing the Bank to be held accountable for its own conduct. In addition, by allowing an investigation of the social and environmental aspects of the project and their adverse consequences, the ombudsman would be able to address at least some

[78] IFI Shihata, *The World Bank Inspection Panel: In Practice* (2nd edn, World Bank 2000).

[79] ibid.

[80] D Hunter and L Udall, 'The World Bank's New Inspection Panel: Will It Increase the Bank's Accountability?' 1 CIEL Brief April 1994 1–6.

[81] D Bradlow, 'Why the World Bank Needs an Ombudsman', *Financial Times* 14 July 1993; and IA Bowles and CF Kormos, 'Environmental Reform at the World Bank: The Role of the U.S. Congress' (1995) 35 Virginia Journal of International Law 777.

of the concerns of the adversely affected complainants about the source of their harm.

Bradlow had an opportunity to present his idea in testimony to the Canadian Parliament[82] and the US Congress.[83] He also presented his ideas to a meeting of the World Bank's Board of Executive Directors and discussed them individually with most of the Executive Directors and with Dr Ibrahim Shihata, who was the Bank's General Counsel at the time.

After a concerted campaign by civil society organizations around the world and the support of key members of the US Congress,[84] who threatened to block financing to IDA, the World Bank Board acknowledged that it had a responsibility to those communities that were being harmed by its operations that was independent of the responsibilities of the project sponsor and its sovereign. In addition, it recognized that it needed some mechanism for investigating claims that the Bank had caused harm by not meeting these responsibilities, at least as defined in its own policies. It therefore decided to establish the Inspection Panel.[85]

The Inspection Panel

The Panel combined elements of all three proposals. It incorporated Bradlow's contention that there was a discrete area of unique Bank responsibility based on its non-compliance with Bank operational policies. It also gave adversely affected communities and groups of individuals the ability to request the panel to investigate claims that they have been harmed by the Bank's non-compliance with its own policies and procedures. It borrowed the idea of a panel to do the investigation from the Hunter–Udall proposal.

[82] D Bradlow, Opening Statement of Professor Daniel Bradlow to the Sub-Committee on International Financial Institutions of the Committee on Finance House of Commons, Parliament of Canada (18 February 1993).

[83] D Bradlow, 'The Case for a World Bank Ombudsman' submitted to the Sub-Committee on International Finance, Trade and Monetary Policy of the Banking, Finance and Urban Affairs Committee, U.S. House of Representatives, May 1993.

[84] The 15th Replenishment of the International Development Association (IDA) And) and the 11th Replenishment of the African Development Fund (AfDF), June 18, 2008 Hearing before the U.S. House of Representative Committee on Financial Services <https://www.govinfo.gov/content/pkg/CHRG-110hhrg44186/html/CHRG-110hhrg44186.htm> (accessed 26 February 2022).

[85] International Bank for Reconstruction and Development International Development Association Resolution No. IBRD 2020-0004 and Resolution No IDA 2020-0003, the World Bank Inspection Panel, 8 September 2020, 1–11.

Following the proposal of the executive directors it allowed a group of board members or the board as a whole to request an investigation.

The Inspection Panel was the first mechanism through which adversely affected communities could seek to hold an international organization accountable for its failure to comply with the policies that it had represented to the world would apply to its operations. This model of accountability mechanism has now been adopted by the largest multilateral development banks and some other international organizations.[86] It is important to note in this regard that the IFC and MIGA have their own mechanism, known as the Compliance Advisor Ombudsman (CAO).[87]

The establishment of the Inspection Panel had a number of implications for the operation of the Bank. The first was that it raised the profile of the Bank's operational policies and procedures. While they are formally only applicable to the Bank staff and management, they have come to be seen as establishing the standards that the Bank is expected to ensure that its clients also meet in their project-related activities. The second is that the risk of being held accountable by an independent body resulted in the Bank staff and management seeking to 'panel-proof' their operations by being able to demonstrate that they had complied with the applicable policies.[88]

Third, the Inspection Panel, in the course of conducting its investigations, needs to interpret these policies and procedures. Consequently, it has become a locus of contestation about the interpretation of the operational policies and about the responsibilities of the Bank. This, in turn, has made the Inspection Panel a channel through which human rights standards have come to be implicitly introduced into the Bank.[89] On rare occasions, the

[86] D Bradlow, 'Private Complainants and International Organizations: A Comparative Study of the Independent Inspection Mechanisms in International Financial Institutions' 36 Georgetown Journal of International Law 405 (2005). See 'CIEL Glass Half Full: The State of Accountability in Development Finance Report 2016' 24–60 <https://www.ciel.org/wp-content/uploads/2021/06/Glass-half-full.pdf> (accessed 26 February 2016).

[87] Compliance Advisor Ombudsman, 'Our Mandate' <https://www.cao-ombudsman.org/about-us> (accessed 26 February 2022).

[88] D Clark et al, *Demanding Accountability: Civil Society Claims and the World Bank Inspection Panel* (Rowman & Littlefield 2003) 1–35.

[89] AN Fourie, *World Bank Accountability: In Theory and in Practice* (Eleven 2016). See also AN Fourie, *The World Bank Inspection Panel Casebook: Cases from Inspection Panel* (Eleven 2014): and D Bradlow and AN Fourie, 'The Multilateral Development Banks and the Management of the Human Rights Impacts of their Operations' in S Deva and D Birchall (eds), *Research Handbook on Human Rights and Business* (Edward Elgar 2020); D Bradlow and MS Chapman, 'Public Participation and the Private Sector: The Role of Multilateral Development Banks in the Evolution of International Legal Standards' 4(2) Erasmus Law Review 92–125 (2011).

Panel has also become a mechanism for providing relief, including compensation, to individuals and groups who had been harmed by the Bank's failure to comply with its own policies and procedures.[90]

Another consequence of the establishment of the Panel was that external stakeholders began to demand the right to have an input into the formulation of the Bank's policies and procedures. This began first with the Board's management of the Panel's own operating policies and procedures.[91] In fact, the Board, in deciding to amend its approach to Panel procedings consulted with a number of stakeholders and changed its proposed amendments in response to the information it learned from these consultations.[92] In addition, the Bank's operational policies, particularly those dealing with environmental and social issues, have become more complex in the sense that they involve both mandatory and discretionary portions. In fact, the Bank followed a transparent and participatory process in formulating the most recent iteration of its environmental and social policies, Thus, the process for formulating the World Bank's current Environmental and Social Framework involved multiple meetings with stakeholders and multiple opportunities for public participation and submission of evidence/statements.[93]

The above developments have had one, perhaps unintended consequence. They have resulted in the World Bank playing a lawmaking role.[94] This follows from the fact that, in conducting its investigations, the Inspection Panel must both interpret and apply the Bank's policies. Since its cases deal largely with environmental and social issues, its reports provide concrete case studies on how a leading financial institution should understand its responsibilities in regard to the impacts of its operations. The issues that arise in these cases, as indicated above, involve such issues

[90] See, eg, Republic of Uganda Transport Sector Development Project—Additional Financing (P121097) Investigation Report 4 August, 2016 <https://www.inspectionpanel.org/sites/www.inspectionpanel.org/files/ip/PanelCases/98-Inspection%20Panel%20Investigation%20Report.pdf> (accessed 26 February 2022).

[91] Bradlow and Schlemmer-Schulte (n 77). See also Bradlow and Hunter, *International Financial Institutions and International Law* (n 11); B Kingsbury, 'Indigenous Peoples in International Law: A Constructivist Approach to the Asian Controversy' (1998) 92 The American Journal of International Law 414–457; and H Cissé, D Bradlow, and B Kingsbury, *International Financial Institutions and Global Legal Governance* (World Bank 2013) 33–57.

[92] D Bradlow, 'Lessons from the NGO Campaign against the Second Review of the World Bank Inspection Panel: A Participant's Perspective' (2000) 7 ILSA Journal of International & Comparative Law 247–257.

[93] P Dann and M Riegner, *The World Bank's Environmental and Social Safeguards and the Evolution of Global Order* (CUP 2019).

[94] JE Alvarez, *International Organizations as Law-makers* (OUP 2005) 235–257.

of international legal interest as compensation for people involuntarily resettled, rights of access to water and land, the meaning of free, prior informed consent in the case of indigenous people, and the appropriate scope and complexity of environmental impact assessments required for different types of projects. While the Panel reports are non-binding and have no formal application outside the context of the specific case, they are public and so influence the way in which these issues are addressed in other contexts. In addition, the procedures that the Bank has followed in updating and amending its policies are influencing the procedures followed by other international organizations in their own rulemaking procedures. In these ways the World Bank is creating the standards to which international organizations, governments, corporations, and civil society groups look in deciding on the appropriate roles and responsibilities of different actors in the development process, the content of the norms and standards that should guide their conduct, and on how to hold these actors accountable when they do not meet these standards.[95]

Conclusion

The above demonstrates that the World Bank has been a significant actor in the evolution of international law. It has impacted international law in three ways. First, it has had an influence on the relationship between international organizations, their member states, and their citizens. In this sense, it is an example of an international organization that is making global administrative law.[96] When the Bank was established, international organizations were viewed as having only a direct relationship with their member states. Outside of the context of contractual relationships, they were not expected to have a direct relationship with non-state actors in these states. Such a relationship was viewed as being tantamount to an inappropriate interference in the domestic affairs of a sovereign state. The evolution in the Bank's operations have however demonstrated that operational international organizations increasingly cannot avoid developing a direct relationship with the citizens of those states in which they operate. Moreover,

[95] EB Weiss, 'On Being Accountable in a Kaleidoscopic World' (2010) 104 American Society of International Law Proceedings 477–490. See O McIntyre and S Nanwani, *The Practice of Independent Accountability Mechanisms (IAMs)* (Brill 2019) 1–4.

[96] B Kingsbury, N Krisch, and RB Stewart, 'The Emergence of Global Administrative Law' (2005) 68 Law and Contemporary Problems 15–61.

it has demonstrated that through their financial power and the terms and conditions on which they lend, they are able to exert authority in such a way as to directly affect the welfare of these non-state actors. Consequently, it is not possible for the Bank, or any comparable international organization, to avoid incurring some degree of responsibility towards those non-state actors who may be harmed by its decisions and operations.[97]

Second, the Bank's operations have demonstrated that the lack of formal legal arrangements to govern its relationship with the non-state actors in its member states is problematic. This follows from the fact that the Bank, like all international organizations, has immunity from the jurisdiction of the domestic courts in its member states. This means that the Bank can avoid any responsibility for its actions, regardless of their impacts. In other words, the evolution in its operations has transformed its immunity from a shield into a sword.[98] The Bank has sought to address the consequences of this lack of immunity by creating the Inspection Panel and the CAO.

Third, the evolution in the Bank's operations has added a new dimension to its operations. In addition to being a source of finance for its borrowers, it is influencing how governments, companies and civil society view the content of the international norms and standards applicable to their rights and responsibilities in connection with the social and environmental impacts of development projects, policies, and activities. In this sense, the Bank is becoming a leading maker of international law, albeit of a soft law nature. However, it is important to note that often its 'soft' law is *de facto* hardened by the sanctions arising from its loan agreement and from the consequences flowing from the work of its independent accountability mechanisms. This in turn, over time, may affect how international lawyers, governments, and other actors view international soft law and its implications.[99]

[97] Bradlow and Hunter, *International Financial Institutions and International Law* (n 11).

[98] S Herz, 'Rethinking International Finance Institution Immunity' in Bradlow and Hunter, International Financial Institutions and International Law (n 11) 137–162; Fourie, 'World Bank Accountability' (n 87); and Bradlow, 'Using a Shield as a Sword' (n 61).

[99] See, eg, D Bradlow and D Hunter (eds), *Advocating Social Change Through International Law: Exploring the Choice between Hard and Soft International Law* (Brill Nijhoff 2020).

6
The Evolution of the International Monetary Fund

The IMF has changed substantially since its establishment in 1944. The most noteworthy development in its history occurred in 1971 when the par value system of fixed but flexible exchange rates that was agreed at the Bretton Woods conference ended. It caused the IMF to make significant adaptations in its functions and set in motion an ongoing process of expansion and evolution in the IMF's operations. This chapter focuses on this evolutionary process and its legal implications. It is divided into three parts. The first part describes some legal issues arising from the IMF's original design. The second part focuses on the legal issues relating to the operations of the IMF during the period in which most IMF member states complied with the requirements of the par value system. The third part discusses legal issues arising from developments in the IMF's functions and operating practices since the end of this system.

The original design of the IMF

When the IMF opened its doors for business in 1946, many of its member states were still recovering from the impacts of the Second World War. As a result, they were not in a position to assume all the obligations of IMF membership set out in the organization's Articles of Agreement. In particular, some of them were not able to comply with the obligation, stipulated in the original version of Article IV,[1] to fix and maintain a par value for their currencies in terms of the US dollar. Many members could also not assume the Article VIII(2)(a)[2] obligation to allow unrestricted payments on all current transactions.[3]

[1] IMF Articles, Art IV Section 3, Note that original Article IV was amended in 1978 to deal with the consequences of the end of the par value system. See discussion infra.

[2] IMF Articles, Art VIII.

[3] Examples of current transactions are payments for exports, and dividend and royalty payments to foreign investors. See IMF *Balance of Payments and International Investment Position Manual* (6th edn, IMF 2009) 222–236.

The drafters of the IMF Articles had anticipated this problem and so they established a transition process that states could follow before assuming the full obligations of IMF membership. Pursuant to Article XIV,[4] member states, after notifying the IMF of their intention, could maintain the restrictions on current transactions that they had in place at the time of joining the IMF. This helped them to protect their balance of payment position and to have the time and policy space they needed to determine a sustainable par value for their currencies and to permit unrestricted payments on current transactions. Article XIV allowed states to adapt their restrictions to changing circumstances but precludes them from introducing new restrictions.[5]

It is important to note in contradistinction to the requirement that states refrain from restricting current transactions, Article VI Section 3[6] of the Articles allowed member states, to impose controls on capital transactions, provided they did not adversely affect the free flow of payments on current transactions. The Articles do not contain definitions of either current or capital transactions.[7] They are usually ascribed their standard economic meanings.[8] However, the lack of precise definitions in the Articles, means that there is some flexibility around their interpretation. As discussed in Chapter 3, pursuant to Article XXIX,[9] the IMF's Executive Board has the authority to interpret the Articles, subject to appeal by dissenting member states to a committee of the Board of Governors.

Over the first approximately fifteen years of the IMF's existence, many of the original member states, in fact, were able to—and did—assume the full obligations of IMF membership.[10] It is important to note that, under Article VIII (2)(a) of the IMF Articles, once a member state accepted the obligations stipulated in Article VIII, it was precluded from imposing any new

[4] IMF Articles, Art XIV.

[5] IMF Articles, Art XIV.

[6] IMF Articles, Art VI Section 3.

[7] See Balance of Payments and International Investment Position Manual 2009, 216–220.

[8] IMF Balance of Payments Manual 1993 51, 77–82. The manual defines 'current transactions' are those transactions that are completed during the current period, usually one year, and 'capital transactions' are those that will take place over a longer period of time. From an economic standpoint, current transactions involve payments which are for the purpose of paying for goods and services and are not for the purpose of transferring capital while capital transactions are payment done with the purpose of transferring capital. See JG Evans Jr, 'Current and Capital Transactions: How the Fund Defines Them' (1968) 5(3) IMF Finance & Development 30–35.

[9] IMF Articles, Art XXIX.

[10] IMF Annual Report of the Executive Directors 1961, 135–137. By about 1958–60 most of the then member states had accepted Art VIII obligations.

restrictions on current transactions.[11] Instead, it was expected to follow monetary policies that were consistent with unrestricted payments on current transactions and the maintenance of the par value of its currency. In the event that it experienced such persistent payments imbalances that it became too difficult to maintain the par value of its currency, it was expected to make use of IMF financial and, if appropriate, technical support to deal with the problem. In the last resort and with prior IMF approval, it could devalue its currency.

The Articles sought to offer additional support to states that had liberalized their current transactions. Article VIII(2)(b)[12] states that:

> Exchange contracts which involve the currency of any member and which are contrary to the exchange control regulations of that member maintained or imposed consistently with this Agreement shall be unenforceable in the territories of any member.

The precise meaning of this provision is unclear because its key terms—such as 'exchange contracts' and 'involve the currency'—are not defined. However, its purpose appears to be to assure member states that if any member state is forced to impost exchange controls on current transactions, and it does so consistently with its IMF obligations, then all 'exchange contracts' which 'involve' the currency of that member state will be unenforceable in all other IMF member states if the contracts are contrary to the member state's exchange control laws.[13] The drafters of the IMF Articles expected that the prospect of having their compliant exchange controls respected by other member states, would incentivize member states to assume the full obligations of IMF membership.

The provision does seem to have had some effect in this regard. There are a number of law cases in which one party sought to justify its failure to pay on a particular contract by arguing that requiring them to make payment

[11] IMF Articles, Art VIII.

[12] IMF Articles, Art VIII(2)(b).

[13] J Gold, 'Article VIII, Section 2(b), of the Fund Agreement and the Unenforceability of Certain Exchange Contracts: A Note' in J Gold, *The Fund Agreement in the Courts*, vol I (1962) 60–69, 82. See also J Gold, *The Fund Agreement in the Courts, vol. IV: Some Problems of the Uniform Interpretation of Multilateral Treaties* (1989) 269–279; and WF Ebke, 'Article VIII, Section 2(b) of the IMF Articles of Agreement and International Capital Transfers: Perspectives from the German Supreme Court' (1994) 28 Journal of International Law 761–771 <https://scholar.smu.edu/cgi/viewcontent.cgi?article=3056&context=til> (accessed 19 May 2022).

would amount to a violation of Article VIII(2)(b).[14] The outcome of these cases tended to depend on how the courts interpret the term 'exchange contracts' or the meaning of the phrase 'involve the currency'. The ambiguity of these terms means that it was difficult to predict how courts would interpret these terms and what sort of evidence they would look at in determining how to interpret them.

It should also be noted that the provision became less relevant after the end of the Bretton Woods system when countries began to switch to floating exchange rates and liberalized their economies and financial systems in order to attract investment and finance. This meant, in fact, that countries tended to remove, or at least loosen, their remaining restrictions on both capital and current payments. As a result, Article VIII(2)(b) became less useful to states and offered less protection for people seeking to avoid making payments on international contracts.[15]

Overseeing the par value system

This period also saw the IMF establish its operational procedures for overseeing the international monetary system. Pursuant to the original Article IV, the member states were obliged to 'collaborate' with the IMF to promote exchange stability and promote orderly exchange arrangements with other member states.[16] In brief, this meant that the member state would adopt and implement policies designed to maintain the par value of its currency and would engage in discussions with the IMF about these polices. The IMF in implementing this mandate, adopted the practice of engaging in regular consultation missions with each of its member states about their policies for

[14] See, eg, *Wilson Smithett & Cope Ltd v Terruzzi* (1976) 1 QB 683 & *Sharif v Azad* [1967] 1 QB 605, (holding Art VIII(2)(b) to be enforceable in English courts); *Libra Bank Ltd v Banco Nacional De Costa Rica*, 570 F. Supp. 870 (S.D.N.Y) 1983; *Southwestern Shipping Corporation v National City Bank of New York* 1 Misc 2d 397 (NY App Div 1958) (holding Art VIII(2)(b) to be enforceable in US federal and New York state courts.) But see, *Batra v Ebrahim* [1982] 2 Lloyd's Rep 11, (holding that Art VIII (2b) is unenforceable in English Courts); *Confederation Life Association v Ugalde*, 164 So. 2d 1—Fla: Supreme Court (1964.) (holding Art VIII(2)(b) to be unenforceable in US sates courts); *Re: Hamburg Londgericht*, Case Chamber 12 for Commercial Affairs, Hamburg Landgericht (Unreported) and *Re: Oberlandesgericht* Judgment of 9 October 1992 [OLG] [Court of Appeals], Hamburg, Get., 39 RIW 68 (1993) (holding Art VIII (2)(b) to be enenforceable in German courts).

[15] This does not mean that the provision became irrelevant. See, eg, Ebke (n 13).

[16] IMF Articles, original Art IV.

maintaining the par value of their currencies.[17] The IMF's purpose in these regular consultations, often referred to as either surveillance or Article IV[18] missions, was to assess those macroeconomic policies of each member state that influenced the ability of the country to maintain the par value of its currency. Thus, the primary focus of the IMF was on such macroeconomic variables as exchange rates, interest rates, inflation rates, the balance of payments, and growth in money supply and credit.[19]

Given the nature of its responsibilities and the scope of its interests, it made sense for the member states to stipulate in the IMF's Articles of Agreement, that the IMF should limit its interactions with its member states to its central bank and ministry of finance. These were the two agencies in the member country that were responsible for its policies regarding the variables of interest to the IMF.

It was also during this period that the IMF developed the Standby Arrangement,[20] the instrument it used, and still uses, to providing financing to its members states. As discussed in an earlier chapter,[21] the IMF adopted the practice of providing its financing to members subject to policy conditionalities.[22] This meant, in practice, that it provided the financing to its members states in tranches with the release of each tranche being dependent on the member state satisfying certain conditions, originally known as performance criteria. These criteria were designed to demonstrate that the member state was making progress in correcting the imbalances in its balance of payments position.[23]

It is important to note that the IMF's articles do not explicitly require that the financing be provided against policy conditionalities. However, after some debate,[24] the IMF derived the legal justification for these conditionalities from the text of the Articles. Article I (iv) provides that

[17] IMF, 'The IMF in History' available at <https://www.imf.org/en/About#:~:text=The%20IMF%20was%20established%20in,staff%20drawn%20from%20150%20nations> (accessed 12 May 2022).

[18] IMF Articles, Art IV is the provision in the IMF Articles that discusses he purposes of these missions.

[19] IMF Articles, Art VIII Section 5.

[20] J Gold, 'The Law and Practice of the International Monetary Fund with Respect to "Stand-by Arrangements"' (1963) 12(1) International and Comparative Law Quarterly 1–30.

[21] See Chapter 3.

[22] IMF Factsheet, 'Conditionality' 22 February 2021 available at <https://www.imf.org/en/About/Factsheets/Sheets/2016/08/02/21/28/IMF-Conditionality> (accessed 13 May 2022). See also M Guitián, 'Conditionality: Past, Present, Future' (1995) 42(4) IMF Staff Papers 792–835.

[23] J Gold, *Conditionality* (IMF 1979) 39–51.

[24] See S Dell, *On Being Grandmotherly: The Evolution of IMF Conditionality* (1981) 1–35.

one of the purposes of the IMF is to give confidence to members by providing them temporarily with financing, subject to 'adequate safeguards' to ensure that the funds would be used to correct the imbalances in their balance of payments.[25] In addition, original Article V Section 7 stipulated that member states shall repurchase any increases in the IMF's holding of their own currency with gold.[26] The IMF interpreted these two provisions as authorizing it to make its extension of financial support to a member state subject to conditionality so that it could ensure that the member state would use the money effectively to correct its balance of payments problem and have the funds to repay the IMF in a timely manner.

The IMF's specialized international monetary mission placed limits on the conditions it would attach to the financing it offered its member countries. These conditions were limited to measures that were aimed at restoring a sustainable balance of payments position and stabilizing the par value of the country's currency. Thus, they focused on such issues as the size of any necessary currency devaluation, the size of the required cut in the budget deficit, and the size of the change in the interest rate and the resulting expected limits on the growth in money supply and credit.[27] The fact that the conditions were focused on macroeconomic issues and framed as numerical targets, in theory, gave the recipient state some policy space to determine for itself which precise policy measures it would adopt in order to meet the IMF's conditionalities.

The Standby Arrangement

In this regard, it is important to recall the particular characteristics of the Standby Arrangement, the basic way in which the IMF provides financing from its general resources. The *sui generis* nature of this arrangement was discussed in an earlier chapter.[28] For present purposes it is only necessary to note that this arrangement is not viewed by the IMF as being contractual in nature.[29] Instead, the IMF understands the transaction to involve

[25] IMF Articles, Art I (iv).

[26] IMF Articles, Art V Section 7. The IMF's holding of a member's currency will increase if it has provided the member state with financing through a Standby Arrangement. The current version of this Article allows the member state to make the repurchase in dollars or another currency acceptable to the IMF rather than in gold.

[27] Gold, *Conditionality* (n 23).

[28] See Chapter 3.

[29] Gold, 'The Law and Practice of the International Monetary Fund' (n 20).

two parallel promises. The first arises from the member state's Letter of Intent in which it spells out the policies it intends to adopt to deal with its balance of payments problem. The second arises from the Board of Directors' Standby Decision indicating that it supports the policy measures that the member state is planning to implement and that it will provide the member state with a stipulated amount of financing to support its efforts to implement the policies. The Decision also stipulates that the financing will be provided in tranches with the member state having to demonstrate that it has met certain performance criteria—such as cutting its budget deficit by a specified amount or has implemented certain specified policy measures—before the next tranche is made available to it. The member state accesses the available funds by swapping its own local currency for an equivalent amount of foreign exchange with the IMF.

It is important to note that, pursuant to the IMF Articles of Agreement, the member state has an obligation to use foreign exchange to repurchase, at a later date, the local currency that it used to access the IMF's resources. This repurchase obligation arises from Art V Section 7 of the IMF Articles and not from the Standby Arrangement itself. Failure to make the repurchase would therefore result in the member state being in breach of its treaty obligations rather than in breach of the Standby Arrangement.

This unusual financing arrangement had a number of benefits for the IMF and the member states. It meant that the IMF could treat the arrangement as *sui generis* and not as contractual.[30] Thus, the IMF could argue that the standby arrangement was not a binding international agreement and so could lawfully be kept confidential.[31] This arrangement made good sense in the days of the par value system when premature public disclosure of a pending devaluation could result in problems for the devaluing member state. Second, it meant that if the member state failed to implement the policy initiatives specified in its Letter of Intent, it would not be viewed as breaching an international agreement which could potentially result in international legal liability for the member state.

[30] ibid.
[31] UN Charter, Art 102.

The principles of uniformity and universality

The IMF developed its operational practices cognizant of the fact that it was designed to be a monetary and not a development institution. It assumed all states were participants in the same international monetary system, that the ability of each state to maintain its par value was influenced by the same variables and that they were all vulnerable to the same types of balance of payments problems.[32] Consequently, there was no need to distinguish between them on the basis of their wealth or level of economic development.

The IMF concretized and operationalized this perception by adopting the principle of uniformity as one of its key operating principles.[33] This principle holds that all IMF member states that are similarly situated in terms of their balance of payments and monetary situations should be treated in a uniform manner. Thus, all states, regardless of their level of economic development, will be able to access IMF financing on the same terms and conditions. This means that the financing will be made available to all member states experiencing similar balance of payments problems subject to the same principle of conditionality. However, the specific policy conditions attached to the financing offered to each member state will vary. In each case, the specific policy conditions and performance criteria will be crafted to help the individual member deal with its particular balance of payments problem in a manner that is consistent with the IMF's Articles.

It must be noted that uniformity does not mean that all states will receive the same amount of IMF financing. While the principle of uniformity ensures that IMF financing is available to all member states subject to the same terms and conditions, the amount of financing that member states receive is based on their quotas.

Uniformity therefore does not mean that the specific policies on which the financing is conditioned will be identical in all cases. It only means that the IMF's financing will be made available to all similarly situated member states and that the associated conditionalities will be aimed at achieving the same objectives. It should also be noted that, during the existence of the par

[32] M Guitian, *The Unique Nature of the Responsibilities of the IMF* (IMF Pamphlet Series No 46, 1992) <https://www.imf.org/external/pubs/ft/pam/pam46/pam46con.htm> (accessed 21 June 2023).

[33] J Gold, 'Uniformity as a Legal Principle of the International Monetary Fund' (1975) 7 Law and Policy in International Business 765–774. See also A Dreher, 'IMF Conditionality: Theory and Evidence' (2009) 141(½) Public Choice 233–267.

value system, uniformity also meant that the IMF's annual consultations with each member state would cover essentially the same issues.

The IMF compliments the principle of uniformity with the principle of universality. This principle means that membership in the IMF is open to all states and that the IMF will not create any distinctions between individual member states or groups of member states. Thus, unlike the World Bank or the United Nations, the IMF does not divide its member states into different groups based on a criterion such as income per capita. During the period of the par value system, it also did not offer different services to different groups of member states. All IMF services and financing facilities supported by its general resources were available to all its member states on the same terms.[34]

Failure to meet IMF obligations

During this early period, the IMF also developed its approach to member states that were not meeting their obligations as IMF member states. In this regard, it is important to note that there is a distinction between a member's commitments under an IMF financing arrangement and its membership obligations.[35] The former related to the terms and conditions associated with the Standby Arrangement through which member states access IMF financing. The latter relates to the obligations of membership spelled out in the Articles of Agreement.

An example of the latter type of breach of obligation is the IMF's dispute with Czechoslovakia. In this dispute, the IMF claimed that the member state had failed to fulfil its obligations under Article XIV Section 4, dealing with transitional arrangements.[36] In particular, the IMF maintained that the member had not provided it with the necessary information to justify its maintenance of exchange restrictions. As a result, the IMF Board of Directors declared Czechoslovakia, pursuant to Article XV Section 2(a), ineligible to use the resources of the IMF. Czechoslovakia, subsequent to this declaration, did not take any actions to provide the requisite additional

[34] See Guitian (n 32) .

[35] IMF Articles, Art V Section 5, discussing the ineligibility to use resources of the IMF, and original Art XV discussing compulsory withdrawal.

[36] IMF, '3. The Compulsory Withdrawal of Czechoslovakia' (1968) Interpretation by the Fund 11–14 <https://www.elibrary.imf.org/view/books/054/14812-9781451939118-en/ch03.xml?language=en> (accessed 14 May 2022).

information to the IMF. Consequently, the Board recommended that, pursuant to Article XV, Czechoslovakia be requested to withdraw from membership, which it eventually did.[37]

This event is noteworthy because it is unusual for an international organization to force a member state to withdraw. In fact, this is the only time that the IMF has taken such an action against a member state. It should be recognized that this event took place within the context of the Cold War, which probably helps explain why the IMF took this action and Czechoslovakia decided to withdraw. It is also worth noting that many years later the IMF amended its Articles of Agreement to allow for intermediate sanctions against non-compliant member states. Pursuant to the current Article XXVI, the IMF can deprive such a member state of its right of access to IMF financing and of its voting rights in the IMF before moving to expel it from the organization.[38]

The era of a functioning Bretton Woods system (1960–71)

By 1960 many of the IMF's original member states had removed the restrictions on their current transactions and were following policies designed to maintain the par value of their currencies. Countries experiencing balance of payments problems during this period were able to take advantage of IMF financing to help them deal with the problems. It is important to note that during this period many member states, including the richest and most powerful member states made use of the IMF's financing facilities.[39]

The General Agreement to Borrow

The decade of the 1960s was marked by three developments that each had legal implications. Chronologically, the first was in 1962, when the IMF's Executive Board approved the terms and conditions for the General Agreement to Borrow (GAB).[40] They did this because the Board was

[37] ibid.

[38] IMF Articles, Art XXIV.

[39] IMF History (n 17).

[40] 'International Monetary Fund General Agreement to Borrow' (2017) <https://www.imf.org/en/Publications/Policy-Papers/Issues/2017/12/26/pp122617-general-arrangements-to-borrow> (accessed 14 May 2022).

becoming concerned that, as more member states assumed the monetary obligations of membership, the organization would be receiving many more requests for IMF financing. This created a risk that the IMF might not have enough funds to meet all the calls on its resources. To address this risk, they decided to make use of the IMF's authority to borrow from its member states.[41] As a result, it was agreed that the G10[42] member states would enter into the GAB, pursuant to which the IMF could borrow from the participating states in the event that one of them needed to access IMF financing.

The GAB was renewed periodically until 2018 when the IMF and the participating states decided it was no longer needed and allowed it to lapse.[43] It was activated 10 times during its life. It is important to note that for the first 20 years of its existence the GAB could only be activated by the IMF in the event that one of the G10 states wished to access IMF financing. In 1983, the G10 agreed to amend the GAB, so that the IMF could borrow under the GAB to support any IMF member state. The GAB was eventually replaced by the New Agreement to Borrow (NAB),[44] which has a similar purpose to the GAB, but involves a larger group of countries.

The GAB, since it initially was only available to the IMF to support financing for the G10, was in effect a deviation from the principle of uniformity. This follows from the fact that at least part of the financial support that the IMF provided G10 countries could come from a different source than the IMF's general resources. However, the form in which the IMF would provide the financing to G10 countries did not differ from standard IMF Standby Arrangements. Nevertheless, the GAB did demonstrate that

[41] IMF Articles, Art V, Section 3.

[42] The member countries are Belgium, Canada, France, Germany, Italy, Japan, the Netherlands, Sweden, Switzerland, the United Kingdom, and the United States. World Population Review (2022) G10 Countries <https://worldpopulationreview.com/country-rankings/g10-countries> (accessed 14 May 2022).

[43] IMF, NAB-GAB Factsheet 'Standing Borrowing Arrangements' (2018) 2 <https://www.imf.org/-/media/Files/Factsheets/English/Standingborrowingarrangement.ashx#:~:text=General%20Agreements%20to%20Borrow%20(GAB),-The%20GAB%20enables&text=The%20GAB%20was%20established%20in,the%20last%20time%20in%201998> (accessed 14 May 2022).

[44] ibid. The member states that participate in the NAB are: Australia, Austria, Banco Central de Chile, Banco de Portugal, Bangko Sentral ng Pilipinas, Bank of Israel, Belgium, Brazil, Canada, China, Cyprus, Danmarks Nationalbank, Deutsche, Bundesbank, Finland, France, Hong Kong Monetary Authority, India, Italy, Japan, Korea Kuwait, Luxembourg, Malaysia, Mexico, National Bank of Poland, Netherlands, New Zealand, Norway, Russian Federation, Saudi Arabia, Singapore, South Africa, Spain, Sveriges Riksbank Swiss National Bank, Thailand, United Kingdom, United States, Greece, Ireland.

the IMF could create special arrangements for particular groups of countries that had special needs.

The growth in IMF membership

The second significant development was that in the wake of the decolonization process that occurred during the 1960s, the membership of the IMF expanded dramatically. In 1960, the IMF had 70 member states, up from 34 in 1946. By 1970, the membership had expanded to 115 with the majority of the new members being the newly independent states.[45]

While, in itself, this increase in membership is not legally significant, it is important to remember that the IMF governance arrangements that were agreed at Bretton Woods were designed for a smaller and relatively more uniform group of states. Their creators did not anticipate that so many new states would gain their independence and seek to join international organizations. They also could not necessarily have appreciated that, because of their colonial histories, these newly independent states would have different needs and interests from those of the original member states. These differences were accentuated by the way in which these new member states had gained their independence from their colonial masters, who were among the original IMF member states. In some cases, countries only won their independence after bitter and sometimes violent struggles. In other cases, the departing colonial powers took resources out of their former colonies as they departed, thereby depriving the newly independent countries of the resources that they would need to develop and become economically independent. In still other cases, the newly independent states were locked into disadvantageous economic relations with their former colonial masters and with companies from these countries.[46] The result was that these IMF member states faced more complex macroeconomic challenges and had more complicated financing needs than the IMF was originally designed to

[45] IMF History (n 17).

[46] See, eg, T Nyamunda, 'British Sterling Imperialism, Settler Colonialism and the Political Economy of Money and Finance in Southern Rhodesia, 1945 to 1962' (2017) 45(1) African Economic History 77, 82–86. See JT Gathii, 'Sovereign Debt as a Mode of Colonial Governance: Past, Present and Future Possibilities' (13 May 2022) Just Money <https://justmoney.org/james-thuo-gathii-sovereign-debt-as-a-mode-of-colonial-governance-past-present-and-future-possibilities/> (accessed 16 May 2022). See also (accessed 18 May 2023). A Mensah, 'The Process of Monetary Decolonization in Africa' 4 Utafiti (1979) p45–63 <https://www.africabib.org/rec.php?RID=185321569> (accessed 21 June 2023).

manage. In particular, many of these new states faced macroeconomic challenges that, at least in part, were structural in nature and required longer periods for resolution than the standard balance of payments problems that the IMF, as a monetary institution, was created to help resolve.[47]

The IMF governance arrangements were not particularly well suited to addressing these needs. The weighted voting and the constituency structure of the IMF Board meant that these new member states often had an attenuated relationship with the decision-making processes in the Board.[48] In addition, Article I of the IMF Articles makes clear that the IMF was designed to be a monetary institution. It was not expected to focus on the challenges of development. These were understood to be the preserve of the International Bank for Reconstruction and Development and the other members of the World Bank Group.[49] However, in order for these newly independent states to join the World Bank and benefit from its development financing, they were required to join the IMF.[50] The result was that the IMF gained a group of member states whose balance of payments problems required primarily medium- to long-term structural support rather than the short-term monetary measures in which the IMF specialized. Nevertheless, the fact that they experienced balance of payments problems made the states eligible for, and interested in, receiving IMF financing. One consequence of this situation is that over time, and particularly in the 1980s, the IMF and the conditionalities attached to its financing became increasingly controversial and a cause of a great deal of tension between the IMF and many of its developing country member states and their residents.[51]

[47] L Taylor, 'Editorial: The Revival of the Liberal Creed — The IMF and the World Bank in a Globalized Economy' (2017) 25(2) World Development 145–152; SC Thacker, 'The High Politics of IMF Lending' (1999) 52(1) World Politics 38–75. See also J Masters, A Chatzky, and A Siripurapu, 'The IMF: The World's Controversial Financial Firefighter' (8 September 2021) Council on Foreign Relations <https://www.cfr.org/backgrounder/imf-worlds-controversial-financial-firefighter> (accessed 17 May 2022)..

[48] D Bradlow, *Stuffing New Wine into Old Bottles: The Troubling Case of the IMF*. <https://ssrn.com/abstract=283288>; <http://dx.doi.org/10.2139/ssrn.283288>. D Bradlow, 'Global Economic Governance and IMF Governance Reform: A Proposal' (2021) III African Sovereign Debt Justice Paper Series, 1–20.

[49] See Chapters 3 and 5 for a discussion of the functions of the World Bank Group.

[50] IBRD Articles, Art 2.

[51] JA Ocampo, 'A Brief History of the International Monetary System since Bretton Woods' in JA Ocampo (ed), *Resetting the International Monetary (Non)System*, (OUP 2017) 1–31. See also R Jolly, 'Adjustment with a Human Face' in R Jolly (ed), *Milestones and Turning Points in Development Thinking* (2012) 172–185. W Easterly, 'IMF and World Bank Structural Adjustment Programs and Poverty' in MP Dooley and JA Frankel (eds), *Managing Currency Crises in Emerging Markets* (University of Chicago Press 2003) 361–391 on the history of IMF of structural adjustment programmes.

This situation raised concerns about the IMF undermining the sovereign prerogatives of at least some of its member states, about the continuing validity of the principle of uniformity and about the governance arrangements of the IMF. While these concerns have been mitigated, they have not been fully resolved.

Special Drawing Rights

The third development was that in 1969, the IMF membership adopted the first amendment to the IMF Articles.[52] This is noteworthy because amending the Articles is not easy. It requires broad member state support. Pursuant to the IMF Articles, an amendment requires approval by a vote of three-fifths of the members holding four-fifths of the total votes.[53] This first amendment established the Special Drawing Rights (SDRs) and the Special Drawing Rights facility in the IMF. SDRs are a form of reserve asset created by the IMF. The SDRs are only issued after the members approve an SDR allocation in a vote that gains 85 per cent support of the votes cast. The SDRs are distributed among the members according to their quotas.[54]

The members are free to hold their SDRs in their reserves or to use them in transactions with prescribed SDR holders. The prescribed holders include the designated holder of SDRs in each of the member states of the IMF and specifically designated holders such as international financial institutions like the World Bank.[55] This means that a member state can use its SDRs to settle outstanding obligations with these holders or it can enter into a transaction with the IMF or another member state to convert the SDRs into a useable currency such as US dollars. The member state will have to pay the IMF an interest charge on the SDRs used in these transactions. The IMF will also pay an identical interest to the member state that has accepted the SDRs. In the latter case, the interest rate is paid on the excess of its SDR

52 Arts XV, XVI, XVII, XVIII, XIX, XX, XXI Articles of Agreement, as amended 2016 <https://www.imf.org/external/pubs/ft/aa/index.htm> (accessed 8 February 2023). See C Wilkie, *Special Drawing Rights (SDRs): The First International Money* (OUP 2009) 45–67 on the history of SDRs,

53 IMF Articles, Art XVII and XXVIII.

54 JM Boughton, P Isard, and M Mussa, '3 The History of the SDR' in *The Future of the SDR in light of Changes in the International Monetary System* (IMF 1996) 25–55..

55 Currently there are 20 international organizations that are presecribed holders of SDRs. <https://www.imf.org/en/About/Factsheets/Sheets/2023/special-drawing-rights-sdr> (accessed 21 June 2023).

holdings above its quota. It is also important to note that when the SDR was created its value was determined according to a specified amount of gold. However, following the end of the Bretton Woods system in 1971, the value of the SDR has been set in terms of a basket of currencies.[56]

The end of the Bretton Woods era and the Second Amendment (1971–1978)

During the course of the 1960s, it became increasingly clear that the Bretton Woods system had a built-in weakness.[57] The fact that the foundation of the system was the link between gold and the US dollar, meant that all participating states needed access to US dollars. They needed the dollars for their international trade and financial transactions and to help preserve the par value of their currencies. This meant that as the global economy expanded, the demand for US dollars increased. The US had to provide states with a way of accessing dollars. However, as the amount of US dollars held outside the US grew, the US promise to always keep the value of the US dollar fixed at $35 per ounce of gold became less credible. The reason was that international holdings of dollars grew at a more rapid rate than the rate at which the US was acquiring gold.

The situation reached a crisis point in the early 1970s with the US experiencing sustained inflation and a growing trade deficit. Eventually, in August 1971, President Nixon unilaterally announced that the US would no longer exchange dollars for gold at $35 per ounce of gold.[58] He supplemented this

[56] The original basket of currencies consisted of the US dollar, UK pound sterling, the French franc, the Deutsch mark, and the Japanese yen. The composition of the basket has changed over time. Since October 2016, it consists of the US dollar, the euro, the yen, the pound sterling, and the Chinese renminbi. See IMF Factsheet 'Special Drawing Rights (SDRs))' (5 August 2021) <https://www.imf.org/en/About/Factsheets/Sheets/2016/08/01/14/51/Special-Drawing-Right-SDR> (accessed 17 May 2022). Currently the weight of each currency in the SDR is: Chinese renminbi 9.067580; €1.279040; ¥171.893000; £1.086580 and US$1.333020. See IMF Currency Unit per SDR May 2022 <https://www.imf.org/external/np/fin/data/rms_mth.aspx?reportType=CVSDR> (accessed 30 May 2022).

[57] R Triffin, 'Gold and the Dollar Crisis: Yesterday and Tomorrow' (1978) 132 Essays In International Finance 1–21. See also MD Bordo and RN McCauley, 'Triffin: dilemma or myth?' (2017) 684 BIS Working Paper 3–31; C Ghymers, 'The Persistence of the Triffin Dilemma Today: A Plan for Overcoming It and Ensuring a Stable International Financial Architecture' in *Reform of the International Monetary System and new global economic governance: how the EU may contribute* (Robert Triffin Internaltional Association 2017) 11–21.

[58] JE Garten, *Three Days at Camp David: How a Secret Meeting in 1971 Transformed the Global Economy* (2021) 33, 245–327.

statement with a range of trade and anti-inflation fighting measures. These actions effectively ended the original Bretton Woods arrangements. They also set off an international effort to create a new basis for the international monetary system. Finally, in 1978, the IMF Articles were amended for the second time and a new international monetary system was created.[59]

This new system effectively moved the world from a commodity linked monetary system to a fiat money system.[60] It also ended the monetary role of gold so that states could no longer set the value of their currency in terms of gold. Each member state now could establish 'by fiat' the value of its currency and determine for itself how to manage the value of its currency. In fact, countries have made use of a variety of policies for managing the value of their currencies. The result is that over time the world has shifted to a market-based international monetary and financial system, in which the value of many countries' currencies are set by the forces of supply and demand.[61]

It is important to note that one consequence of this development was to simultaneously reduce the IMF's role as the overseer of the international monetary system and make its role in global economic governance more complicated. If the member states were not expected to maintain any particular value for their currencies and could choose their own exchange rate policies, then what was the IMF supposed to be monitoring in its annual consultations with the country?

The amended Article IV provides only limited guidance.[62] It requires each member state to 'endeavour to direct its economic and financial policies toward … fostering orderly economic growth' and to 'seek to promote stability by fostering orderly underlying economic and financial conditions' and to 'follow exchange rate policies compatible with the undertaking' of Article IV. The lack of specificity of this language suggests, as in fact has become the case, that the IMF needs to look at any aspect of the member state's economic and financial policies that could affect its 'orderly economic growth', its external balance of payments and the value of its currency. In

[59] 'A General View', in the IMF, *The Second Amendment of the Fund's Articles of Agreement* (IMF 1978).

[60] KF Israel, 'The Fiat Money Illusion: On the Cost-Efficiency of Modern Central Banking' (2021) 44 World Economy 1701–1719. See also IMF, 'Some First Effects of the Second Amendment' in *The Second Amendment*, ibid.

[61] JO Grabbe, *International Financial Markets* (3rd edn, Pearson Education 1995).

[62] IMF Articles, Art IV.

other words, the Second Amendment resulted in the IMF dramatically expanding the scope of its Article IV consultations.[63]

It also has resulted in an expansion in the range of conditions that the IMF attaches to the financing it provides to member states. This follows from the fact that the international monetary system gives individual countries the flexibility to determine for themselves how to manage their currency and to determine their own monetary and macroeconomic policies. Since almost any domestic or international economic issue can influence the efficacy and sustainability of these policies, almost any economic issue can affect the country's balance of payments. Consequently, almost any economic issue can be relevant to both the IMF's surveillance function and to the conditionalities it attaches to its financing. The result is that the range of issues addressed by the IMF in its discussions with its member states and in its conditionalities have expanded. In fact, in some cases, IMF financing arrangements have contained over 100 conditions covering such issues as privatization, reform of tax administration, adoption of new laws such as bankruptcy codes, allocations of resources for social safety nets and other budgetary purposes, and banking law reform, in addition to the more standard IMF macroeconomic conditions.[64] The specificity and, at times, micro nature of these requirements highlight the evolution of the IMF from a purely monetary institution to a more general macroeconomic-focused institution.

A consequence of the Second Amendment

One unintended consequence of these developments was that the relationship between the IMF and its member states began to change. The IMF's original governance structure was designed on the assumption that in an

[63] JM Boughton, *The IMF and the Silent Revolution: Global Finance and Development in the 1980s* (IMF 2000). See also MS Edwards, KA Coolidge, and DA Preston, 'Who Reveals? Transparency and the IMF's Article IV Consultations' (2012) 1–44 <https://www.peio.me/wp-content/uploads/2014/04/Conf5_Edwards-30.09.11.pdf> (accessed 18 May 2022).

[64] See IMF, 'Recovery from the Asian Crisis and the Role of the IMF' (IMF 2000) <https://www.imf.org/external/np/exr/ib/2000/062300.htm> (accessed 18 May 2022). An example of a standby arrangement with over 100 conditions is the standby arrangements with Indonesia from November 1997. It is also important to note that the IMF has subsequently made efforts to place some constraints on the scope of IMF conditionality. See, for example, 'IMF Guidelines on Conditionality' (2002 pp 1–11). See also IMF, *Review of Program Design and Conditionality* (IMF 2018) for the latest IMF policy/guidelines on conditionality. These guidelines are periodically reviewed and updated.

international monetary system based on par values all countries could potentially run into balance of payments problems and need to make use of the IMF's financing facilities. Thus, even though the IMF's system of weighted voting meant that some countries had more influence in the IMF than others, they all had an interest in developing policies that were acceptable to states that actually used the IMF's services. This meant that because even the most powerful states could one day need the IMF's support—and in fact had utilized IMF financial facilities—they were less likely to advocate policies that were unduly burdensome for member states. They understood that the policies they supported in the IMF could one day directly affect their own societies and they could be held accountable for them.

The Second Amendment challenged this assumption. It had disparate impacts on different groups of IMF member states.[65] The first group, which can be called 'IMF supplier states', consists of those countries which, because of their wealth and position in the global economy, determined that they could meet all their foreign exchange needs from their own resources and the private financial markets. The fact that these countries did not intend using the IMF's financing facilities freed them from any need to defer to any advice the IMF may offer them in their annual consultations.[66] As a result, they regained a large measure of their monetary sovereignty from the IMF. Moreover, given their dominance in the governance of the IMF, their

[65] D Bradlow, 'Stuffing New Wine into Old Bottles: The Troubling Case of the IMF' (2001) 3(9) Journal of International Banking Regulation 9–36 <https://link.springer.com/article/10.1057/palgrave.jbr.2340102> (accessed 28 June 2022).

[66] ibid. This does not, however, mean that they have regained full monetary sovereignty. The world's economy has become too integrated for that. Instead, these countries, particularly the G7, have, in effect, agreed to resolve all monetary and financial issues that may arise between them in an alternate set of international fora. These issues are now resolved through such entities as the G20, the G7, the Organization of Economic Cooperation and Development (OECD), and the Bank for International Settlement (BIS). When these are not deemed adequate, the G7 have been willing to create additional fora. For example, after the Asian financial crisis and the near bankruptcy of Long Term Capital Management, the G7 became concerned about the regulatory framework for international financial markets. These countries decided that they needed a mechanism through which they could coordinate national regulation of financial markets and financial institutions. Consequently, they created the Financial Stability Forum in which the regulators of the banking, securities, and insurance industries of major industrial countries and financial centers could meet together with representatives of the IMF, the World Bank, and the BIS to discuss regulatory issues of mutual concern and to ensure that the regulatory frameworks existing in all countries that participate in the international financial markets are consistent with the demands of the increasingly integrated international financial market. See FSB, 'About the FSB' <https://www.fsb.org/about/> (accessed 18 May 2022). They also created the G20, which consists of the G7 plus some other key industrial and emerging market countries. The original purpose of this group was to provide a forum in which these states could meet to discuss matters of common economic and financial interest. See 'About G20', available at: <https://www.g20.org/en/about-g20/> (accessed 16 March 2023).

newly gained monetary independence meant that they acquired new capacity to use the IMF to impose their views of good political and economic policies on poorer and smaller countries. This development has politicized the IMF and caused many observers to see the IMF more as a political organization that is biased in favour of the rich countries and their interests than as the technically specialized and politically neutral organization that it was supposed to be.[67]

The second group consists of those member states that need or know they may need IMF financing and other services in the foreseeable future. They can be called the 'IMF consumer member states'. These states must pay careful attention to the views of the IMF because they will influence the conditions that the IMF will attach to the funds it provides to any of these states that need its financial support. Given the broadening range of topics of interest to the IMF, its role in the consumer member states began to grow. It became an important source of information on and advice to the member state on any macroeconomic issue that the member state or the IMF decided was relevant to its monetary or balance of payments situation. In other words, following the Second Amendment, the IMF, *de facto,* became an important participant in the policy-making process of these IMF consumer member states. In fact, because of its financing role, the IMF can be the decisive voice in these countries' policy-making processes. This is particularly likely to be the case in those member states where the IMF can influence their access to other sources of funds. This follows from the way in which other potential funders of the state react to the IMF's willingness to provide financing to the country.[68] The combination of the IMF's *de facto* role in national policy-making and its gatekeeping role in regard to international finance can further tip the balance of bargaining power in favour of the IMF in both the annual consultations and in the negotiations over the policy conditions to be attached to IMF financing for these consumer member states.

The IMF's expanded role in its developing country member states has also changed the range of actors with whom it must directly interact in these

[67] D Lombardi and N Woods, 'The Politics of Influence: An Analysis of IMF Surveillance' (2008) 15 Review of International Political Economy 711–739; T Oatley and J Yackee, 'American Interests and IMF Lending' (2004) 41 International Politics 415–429; Thacker (n 47) 38–75.

[68] S Zwart, 'The Mixed Blessing of IMF Intervention: Signalling versus Liquidity Support' (2007) 3 Journal of Financial Stability 149–174; T Krahnke, 'Doing More with Less: The Catalytic Function of IMF Lending and the Role of Program Size' (2020) No 18/2020 Deutsche Bundesbank Discussion Paper 1–44.

states. Prior to 1978, the IMF could reasonably limit its direct interactions to the makers of monetary and macroeconomic policy in the member states, namely to the central banks and the ministries of finance. Today, however, the IMF's operations directly affect many, if not all, government ministries and the lives of all those people who will be governed by the policies that the IMF helps make. This means that it is no longer feasible for the IMF to limit its interactions to the central bank and the ministry of finance. In fact, without directly interacting with a broader range of both governmental and non-governmental actors in the member states, the IMF is unlikely to obtain all the information it needs to play an effective policy making role. For example, it may need to consult with government ministries whose budgets and policies will be affected by the IMF's funding conditionalities. It also may find it useful to consult with the legislators who must pass the laws that the IMF policies require. To be an effective and credible policymaker, the IMF also should hear the views of all those stakeholders—such as business, labour, and civil society organizations—who will be affected by the specific policy decisions it is influencing. These stakeholders have the ability to influence the success or failure of those policy decisions. To date, the IMF, utilizing informal procedures has consulted with some of these actors. However, it has not yet developed formal procedures for ensuring that all relevant stakeholders are consulted.[69]

The changes in the IMF's relations with its member states have also had legal ramifications. As was explained above, the IMF, in implementing its mandate, developed the principles of uniformity and universality. These principles require the IMF to grant all states access to its financing and other services without drawing any distinctions between member states based on their wealth, size, level of development, or importance in the international monetary system. The lack of such a distinction made sense when the IMF functioned purely as a monetary institution and all its member states, in fact, were utilizing its services.

However, it does not make sense when its services are being utilized primarily by its developing country member states. It means, for example, that the IMF can only meet the special needs of a subset of its member states by creating special mechanisms that operate outside the general resources of the IMF. Thus, in order to provide low-income countries with

[69] D Bradlow, 'Operational Policies and Procedures and an Ombudsman' in B Carin and A Wood (eds), *Accountability of The International Monetary Fund* (Ashgate Publishing 2005) 88–108, available at SSRN <https://ssrn.com/abstract=805805>.

long-term concessional financing, it had to create a special trust, the Poverty Reduction and Growth Trust (PRGT).[70] This trust could only be funded with donations from richer member states.

This has two consequences. First it means that the amount of funding that the IMF can provide is dependent on the generosity of the donor states. Second, it means that the PRGT, like the International Development Association, is always vulnerable to being used by the richer states to advance their own economic and political agendas. This follows from the fact that the donor member states can always use their contributions to the PRGT to require the IMF to attach specific conditions to the use of its funds. It, therefore, also creates a risk of the PRGT becoming subject to multiple demands from its donor states. It also means that the poorest and weakest IMF member states are at risk of being required to comply with the most onerous conditions in order to access IMF financing.

In 2022, the IMF created a new trust, the Resilience and Sustainability Trust.[71] This trust is funded primarily by IMF member states through their share of the SDR allocations that the IMF made in 2022. Its resources are being used to support countries working to enhance their capacity to respond to new pandemics and climate emergencies. The trust, which has limited resources, is used to supplement standard IMF programmes.

This suggests that the IMF would be better off if it could treat different categories of its member states differently in regard to all its services and resources. This would enable the IMF to more easily design facilities that are only suitable for certain member states. It would also allow it to consider whether or not it needs to restructure some of its decision-making procedures to make them more responsive to the needs of its poorer and weaker member states.

The Articles of Agreement require the IMF, when conducting its annual consultations with its member states and when designing the conditions it attaches to its funding, to pay due regard to social and political conditions in the country.[72] The IMF has historically interpreted this requirement as

[70] IMF Factsheet, 'IMF Support for Low-income Countries' (5 January 2022) <https://www.imf.org/en/About/Factsheets/IMF-Support-for-Low-Income-Countries> (accessed 18 May 2022). See also T Stubbs, W Kring, C Laskaridis, A Kentikelenis, and K Gallagher, 'Whatever It Takes? The Global Financial Safety Net, Covid-19, and Developing Countries' (2021) 137 World Development 1–8.

[71] For more information on the Resilience and Sustainability Trust, see: <https://www.imf.org/en/Topics/Resilience-and-Sustainability-Trust> (accessed 21 June 2023).

[72] IMF Articles, Art IV Section 3(b) See also D Bradlow, 'The World Bank, the IMF, and Human Rights' (1996) 6(47) Transnational Law & Contemporary Problems 49–60, available at <https://ssrn.com/abstract=1710636>.

prohibiting it from being influenced by political (that is non-economic) considerations in its dealings with its member states.[73] This interpretation of the requirement that it pay due regard to social and political conditions in its member countries may have made sense when the IMF's operations were limited to monetary issues. However, it is neither prudent nor principled for an organization that attaches conditions to its funding that relate to such issues as governance, corruption, budgetary allocations, and privatization to pretend that it can avoid being influenced by social and political considerations. The only function that the current interpretation serves is to obscure what political considerations the IMF does view as relevant to its operations, what principles it applies in making these judgements, and what process it follows in reaching these decisions.

The IMF and human rights

A good example of the problems that can arise in this regard is human rights issues.[74] These issues can arise in two ways in the context of the IMF's operations. The first is that a member state may be responsible for human rights violations in its domestic governance. These violations may be adversely affecting its macroeconomic situation. For example, the government of the country may be spending an undue share of its foreign exchange reserves on purchasing equipment that its military and police forces can use to repress political opposition rather than on developing the infrastructure of the country or on purchasing necessary medical supplies for its citizens.

[73] F Gianviti, 'Economic, Social and Cultural Rights and the International Monetary Fund' (2002) 1–45 <https://www.imf.org/external/np/leg/sem/2002/cdmfl/eng/gianv3.pdf> (accessed 19 May 2022). Morgan-Foster, 'The Relationship of IMF Structural Adjustment Programs to Economic, Social, and Cultural Rights: The Argentine Case Revisited' (2003) 24 Michigan Journal of International Law & Policy 577–630 J Gold, *Legal and Institutional Aspects of the International Monetary System: Selected Essays* vol II (IMF 1984) 947. See also, A Ansong, 'Decision-Making in the International Monetary Fund: Implications for Sovereign Equality of States' (2018) <https://ssrn.com/abstract=3289151> (accessed 18 May 2022).

[74] Bradlow, 'The World Bank, the IMF, and Human Rights' (n 72). See also JP Bohoslavsky and F Cantamutto, 'The IMF and Human Rights: Interviews' Speak out at the Laboratory for Advanced Research on the Global Economy' (2021) LSE Human Rights 1–49 <https://www.lse.ac.uk/sociology/assets/documents/human-rights/IMF-HRs-LSE-final.pdf>. E Toussaint, 'The World Bank, the IMF and the respect of human rights' (25 October 2020), CATDM, <https://www.cadtm.org/The-World-Bank-the-IMF-and-the-respect-of-human-rights> (accessed 19 May 2022); B Ghazi, *The IMF, the World Bank Group and the Question of Human Rights* (Brill 2005) 468.

The second way in which human rights issues can arise is through the impacts of the conditionalities that the IMF attaches to its financing. Given the fact that the IMF is providing financing to member states facing balance of payments and budget deficits, there is a strong possibility that its conditionalities will require the recipient member state to reduce its budget deficits by either cutting expenditures or raising new revenues from its citizens. These policy options will inevitably have distributional impacts that can adversely affect the physical and political environment in the country and the social and economic situation of at least some residents of the country. For example, it could result in some residents becoming unable to afford health or education services. If the IMF does not adequately account for these impacts in its own operations, there is a risk that it inadvertently becomes a contributor to human rights violations in the country.

This brief discussion of the IMF and human rights demonstrates that the IMF's lack of a clear policy that explains its understanding of its responsibilities in regard to environmental, political, and social issues and that provides guidance to its staff on how they should deal with these issues in IMF operations is problematic. It creates risks for the IMF. For example, by failing to demonstrate how it defines and intends meeting its responsibilities in regard to these human rights and social impacts, the IMF creates reputational risk for itself and even risks undermining its legitimacy.[75]

The legal nature of the Standby Arrangement and its consequences

A third legal problem for the IMF arises from the IMF's characterization of the legal nature of the Standby Arrangement through which it provides much of its financing to its member states. The IMF's formalistic interpretation of the nature of this transaction had a utilitarian value when the IMF functioned as the manager of the par value system, and the conditions attached to the financing included a relatively permanent change in the par value of a currency. In this case, there would be negative consequences if news about the change were released prematurely.

It is not, however, clear that the same considerations apply in the post-Bretton Woods era. In fact, the IMF seems to have recognized as much. In

[75] Bradlow, 'Operational Policies and Procedures and an Ombudsman' (n 69).

recent years, as part of its efforts to promote transparency, it has encouraged its member states to publish their Letters of Intent. Nevertheless, the IMF has not yet reviewed its decision regarding the nature of the transaction. The result is that the transactions are still not viewed by the IMF as contractual and, therefore, are still not considered as international agreements. This is problematic for two reasons. First, if the arrangements, like World Bank loan agreements,[76] were classified as international agreements, they would be registered with the United Nations and would become public documents. Consequently, the IMF could require, rather than encourage, member states to publish their Letters of Intent and any related documents. This would more effectively advance the IMF's goal of promoting transparency than the current arrangements.

Second, as IMF transactions became more complex there is a greater need for the documentation associated with IMF financing to be subjected to predictable principles of interpretation. The reason is that, as the complexity of the conditions attached to IMF financing increases and their scope broadens beyond issues that are easily tested against a numerical or objective standard, it is possible for disagreements to arise about whether the member state has sufficiently complied with the conditionalities associated with the IMF financing to justify the member state gaining access to the next tranche of the funds. If these transactions were viewed as international agreements, they would be subject to public international law rules for interpreting international agreements.[77] Under the current IMF view that the transactions are *sui generis*, there are no obviously applicable rules of interpretation. Consequently, the transactions are amenable to ad hoc and arbitrary interpretation.

The changing balance of power in the IMF

An additional, though perhaps unintended, impact of the Second Amendment was that it resulted, *de facto*, in the rich countries gaining

[76] A Broches, *Selected Essays: World Bank, ICSID and other Subjects of Public and Private International Law* (Martinus Nijhoff 1995) 161. See also, 'IMF Guidance Note On The Fund's Transparency Policy' (2013) p 4–25 <https://www.imf.org/external/np/pp/eng/2013/112613.pdf> (accessed 30 May 2022). See also A Broches, 'The Convention on the Settlement of Investment Disputes Between States and Nationals of Other States' (1972) 136 The Hague Academy of International Law 331–410.

[77] See, eg, 'Vienna Convention on the Law of Treaties Between States' <https://legal.un.org/ilc/texts/instruments/english/conventions/1_1_1969.pdf> (accessed 8 February 2023).

increased voice and influence in the governance of the IMF. This is in part due to the Second Amendment's impact on their monetary sovereignty, discussed above, and in part due to the increase in the number of IMF member states.

The latter development had significant implications for the relative position of IMF member states in the governance of the institution. This follows, firstly, from developments in the composition of the voting rights of each member state. Each state's vote consists of 250 basic votes plus one vote for each SDR100,000 it contributes to the IMF's general resources.[78] The basic vote is intended to reflect the general principle of the sovereign equality of states. The remaining portion of the vote is intended to reflect the size of the country and its importance in the world economy. Since the establishment of the IMF in 1946, the number of total votes in the IMF have been increasing, in part due to the IMF membership growing from thirty-nine states in 1946 to 189 states today. They have also been increased as a result of the periodic reviews of the IMF quotas that are required by the IMF Articles and are motivated by the need for the IMF's resources to increase in response to the growth of the global economy.[79]

However, until recently there had not been a commensurate change in the number of basic votes. Consequently, over time the basic votes have become a significantly smaller portion of the total vote than was the case in 1946. In 1946 the basic votes accounted for 11.3 per cent of the total vote. They eventually fell to 2.2 per cent of the total vote. In 2008, he IMF membership agreed, to increase the basic vote and to always maintain the total of the basic votes as equal to 5.502 per cent of the total votes.[80] This means that, over time, the portion of the IMF's voting system that offered the smaller and weaker states some counterweight to the dominance of the richest and biggest countries in the IMF has been reduced in importance and the dominance of these richer and bigger countries has been correspondingly enhanced.[81] The 2008 decision to increase the basic votes has only partially addressed this problem.

[78] IMF Articles, Art XII, Section 5.

[79] IMF Articles Art 3, Section 2.

[80] IMF, 'IMF Quota' 4 March 2021 <https://www.imf.org/en/About/Factsheets/Sheets/2016/07/14/12/21/IMF-Quotas> (accessed 19 May 2022). See also 'IMF Members' Quotas and Voting Power, and IMF Board of Governors' (updated 29 June 2022) <https://www.imf.org/en/About/executive-board/members-quotas> and IMF Factsheet, 'How the IMF Makes Decisions' (23 February 2021) <https://www.imf.org/en/About/Factsheets/Sheets/2016/07/27/15/24/How-the-IMF-Makes-Decisions> (accessed 29 June 2022).

[81] IMF Articles, Art XII Sections 1–5.

The second development is that the number of IMF Executive Directors has grown more slowly than the number of IMF member states. The original thirty-nine member states were represented by a twelve-member board of directors.[82] Today the 190 members are represented by a board of twenty-four members. Originally, the five biggest shareholders had their own Executive Directors and the remaining thirty-four member states were represented by the other seven directors. This meant that each of these seven directors represented constituencies consisting of, on average, slightly less than five states. Today, of the twenty-four members of the Executive Board, eight Executive Directors represent single-state constituencies. Five of these eight Executive Directors represent the five states with the largest quotas. The other three represent states which for a variety of historical reasons have acquired direct representation on the Board. The remaining sixteen directors represent a total of 182 member states. This means that each of these directors represents on average slightly more than eleven states. In fact, some Executive Directors, for example the two directors representing sub-Saharan Africa, represent considerably more than eleven states.[83]

This change in the average size of the constituencies represented by the Executive Directors has an important impact on the power relations in the IMF's decision-making process. It means that those states that have permanent representation on the Board have a distinct advantage in having their views heard in the Board. They are also able to develop expertise in how to function effectively in the IMF. It is unlikely that a director who represents eleven or more states can advocate for the views of each of those states as effectively as a director who only represents one state. It is also unlikely that such a director can play the same active role in policy issues in the IMF as an Executive Director who represents only one state. In this regard, it is noteworthy that each of the G7 countries always has a national of their country on the Executive Board.

The numerical advantage of the industrialized countries on the Executive Board and the permanency of the G7's representation is significant even though the Board always operates by consensus. The reason is that these countries, because of their permanent presence on the Board, are able to

[82] IMF Articles, Art XII Section 3.

[83] The Executive Director of the Africa Group 1 (AfG1) Constituency, represents a constituency comprising of 22 African states. The Executive Director representing the Africa Group 2 (AfG2) constituency represents 23 African states. See 'IMF Executive Directors and Voting Power' (updated 29 June 2022) <https://www.imf.org/en/About/executive-board/eds-voting-power> (accessed 29 June 2022).

develop institutional memories and expertise in how to function in the IMF. This enhances their ability to negotiate effectively and to shape the issues and the decisions around which the consensus must form.

On the other hand, the practice of decision-making by consensus mitigates to some extent the imbalance in power on the Executive Board. The reason is that because the Board members meet regularly and get to know each other, a well-respected Board member will be listened to carefully regardless of their actual vote. Thus, they can have an influence that is greater than their vote would suggest.[84]

The result of these developments is that, *de facto*, the G-7 countries control the policy agenda in the IMF to a considerable extent. However, because these countries are effectively independent of the IMF, their citizens don't have to live with the consequence of the policies that they make for the IMF's operations. This means that the Executive Directors from these countries can make IMF policy that is only of limited interest to their own citizens. The policy is, of course, of immense interest to people in developing countries who have no ability to hold them accountable for their decisions or actions. This situation of decision makers having power with accountability to people who do not have to live with the consequences of their decisions but without accountability to those most affected by their decisions is a situation ripe with potential for abuse.[85]

The principles of good governance that the IMF advocates require that all players in the policymaking process should be held accountable for their actions and decisions. To date, the IMF has not established any mechanism through which the residents of its member countries can hold the IMF accountable for its actions in the policy-making process. In other words, the changes in the IMF's functions have resulted in the IMF being an influential part of the policy-making process of its member states but being effectively unaccountable to many of its developing country member states or the people living in these states.[86]

This governance challenge is being accentuated by the growing range of issues that the IMF views as relevant to its macroeconomic mandate. Examples of these 'new' issues are climate change, gender, inequality, and

84 IMF Articles, Art XII Section 3(c).

85 Bradlow, 'Operational Policies and Procedures and an Ombudsman' (n 69).

86 ibid. See also D Bradlow, 'The IMF Needs an Ombudsman with Clout' (6 October 2021) Financial Times Alphaville <https://www.ft.com/content/1c4ce23e-15f2-4461-b9f7-48a198276fe1> (accessed 30 May 2022).

public health.[87] They require changes in the IMF's usual operating practices because they blur the boundaries between the macro- and micro-impacts of economic, social, and environmental policies. They also operate over longer time periods than the usual IMF operations. For example, a full understanding of the impacts of climate policies includes assessing both their macro-level financial and fiscal implications, and their differential impacts on subsets of sub-national governments, businesses, communities, regions, and social groups. These impacts can both affect the success of the climate policy and have implications for the level of inequality and discrimination in the member state. The IMF, therefore, can only fully assess the likely success of its proposed policies if it engages more directly with all the affected state and non-state actors about how it will respond to these impacts than it historically has done.

The IMF's relations with other international organizations

The original conception of the creators of the specialized agencies of the United Nations (UN) system was that each agency would exercise its authority within the limited scope of its specialization and that the UN Economic and Social Council would be the forum in which their activities would be coordinated.[88] Each specialized agency, in part to facilitate co-ordination, entered into a relationship agreement with the UN.[89] This relationship agreement ostensibly clarified the fact that the specialized agency was subordinate to the UN and clarified how it would relate to the UN. The relationship agreement between the IMF and the UN, however, amounts in effect to a declaration of independence. While it acknowledges that the IMF is a specialized agency of the UN, it relieves the IMF of any significant responsibilities to the UN and denies the UN any meaningful role in the affairs of the IMF.[90]

[87] K Georgieva and R Weeks-Brown, 'The IMF's Evolving Role Within a Constant Mandate' (2023) 26 Journal of International Economic Law17–29 available at <https://doi.org/10.1093/jiel/jgac064> (accessed 16 March 2023); AM Trevelyan, 'Advancing Gender Equality Through Climate Action' (September 2021) IMF Finance & Development 1.

[88] IMF Articles, Art X.

[89] Agreement Between the United Nations and the International Monetary Fund, 16 UNTS 328, 332 (1948).

[90] R Mikesell, *The Bretton Woods Debates: A Memoir (Essays in International Finance: No 192)* (Princeton University Press 1994) 34–60.

The effective independence of the IMF from the UN has become a problem as the scope of the IMF's operations has expanded beyond its original monetary function. Now that the IMF is involved in such issues as law reform, corruption, inequality, gender, environment, and trade liberalization, its operations are encroaching into the jurisdiction of other specialized international organizations like the World Bank, the ILO, WTO, WHO, and UNICEF, as well as other UN programmes and entities like the UN Human Rights bodies and the UN Environment Program.[91] It is doing so without any formal obligations to defer to these other organizations and entities in their areas of specialization. It should be noted, however, that the IMF is not insensitive to the governance and policy challenges that this can create. As a result, it does collaborate with these other bodies and in some cases has entered into formal arrangements with them. For example, it has signed formal cooperation agreements with the World Bank[92] and the World Trade Organization.[93]

Conclusion

The end of the par value system initiated an expansive evolutionary process in the IMF that has not ended. This process has had operational as well as legal consequences for the IMF. It expanded the scope of the IMF's areas of interest in its member states. This altered both the range of issues that it discusses with the member states in its annual surveillance missions and the nature and scope of the conditionalities that it attaches to the financing it provides to the member states. It also, *de facto*, has led the IMF to begin differentiating between member states, with some states being viewed primarily as suppliers of resources to the IMF and others as consumers of its services.

[91] D Bradlow, 'The Governance of the IMF: The Need for Comprehensive Reform (September 2006)' G24 Technical Committee Meeting, Singapore, Available at SSRN: <https://ssrn.com/abstract=928467> or <http://dx.doi.org/10.2139/ssrn.928467>; D Dodge and J Murray, 'The Evolving International Monetary Order and the Need for an Evolving IMF' (2006) 12(4) Global Governance 361–372; H van Zyl, 'A Historical Perspective on the Changing Role of the International Monetary Fund' (1994) 9 South African Journal of Economics 65–78.

[92] For information on IMF-World Bank cooperation see, IMF Factsheet 'The IMF and the World Bank' (3 March 2021) available at <https://www.imf.org/en/About/Factsheets/Sheets/2016/07/27/15/31/IMF-World-Bank> (accessed 22 June 2022).

[93] See 'Press Release: WTO and IMF Sign Cooperation Agreement' (16 December 1996) available at <https://www.imf.org/en/News/Articles/2015/09/14/01/49/pr9661> (accessed 22 June 2022).

While these changes in IMF operations have legal implications, they have not led to significant formal legal changes in either the Articles of the IMF or its operating principles. Thus, it still maintains that it operates on the basis of the principles of uniformity and universality even though, in many situations, it does in fact distinguish between different groups of countries. It now also is pushing its member states to undertake reforms that clearly have social and political implications but it continues to maintain that it is a technocratic organization which is precluded from taking political factors into consideration. This results in it avoiding having to establish rules and procedures for engaging with all relevant stakeholders in a society. In addition, it enables it to avoid acknowledging all the implications of its growing *de facto* role in the policy making process of many of its member states. . Finally, the IMF has changed the substance of its relationship with those states to whom it provides financing but not the form. Thus, the IMF still relies on the standby arrangement even though the benefits that this legal form provided during the era of the par values are no longer applicable and a new legal form for this financing would be more appropriate.

7
The Other International Financial Institutions

In the years following the establishment of the World Bank Group (WBG) and the International Monetary Fund (IMF), states have created a number of other international financial institutions (IFIs). These have all been 'sub-universal' in the sense that they are only intended to provide benefits to a specifically designated group of states. These groups are characterized either by geography or some other salient factor. The majority of these entities, like the WBG, are multilateral development financing institutions but there are a few entities that, like the IMF, have an international financial stability and monetary mandate.

One indicator of the number of IFIs that have been created over the past seventy years is that in 2017, there were eighty IFIs that were accorded legal recognition under United Kingdom's International Organizations Act of 1968.[1] While it is likely that this is not a full accounting of all international financial institutions in the world, it is a meaningful indicator. The reason is that because of London's status as an international financial centre, there are some IFIs, in addition to those in which the United Kingdom is a member state, that wish to have a presence in London and so seek recognition from its government.

The purpose of this chapter is to provide an overview of these different entities and to discuss some of the international legal issues that they raise. It is divided into two sections. The first focuses on the multilateral development financing institutions. The second section concentrates on the multilateral entities with international financial stability and monetary

[1] C Chance, 'Briefing Note: The Status of Multilateral Financial Institutions in English Law' (2017) 1–4 <https://www.cliffordchance.com/content/dam/cliffordchance/briefings/2017/06/the-status-of-multilateral-financial-institutions-in-english-law.pdf> (accessed 23 May 2022). United Kingdom International Organizations Act 1968, https://www.legislation.gov.uk/ukpga/1968/48/introduction (accessed 22 June 2023).

mandates. Both of these sections are divided into two parts. The first part is a brief overview of the relevant entities. The second discusses the specific international legal issues that they raise.

Sub-universal development financing institutions

As was discussed in Chapter 5 the World Bank's first loans were to European countries seeking financing for their post-Second World War reconstruction efforts.[2] Following the establishment of the Marshall Plan and the beginning of growth in European economies, the World Bank's focus shifted to financing projects in developing countries. The demand for its loans grew as the number of its member states increased following the period of decolonization in Africa and Asia.[3] These newly independent states, while interested in borrowing from the World Bank, were also concerned that their particular needs would not be optimally served in an institution that was global in focus and was controlled by a small group of richer states that included their former colonial masters.

As a result, beginning in the late 1950s, regional groupings of developing countries began efforts to establish new development banks that would be more responsive to their needs and would give them a greater voice and vote in the governance of the institutions. This resulted in 1959 in the creation of the first regional development bank, the Inter-American Development Bank (IDB).[4] It was followed by the establishment of the African Development Bank (AfDB) in 1964,[5] and the Asian Development Bank (ADB) in 1966.[6] States also formed sub-regional development banks, such as the Corporación Andina de Fomento (CAF) in 1966,[7] the East

[2] See Chapter 5.

[3] MJ Hogan, *The Marshall Plan: America, Britain, and the Reconstruction of Western Europe, 1947–1952 (Studies in Economic History and Policy: USA in the Twentieth Century)* (CUP 1989) 1–125; B Steil, *The Marshall Plan: Dawn of the Cold War* (Council of Foreign Relations 2019).

[4] Agreement establishing the Inter-American Development Bank, 8 April 1959 (389 UNTS 69, UN Reg No I-5593), entered into force 30 December 1959 <https://treaties.un.org/pages/untsonline.aspx?id=3&clang=_en> (accessed 23 May 2022) (IIDB Articles).

[5] Agreement establishing the African Development Bank, 4 August 1963 (510 UNTS 46, UN Reg No I-7408), entered into force 7 May 1982 <https://treaties.un.org/pages/untsonline.aspx?id=3&clang=_en> (accessed 23 May 2022) (AfDB Articles).

[6] Articles of Agreement establishing the Asian Development Bank, 4 December 1965 (1887 UNTS 454, UN Reg No I-8303) entered into force 22 August 1966 <https://treaties.un.org/pages/untsonline.aspx?id=3&clang=_en> (accessed 23 May 2022) (ADB Articles).

[7] CAF, 'About CAF' <https://www.caf.com/> (accessed 23 May 2022).

African Development Bank in 1967,[8] and the Caribbean Development Bank in 1969.[9]

The international community created a second generation of regional multilateral development banks (MDBs) following the end of the Cold War. In 1991, acting on a proposal from the French President, the international community established the European Bank for Reconstruction and Development (EBRD).[10] Its original purpose was to develop market economies and promote private sector development in former Soviet bloc states that were committed to 'the principles of multiparty democracy, pluralism and market economies'.[11]

More recently, China has been a driving force behind the establishment of two new multilateral development banks. Working with the other member states in the BRICS—Brazil, Russia, India, China, and South Africa—it established the New Development Bank (NDB) in 2014.[12] It also led the initiative to establish the Asian Infrastructure Investment Bank (AIIB),[13] which opened for business in 2016 with fifty-seven member states, thirty-seven of which were regional member states.[14]

These three generations of sub-universal development banks share a number of common characteristics but also have some important differences. They can be divided into three categories.

[8] Treaty and Charter of the East African Development Bank 6 June 1967. This treaty is part of the Treaty for East African cooperation, 6 June 1967 (UN Reg No 1-34026), entered into force 1 December 1967 <https://treaties.un.org/pages/untsonline.aspx?id=3&clang=_en> (accessed 23 May 2022).

[9] Treaty establishing the Caribbean Development Bank, 18 October 1969 (712 UNTS 217, UN Reg No I-10232), entered into force 26 January 1970 <https://treaties.un.org/pages/untsonline.aspx?id=3&clang=_en> (accessed 23 May 2022).

[10] Agreement establishing the European Bank for Reconstruction and Development (EBRD) 29 May 1990 (OJ L 372, 31.12.1990, 4–26), entered into force 28 March 1991 <https://eur-lex.europa.eu/legal-content/EN/TXT/PDF/?uri=CELEX:21990A1231(01)&from=EN> (EBRD Articles). See EBRD, 'The History of the EBRD' <https://www.ebrd.com/who-we-are/history-of-the-ebrd.html> (accessed 23 May 2022). See S Weber, 'Origins of the European Bank for Reconstruction and Development' (1994) 48 International Organization 1–38.

[11] EBRD Articles, Preamble and Article 1.

[12] 'Agreement on the New Development Bank' (15 July 2014) <https://www.ndb.int/wp-content/themes/ndb/pdf/Agreement-on-the-New-Development-Bank.pdf> (accessed 23 May 2022) (NDB Articles).

[13] Agreement establishing the Asian Infrastructure Investment Bank 22 May 2015, entered into force 29 June 2015 <https://www.aiib.org/en/about-aiib/basic-documents/_download/articles-of-agreement/basic_document_english-bank_articles_of_agreement.pdf> (AIIB Articles).

[14] N Lichtenstein, *A Comparative Guide to the Asian Infrastructure Investment Bank* (OUP 2018)

Regional development banks modelled on the WBG

The first category consists of development banks that are regional in focus and are modelled on the World Bank. The AfDB, ADB, and IDB are the leading examples of these regional development banks. Each of these banks, like the World Bank, has a capital structure that is based on a mix of paid-in and callable capital.[15] The capital is divided into shares with each member state allocated shares according to a formula that is based on the size of their economies. Thus, member states have weighted votes, with each of their votes depending on the size of their capital contribution.

Each of these banks also has both regional member states and non-regional member states.[16] The latter group of states cannot borrow from these banks but are eligible to compete for procurement contracts on the projects the banks finance. The non-regional member states are also represented on the boards of the regional development banks and have a vote that reflects their investments in the relevant bank. Each of the banks also seeks to ensure that the regional member states have a leading voice in the governance of the institution. Consequently, they limit the total vote of non-regional member states. This is expected to limit the role that the non-regional member states as a group can play in the governance of the institutions.[17]

The AfDB provides a good example of the efforts that regional development banks have made to limit the role of non-regional member states. Originally, membership in the bank was limited to African states.[18] However, the exclusion of non-regional members proved to be unsustainable for financial reasons. As a result, the AfDB decided to offer membership to non-regional states that were willing to contribute capital to the bank. Today, twenty-seven of the AfDB's eighty-seven member states are non-regional member states.[19] In order to preserve Africa's voice in the affairs of the bank, the Articles provide that more than 50 per cent of the members of the Board of Executive Directors must represent African states.[20] Analogous efforts to ensure that regional member states have a

[15] AfDB Articles, Art 5; ADB Articles, Art 4; IDB Articles, Article II Section 2.

[16] AfDB Articles, Art 3(3); ADB Articles Art 3(1); IDB Articles, Art II(b).

[17] AfDB Articles, Art 35; ADB Articles, Art 11; IDB Articles, Art VIII(4).

[18] ADB Articles, Arts 1 and 2.

[19] AfDB member countries <https://www.afdb.org/en/about-us/corporate-information/members> (accessed 25 May 2022).

[20] AfDB Articles, Art 33(1).

leading voice in the governance of their institutions were made at the ADB and the IDB.[21]

These regional development banks share a number of characteristics with the World Bank in addition to their capital and governance structures. First, they have both a non-concessional and a concessional financing window. The AfDB has the African Development Fund[22] to provide concessional financing to low-income African countries; and the ADB has the Asian Development Fund for the same purpose.[23] The IDB had the Fund for Special Operations, which offered concessional financing to low-income member states. In 2017, the fund was merged with the IDB's capital and replaced by a blended financing option that provides consessional financing to qualifying borrowers.[24]

Second, like the World Bank Group, these regional banks provide financing to both public and private sector borrowers. However, unlike the World Bank, they do not necessarily provide this financing through a separate entity. The AfDB and the ADB both provide this financing through their general bank operations.[25] The IDB, on the other hand, has created a separate entity to fund the private sector, which is comparable in structure and function to the World Bank Group's, International Finance Corporation.[26]

Third, all these entities are designed to be technocratic financial institutions. Consequently, like the World Bank, they are expected to base their lending decisions on economic and not political criteria. Their Articles of Agreement contain the identical political prohibition clause as the World Bank entities.[27]

[21] AfDB Articles, Art 30(1)(a); ADB Articles, Art VIII(3)(b)(ii) ADB Articles.

[22] Agreement establishing the African Development Fund <https://www.afdb.org/fileadmin/uploads/afdb/Documents/Legal-Documents/Agreement_establishing_the_African_development_fund_2016_edition.pdf> (accessed 17 March 2023). It should be noted that the AfDB has a second concessionary window, the Nigerian Development Fund. See Agreement establishing the Nigeria Trust Fund and Technical Cooperation Agreement Between the Federal Republic of Nigeria and the African Development Bank and the African Development Fund 2004 available at <https://www.afdb.org/fileadmin/uploads/afdb/Documents/Legal-Documents/00157770-EN-NTF-AGREEMENT.PDF> (accessed 17 March 2023).

[23] 'ADB Asian Development Fund overview' <https://www.adb.org/what-we-do/funds/adf/overview> (accessed 25 May 2022).

[24] 'Concessional Financing', <https://www.iadb.org/en/idb-finance/concessional-financing> (accessed 22 June 2023).

[25] AfDB Articles, Article 11 , ADB Articles, Article 2.

[26] Agreement establishing the Inter-American Investment Corporation [MS No 7/2018]. See also <https://idbinvest.org/en> (accessed 26 May 2022).

[27] Art IV (10) International Bank for Reconstruction and Development Articles of Agreement Article (as amended effective 27 June 2012). For comparable provisions, see AfDB Articles, Art 38; ADB Articles, Art 36; IDB Articles, Art III.

Finally, all three regional development banks have independent accountability mechanisms, comparable to the World Bank's Inspection Panel, to enhance their accountability to communities and individuals who may have been adversely affected by their failure to comply with their own operational policies and procedures.[28]

Another important regional development bank that belongs in this first category is the European Investment Bank (EIB).[29] This bank was created in 1957 by the Treaty of Rome[30] to promote investment in the undeveloped regions of the member states of the European Economic Community.[31] Subsequent to its establishment, the EIB acquired a mandate to invest at least some of its funds outside the member states of the European Union.[32] As a result, it now has financed a portfolio of projects in developing countries.[33] Its operations in these countries have sometimes been as controversial as those of the other development banks. It is important to note that since the EIB is a European institution, its operations fall under the jurisdiction of the European Ombudsman.[34] Consequently, non-state actors who allege they have been harmed by the operations of the EIB, provided their complaints meet the requirements for submission to the European Ombudsman, can complain to the European Ombudsman.

[28] Eg, 'What is MICI?' <https://www.iadb.org/en/mici/mici-independent-consultation-and-investigation-mechanism> MICI in IDB, Independent Review Mechanism in the AfDB <https://www.afdb.org/en/independent-review-mechanism-irm#:~:text=The%20mandate%20of%20the%20IRM,its%20own%20policies%20and%20procedures>; Accountability Mechanism at the ADB <https://www.adb.org/who-we-are/accountability-mechanism/main#:~:text=ADB's%20Accountability%20Mechanism%20provides%20a,ADB's%20operational%20policies%20and%20procedures> (all accessed 26 May 2022).

[29] EIB, 'European Investment Bank is the Bank of the European Union' <https://www.eib.org/en/index.htm> (accessed 26 May 2022).

[30] European Union, 'Treaty establishing the European Community (Consolidated Version)' (25 March 1957) <https://www.refworld.org/docid/3ae6b39c0.html> (accessed 29 June 2022) (Rome Treaty).

[31] Rome Treaty, Arts 129 and 130.

[32] EIB, 'Our region of activities' <https://www.eib.org/en/projects/regions/index.htm> and <https://european-union.europa.eu/institutions-law-budget/institutions-and-bodies/institutions-and-bodies-profiles/eib_en> (accessed 26 May 2022).

[33] The EIB is an important development financing institution. For example, in 2021 it made €1.6 billion in new commitment to developing countries, €8.9 billion in disbursements and its total stock of outstanding loans to developing countries was €9.3 billion. See Global Solutions, 'International Partnerships', The European Investment Bank Development Report 2021 69.

[34] See European Ombudsman <https://www.ombudsman.europa.eu/en/home> (accessed 27 May 2022).

Development financing institutions with a political/ideological purpose

The second category of development financing institutions are those that have a political or ideological character as well as an economic one. The most prominent examples in this category are the EBRD[35] and the Islamic Development Bank (IsDB),[36] which was established in 1975. As discussed above, the EBRD, pursuant to its Articles of Agreement is mandated to promote market-based economies.[37] As a result, the EBRD tends to focus on private sector development. The bank is also authorized to promote multiparty democracies but this has not been a clear and substantial part of its operations.[38] One indicator that the bank does have a political as well as economic agenda is that after the Arab Spring in 2011, the Articles of the Bank was amended to allow it to accept the states in the Middle East as member states in which it could fund projects and to which it could provide technical support.[39] It is important to note that in other respects the EBRD is modelled on the IBRD. Thus, its members' contributions to the bank's capital are based on a formula and they have weighted votes in its governance structure.[40] Unlike the first group of regional development banks, the EBRD does not to have a concessional financing window. It does however have an independent accountability mechanism.[41]

The IsDB has a similar development mission to the IBRD and the regional development banks. However, its focus is on providing development finance to Islamic member states, defined in terms of membership of the Organization of Islamic States.[42] The Bank is also concerned with

[35] EBRD Articles.

[36] Islamic Development Bank (IsDB) 'Articles of Agreement' (12 August 1974) available at <https://www.isdb.org/sites/default/files/media/documents/2019-10/IsDB%20Articles%20of%20Agreement.pdf> (accessed 17 March 2023) (IsDB Articles).

[37] EBRD Articles, Article 1

[38] ibid. 'Political Aspects of the Mandate of the European Bank for Reconstruction and Development' (2013) <https://www.ebrd.com/news/publications/instituational-documents/political-aspects-of-the-mandate-of-the-ebrd.html> (accessed 27 May 2022). See S Shields, 'The EBRD, Fail Forward Neoliberalism and the Construction of the European Periphery' (2020) 31(2) The Economic and Labour Relations Review 230–248.

[39] EBRD Articles, Arts 1, 61; 'The History of the EBRD' (n 10).

[40] EBRD Articles, Art 5 and Annex A: Initial subscriptions to the authorized capital stock for prospective members which may become members in accordance with Article 61, Basic Documents of the EBRD 2013, <www.ebrd.com> (accessed 24 June 2023).

[41] EBRD Independent Project Accountability Mechanism (last updated: 1 July 2020) <https://www.ebrd.com/what-we-do/independent-project-accountability-mechanism.html> (accessed 27 May 2022).

[42] IsDB Articles, Arts 1, 2, and 3.

promoting Islamic principles and values as part of the development activities that it finances. This means that the bank provides financing in accordance with Islamic banking principles, which prohibit the payment of interest. The ISDB therefore provides financing to its member states on a risk sharing basis rather than by making loans that carry a contractually enforceable interest rate. It is important to note that the bank's Articles contain a similar political prohibition to the other development banks.[43] This is interesting because of the banks' explicit focus on promoting development consistent with Islamic principles, which means that its operations have a moral as well as an economic content.[44]

The fact that the bank operates on Islamic banking principles has a number of ramifications. First, it means that the bank only funds projects that are amenable to risk and profit-sharing arrangements. This means that the IsDB tends to favour projects that have relatively predictable revenue flows. As a result, it is a relatively conservative lender.[45] Second, it means that the legal contracts involved in its financing arrangements are Sharia-compliant. As a result, they contain some different provisions from those used by the World Bank and the regional development banks. In particular, since the borrower does not have an obligation to pay interest, the provisions dealing with the security arrangements and the events of default will differ from the more standard MDB contracts.[46]

Another interesting difference between the IsDB and the other MDBs, which is unrelated to its Islamic character, is that the IsDB is authorized to accept deposits from its member states. In this respect, the bank functions more like a commercial bank than the other development banks.[47]

[43] ISDB Articles, Art 37.

[44] IsDB, *The Road to the SDGs: The President's Programme A New Business Model for a Fast-Changing World* (2019) 9, 87–89.

[45] M Tabash and R Dhankar, 'The Relevance of Islamic Finance Principles in Economic Growth' (2014) 3 International Journal of Emerging Research in Management & Technology 49–52; S Franzoni and AA Allali, 'Principles of Islamic Finance and Principles of Corporate Social Responsibility: What Convergence?' (2018) 10 Sustainability 637, 638–643.

[46] M Hussain, A Shahmoradi, and R Turk, 'An Overview of Islamic Finance' (2015) IMF *WP* Working Papers 15/120 5–16; N Alam, L Gupta, and B Shanmugam, *Islamic Finance: A Practical Perspective* 35–55, 1st edn (Palgrave Macmillan 2017).

[47] IsDB Articles, Art 8.

Development banks created by the Global South

The third category of development banks consists of banks that have been created by the countries in the Global South, although they may accept other countries as member states. These banks have been established with the objective of financing development in a way that is more responsive to the needs and concerns of the countries of the Global South. The most prominent examples of this category are the AIIB and NDB.

China intended the AIIB to be both a new source of funding for infrastructure in Asia and to offer an alternate development financing model from the Western led institutions such as the World Bank and the ADB.[48] In particular, the AIIB promised to reduce the upfront costs and lead time involved in development bank financing.[49] It is interesting to note, therefore, that the bank relied on a number of former World Bank officials to draft its Articles of Agreement and its operating principles and practices.[50]

Since it began operations in 2016, both the AIIB's membership and the scope of its operations have grown. Its 105 member states now include a number of Western countries and emerging markets and developing countries from outside the Asian region.[51] It has also expanded the scope of its financing operations to include projects in non-Asian countries.[52] In order to preserve the Asian character of the Bank, its Articles provide that non-regional members cannot own more than one third of the shares in the bank and that the regional members will always have at least 75 per cent of the total vote in the bank.[53]

The NDB was established initially to fund development in the five BRICS member states—Brazil, Russia, India, China and South Africa—although its Articles provide that the member states can allow other states to join the bank. Each of these states contributed an equal amount to the bank's capital.[54] They also each have an equal vote in the bank's governance. Since it was created

[48] Lichtenstein, *A Comparative Guide* (n 14) 4–7.

[49] Id. at 15-19. See, for example, Statement by J Liqun at a Press Conference in Tbilisi (26 August 2015) <https://www.aiib.org/en/news-events/news/2015/Statement-by-Jin-Liqun-at-a-Press-Conference-in-Tbilisi.html> (accessed 29 May 2022). (Bank President states that bank would be managed as a 'lean, green and clean' organization.)

[50] Lichtenstein, *A Comparative Guide* (n 14) 12–13.

[51] 'AIIB Members and Prospective Members of the Bank' <https://www.aiib.org/en/about-aiib/governance/members-of-bank/index.html> (accessed 27 May 2022).

[52] 'AIIB Financing Operations' <https://www.aiib.org/en/about-aiib/who-we-are/financing-operations/index.html> (accessed 27 May 2022).

[53] AIIB Articles, Art 5(2) and (3).

[54] N Duggan, JC Ladines Azalia, and M Rewizorski, 'The Structural Power of the BRICS (Brazil, Russia, India, China and South Africa) in Multilateral Development Finance: A Case

as a BRICS institution, the bank has an implicit mission to promote reform of the arrangements for global economic governance.[55] In particular, they seek to promote global governance arrangements that are more responsive to the concerns and interests of the BRICS and other countries in the Global South. Interestingly, while the BRICS are concerned about their lack of voice in global economic governance, they provided in the NDB's Articles that the five founding states would always have a combined vote in the affairs of the bank equal to 55 per cent.[56] Recently, four additional states—Bangladesh, Ecuador, Egypt, and the United Arab Emirates—have joined the NDB.[57] The NDB expects more states to join the bank over time. However, regardless of how many join the Bank, without amending the Articles, the BRICS will always collectively have the controlling voice in its affairs.

These two banks have characteristics that distinguish them from the Western-backed development banks. First, they, unlike the first two categories of development banks, do not have a resident board of directors. Instead, their directors serve the banks on a part time basis and only meet periodically during the year.[58] As a result, they play a much less active role in the development bank's affairs than is the case in the other multilateral development banks. Second, these banks were intended to respond to their member states concerns about the slow pace of transactions with the earlier multilateral development banks. In the case of this latter group of banks, it is not uncommon for there to be a period of two years between the time when a country first approaches the MDB for financing and the time when the funds are disbursed, and the project can begin.[59] The AIIB and the NDB seek to be much quicker in providing financing. This, of course, has implications for the social and environmental impacts of the projects funded by

Study of the New Development Bank' (2021) International Political Science Review 1–13. Also see NDB Articles.

[55] S Griffith-Jones, 'A BRICS Development Bank: A Dream Coming True?' (2014) 215 United Nations Conference on Trade and Development Discussion Paper 1–12; G Mostafa, 'The Rise of the BRICS and Their Challenge to the G7' (2015) International Journal of Emerging Markets 156–170.

[56] NDB Articles, Art 8.

[57] New Development Bank <https://www.ndb.int/> (accessed 27 May 2022). The most recent country to join the Bank was Egypt, which joined the Bank on 29 December 2022. See <https://www.ndb.int/press_release/ndb-admits-egypt-as-new-member/> (accessed 22 June 2022).

[58] AIIB Articles, Arts 12(g) and 25; NDB Articles, Art 12(g).

[59] M Hinds, 'Role of Regional Development Banks in Rebuilding the International Financial Architecture' (2002) 179–200 <https://www.cgdev.org/sites/default/files/9780881323535-FinDev5.pdf> (accessed 28 May 2022).

these banks. This is explored below. It should be noted in this regard, that the AIIB has established an accounability mechanism which reports to the presidents of the bank.[60]

International legal issues

The MDB s in all three categories were created by treaties. This means that they are subjects of international law.[61] Their rights and obligations as subjects of international law are, in principle, the same as those of the entities in the World Bank Group. Thus, they have comparable privileges and immunities to these World Bank entities. In short, they are immune from the jurisdiction of their member states and cannot be sued in these states unless they waive that immunity. However, because they all have less than universal membership, their privileges and immunities are only necessarily recognized in their member states. Their legal status and privileges and immunities in non-member states will depend on the domestic law in those non-member states.[62]

One area in which these sub-universal MDBs differ from the World Bank is in the approach they take to the sovereignty and policy prerogatives of the member states. Many of the World Bank's borrower member states view the World Bank as being too intrusive into their policy prerogatives. They maintain that the World Bank's governance arrangements provide non-borrower states with a disproportionately powerful voice. In addition, they argue that the conditions that the World Bank attaches to its financing are burdensome and tend to slow down and complicate projects financed by the World Bank.

The regional development banks sought to address the first issue by ensuring that their regional member states, the actual consumers of their services, had more voice and vote in the governance of the banks.[63] This has contributed to each of the banks being more responsive to the concerns of their regional member states. However, it has not necessarily led to the

[60] See Project-affected People's Mechanism, https://www.aiib.org/en/about-aiib/who-we-are/project-affected-peoples-mechanism/how-we-assist-you/index.html (accessed 22 June 2023).
[61] See Chapter 4.
[62] See, eg, *The Arab Monetary Fund v Hashim & Others* [1997] EWCA Civ 1298 (21 March 1997).
[63] NDB Articles, Art 6.

bank's financing being available more quickly and subject to less conditions than the World Bank.[64]

The AIIB and the NDB the banks have sought to differentiate themselves by having lending practices that are nimbler and simpler than the older development banks.[65] They have sought to do this by deferring more to their member states both in regard to the planning of projects and to the assessment and management of the environmental and social impacts of the project. Thus, they have adopted in a more vigorous form of the 'country systems' approach that that the World Bank pioneered.[66]

The country systems approach, in brief, is premised on the principle that the bank should, whenever possible, defer to the borrowing country's own regulatory regimes, particularly dealing with environmental and social issues, in regard to the projects they finance. This means that, wherever feasible, they will utilize the country's own laws and regulations (the 'country system') in their assessment and management of the project's environmental and social impacts rather than the bank's own policies. The proponents of a country system approach maintain that it is more respectful of the country's sovereignty and its environmental and social policy choices relating to development projects. They further contend that this country systems approach promotes development because it incentivizes the country to improve and implement its own management and regulatory approaches to these issues. In addition, they maintain that this approach should result in projects that are more consistent with local conditions than would be the case if the development bank insists on the borrower applying the bank's environmental and social policies.[67]

[64] Hinds, 'Role of Regional Development Banks' (n 59).

[65] AIIB, 'Who We Are Infrastructure For Tomorrow' <https://www.aiib.org/en/about-aiib/who-we-are/infrastructure)-for-tomorrow/overview/index.html>. Also see Statement by J Liqun at a Press Conference in Tbilisi (26 August 2015) <https://www.aiib.org/en/news-events/news/2015/Statement-by-Jin-Liqun-at-a-Press-Conference-in-Tbilisi.html> (accessed 29 May 2022) (Bank President states that bank would be managed as a 'lean, green and clean' organization).

[66] See, for example. AIIB, Environmental and Social Framework, <https://www.aiib.org/en/policies-strategies/_download/environment-framework/AIIB-Environmental-and-Social-Framework_ESF-November-2022-final.pdf> (accessed 22 June 2023); New Development Bank webpage on Environment and Social Sustainability available at: <https://www.ndb.int/projects/environment-and-social-sustainability/> (accessed 22 June 2023). On World Bank approach to country systems, see 'World Bank Frequently Asked Questions on the use of Country Systems in Bank-supported Operations' (18 October 2004) <http://www1.worldbank.org/publicsector/pe/befa05/usecountrysystems.pdf> (accessed 29 May 2022).

[67] See E Rosenthal, 'The Use of Country Systems in World Bank Lending: A Summary of Lessons from the Pilot Projects and Recommendations for a Better Approach' (CIEL, 2008) 1–6. See also CL Pallas and J Wood, 'The World Bank's Use of Country Systems for Procurement: A Good Idea Gone Bad?' (2009) 27 Development Policy Review 215, ,217–226;

While this seems reasonable in principle, the country systems approach raises a number of difficult issues for the development banks. These include the following: what happens if the domestic law is less rigorous in its requirements than the bank's own policies? What happens if the domestic law would lead to the lenders having to assume less responsibility, and therefore risk, concerning the social and environmental aspects of the projects they finance than would be the case if the bank applied its own policies? What happens if there are complaints that the project is failing to comply with the applicable law? These questions highlight the risks that the country system approach can create for an MDB. They suggest that the country system approach can expose, for example, the AIIB and the NDB to greater risk of reputational damage if serious social or environmental problems arise in a project that they finance than is the case with an MDB that applies its own operational policies. Given that, at the time of writing, the banks only began operating relatively recently and are still learning how to apply their operational policies and practices, it is not yet clear how they will manage these risks or how they react if the risks actually materialize and cause serious operational, reputational or financial challenges for the banks.

An analogous situation has arisen in regard to the EBRD's political mandate. The EBRD has been reluctant to discipline countries that are not complying with its political mandate. This is often on the grounds that each country has the sovereign right to decide how to structure its own internal politics and their decision should be respected by outside actors like the EBRD. However, this leaves open the question of whether or not the EBRD is fulfilling its responsibilities in regard to its political mandate.[68]

Sub-universal international monetary and financial stability entities

During the period that the Bretton Woods system functioned, the IMF was able to provide the financial safety net that its member states around the

S Knack, 'Building or Bypassing Recipient Country Systems: Are Donors Defying the Paris Declaration?' (2014) 50 The Journal of Development Studies 839–854. For an African Use perspective on the use-of-country system, see C Prinsloo, C Markowitz, EM Jamea, and K Owino, 'Informing the Approach of Multilateral Development Banks to use of Country Systems' (2017) *Global Economic Governance Discussion Paper* 5–23.

[68] Political Aspects of the Mandate of the European Bank for Reconstruction and Development 2013, <https://www.ebrd.com/news/publications/instituational-documents/political-aspects-of-the-mandate-of-the-ebrd.html> (accessed 24 June 2023).

world needed. This was related to the fact that the par value system imposed some constraints on the macro-economic policies of member states and on the size of the imbalances that could arise between countries. As a result, in fact, the IMF was able to meet the financing needs of most countries facing payments challenges.[69] However, when the Bretton Woods system ended, the situation changed and the volatility in the international monetary system increased. The international monetary situations of states became less predictable. They also became less confident that the IMF would have adequate resources to meet their needs in case of a crisis. In addition, the policies adopted by the IMF in the post-Bretton Woods era and the conditionalities it attached to its financing became more controversial.[70] This led some states to decide that establishing alternate sources of financial support in cases of payments crises would be desirable.

The first regions in which states established alternative sources of support were the Middle East and South America. In 1976 the states of the Middle East created the Arab Monetary Fund.[71] It became operational in 1977 and has twenty-two member states.[72] Its objective is to promote monetary and financial stability in the region. Its mandate and operating approach are similar to the IMF. Its governance structure is also similar to the IMF's.[73]

In 1978, five South American countries created the Andean Reserve Fund[74] to help them deal with their external payments imbalances and to promote regional integration. In 1989, these five countries, interested in expanding their fund to the rest of Latin America, converted the fund into the Latin American Reserve Fund.[75] In the ensuing years, four more countries

[69] It is important to note that the one qualification on this statement is that the IMF established the General Agreement to Borrow to deal with possible financing challenges that could arise following financing requests from the G10 countries; see Chapter 6.

[70] There is an extensive literature on IMF Conditionality. See, eg, J Williamson, 'On Seeking to Improve IMF Conditionality' (1983) 73 American Economic Review 354–358; R Jolly, 'Adjustment with a Human Face: A UNICEF Record and Perspective on the 1980s' (1991) 19 World Development 1807–1821; JB Zulu and SM Nsouli, 'Adjustment Programs in Africa: The Recent Experience' (1985) 34 IMF Occasional Papers 1–40; and JR Vreeland, *The International Monetary Fund: Politics of Conditional Lending* 5–73 (Routledge 2007).

[71] The Articles of Agreement of the Arab Monetary Fund official English translation (27 April 1976).

[72] AMF, 'About us'<https://www.amf.org.ae/en/about-us> (accessed 29 May 2022).

[73] ibid.

[74] Andean Group: Treaty for the Creation of the Andean Reserve Fund (12 November 1976) entered into force 8 June 1978.

[75] 'Treaty establishing the Latin American Reserve Fund' (1989) ILM 1219.(original signatories of the treaty are Bolivia, Colombia, Ecuador, Peru, and Venezuela).

joined the organization.[76] The purpose of the organization is to support member states facing balance of payments problems either by providing them with loans or loan guarantees, improve investment opportunities for the foreign reserves of the member countries and to help harmonize their exchange rate and monetary and financial policies.[77] Thus, this Fund has a broader mandate than the IMF. Its governance structure is also a bit different in that the central bank governors of the member states serve as the board of directors of the Fund and the ministers of finance are the board of governors.[78] In addition, the Fund has a small secretariat for doing technical work and implementing the policies adopted by the boards of governors and directors. The Fund is fully operational. On a number of occasions, it has responded to requests from its member states and provided them with financial support to deal with their financial and monetary problems.[79]

Following the Asian financial crisis in the mid-1990s, the countries in theAssociation of Southeast Asian Nations (ASEAN)countries began to consider the possibility of creating a regional financial institution. They eventually worked together with China, Japan, and South Korea to establish the Chiang Mai Initiative.[80] This was initially a series of bilateral swap arrangements between the participating central banks. It enabled each of them to swap their currency for stipulated amounts of foreign exchange with each of the other participating central banks with which they had bilateral swap arrangements. Interestingly, the participants agreed that they could only swap a stipulated fraction of the agreed total amount for the swap arrangement without conditions. In order to access the additional funding, the state would have to also enter into a financing programme with the

[76] FLAR, 'About FLAR' <https://flar.com/en/about-flar> (accessed 29 May 2022).

[77] Preamble and Art 3 Treaty establishing the Latin American Reserve Fund 1989. See B Turner, 'Latin American Reserve Fund' in B Turner (ed), *The Statesman's Yearbook: The Politics, Cultures and Economies of the World* (2002) 84; D Titelman, C Vera, P Carvallo, and EP Caldentey, 'A Regional Reserve Fund for Latin America' (2014) 112 CEPAL Review 8–27.

[78] ibid.

[79] See FLAR, 'Regional institutions' deposits' <https://flar.com/en/what-we-do/other-services> (accessed 30 May 2022).

[80] ADB Asia Regional Integration Center, Money and Finance Chiang Mai Initiative [Multilateralisation] <https://aric.adb.org/initiative/chiang-mai-initiative> and AMRO, Overview of CMIM <https://www.amro-asia.org/about-amro/amro-and-the-cmim/>. See also C Sussangkarn, 'The Chiang Mai Initiative Multilateralization: Origin, Development and Outlook' (2010) 6(230) Asian Development Bank Institute, Working Papers 1–19. See also BSP Research Primer, 'Chiang Mai Initiative Multilateralization' (October 2021) <https://www.bsp.gov.ph/Media_and_Research/Primers%20Faqs/Chiang_Mai_Initiative_Multilateralization_FAQ.pdf>; JT Chow, 'Chiang Mai Agreement' (2015) in Encyclopedia Britannica, <https://www.britannica.com/event/Chiang-Mai-Agreement> (accessed 30 May 2022).

IMF.[81] The central bank's access to the remaining amount from its Chiang Mai counterpart would therefore be subject to the same conditionalities as applied to the IMF's financing.

Eventually, the parties agreed to multilateralize the arrangement, renaming it as the Chiang Mai Initiative Multilateralization (CMIM).[82] This meant that the swap arrangements were no longer only bilateral. A participant could now engage in a swap transaction with all its counterparties in the CMIM rather than just one at a time. The arrangement however retained its link to an IMF programme, although the percentage of the total swap amount that a participant could access before having to go to the IMF was increased. In addition to multilateralizing the swap arrangements, the agreement on CMIM also resulted in the creation of the ASEAN + 3 Monetary Research Office (AMRO).[83] This office monitors macroeconomic conditions in the participating states. It can also provide advice to states on their macroeconomic and monetary situations.

Following the establishment of the CMIM two other groups of countries established inter-central bank swap arrangements. First, a number of central banks from the member states of the South-East Asian Association for Regional Cooperation (SAARC) entered into bilateral swap arrangements.[84] It is important to note that these swap arrangements are not subject to a link to IMF financing as is the case with the CMIM. However, swap arrangements exist only among some of the SAARC member states. These swap arrangements have, in fact, been activated. In 2022, two SAARC member states entered into a central bank swap transaction. In this case, the Sri Lankan central bank engaged in a swap transaction with the Reserve Bank of India.[85]

[81] See JD Ciorciari, 'Chiang Mai Initiative Multilateralization: International Politics and Institution-Building in Asia' (2011) 51 (5) Asian Survey 926–952.

[82] ibid.

[83] AMRO, 'About AMRO: Who we are' <https://www.amro-asia.org/about-amro/who-we-are/> (accessed 30 May 2022).

[84] SAARC, 'About SAARC' (12 July 2020) <https://www.saarc-sec.org/index.php/about-saarc/about-saarc>. MFAsia, South Asian Association for Regional Cooperation (SAARC) <https://mfasia.org/mfa_programs/advocacy/south-asian-association-for-regional-cooperation/#:~:text=The%20South%20Asian%20Association%20for,Lanka%20formally%20adopted%20the%20charter> (accessed 30 May 2022).

[85] Reserve Bank of India, <https://www.rbi.org.in/Scripts/AboutusDisplay.aspx> (accessed 30 May 2022).

In 2012, the BRICS building on the model of the CMIM, created the Contingent Reserve Arrangement (CRA).[86] The CRA is structured as a treaty between the BRICS states supplemented by an inter-central bank operational agreement.[87] The central bank agreement allows any of the participating banks to enter into swap transactions with the other central banks up to stipulated amounts. It is important to note that, as with the CMIM, the central banks can only enter into these swap arrangements for a portion of the stipulated amount before they need to enter into a financing arrangement with the IMF.[88] After they have entered into this arrangement with the IMF, they can access the remaining CRA funds through swap transactions with their counterpart central banks. Access to this second tranche, therefore, is effectively subject to the same conditionalities as the IMF transaction.

It is important to note that, as of the time of writing, neither the CMIM nor the CRA has ever actually been used by any of their participants. However, they have both run tests to ensure that the arrangement will work if it ever is required.[89]

Another example of a regional financial arrangement is the European Stability Mechanism.[90] This was established after the European financial crises in 2012. Its purpose is to help the Eurozone countries avoid financial crises and maintain financial stability. It provides financing to its member states when this is necessary to maintain financial stability in the Euro area.

[86] A Mazenda and R Ncwadi, 'The Rise of BRICS Development Finance Institutions: A Comprehensive Look into the New Development Bank and the Contingency Reserve Arrangement' (2016) 3 African East-Asian Affairs 96–123.

[87] 'Treaty for the Establishment of a BRICS Contingent Reserve Arrangement entered into force 15 July 2014' <https://web.archive.org/web/20150925234418/http://brics.itamaraty.gov.br/media2/press-releases/220-treaty-for-the-establishment-of-a-brics-contingent-reserve-arrangement-fortaleza-july-15> (accessed 30 May 2022).

[88] N Cattaneo, M Biziwick, and D Frye, 'The BRICS Contingent Reserve Arrangement and its position in the Emerging Global Financial Architecture' (2015) 10 SAIIA Policy Insights 1–7.

[89] Y Kadogawa, V Khut, LL Ong, C Poonpatpibul, J Shimizu, and H Wang, 'Asia and the CMIM in the Evolving International Monetary System' (2018) 18/01 AMRO Working Paper 21–26. See IMF, *Collaboration Between Regional Financing Arrangements and the IMF - Background IMF Paper Policy* (2017) 3–25; and AI Würdemann, 'The BRICS Contingent Reserve Arrangement: A Subversive Power Against the IMF's Conditionality?' (2018) 19 The Journal of World Investment & Trade 570–593. See R Singhal, 'NDB: A pivot to financial alternatives' (2015) 4–7 <https://www.gatewayhouse.in/wp-content/uploads/2015/10/Rishi_Fudan-full-report.pdf> (accessed 30 May 2022).

[90] European Stability Mechanism, 'Who we are' <https://www.esm.europa.eu/about-us> (accessed 30 May 2022).

Finally, the Eurasian Fund for Stabilization and Development[91] was established in 2009 by Russia and five former Soviet states to both help the countries maintain financial and monetary stability and to help them raise funds for development. Thus, the Fund operates as both a development bank and a monetary fund.

As can be seen from the above, the IMF has been supplemented by a set of sub-universal, primarily regional, financial arrangements. While these arrangements differ in form and mandate, they are all designed to help support the states participating in the arrangement deal with monetary imbalances and financial instability. However, the arrangements are not large enough to eliminate the need for their participating states to draw on IMF financial and policy support. In fact, in some cases, their support is explicitly linked to support from the IMF. Nevertheless, these arrangements are significant. Their existence is a symptom of declining global confidence in the IMF and, arguably, its capacity to effectively address any monetary or financial crises that its member states may experience. It is also arguably an expression of the participating states concerns about the current arrangements for global economic governance and the international economic order that it helps support.[92]

Another important feature of all these regional arrangements is that they are evidence of the dominant role that the US dollar plays in international finance.[93] All these arrangements are essentially arrangements to either directly provide the participating state with US dollars or to help them deal with a balance of payments crisis that arises in some way from their limited access to US dollars.

The fact that the currency of one state is playing such an important and dominant role in the international monetary system, while important in economic and financial terms, is not per se an international legal issue. This follows from the fact that it does not affect the legal status of any of these entities or of the legal forms of their transactions with their participating states. However, it does raise important questions, which are outside the

[91] See Eurasian Fund for Stabilization and Development (EFSD) <https://www.devex.com/organizations/eurasian-fund-for-stabilization-and-development-efsd-65527> (accessed 30 May 2022).

[92] Fiscal Policy Research Institute, *The Role of Regional Financial Safety Nets in the Global Architecture* (FPRI 2012) 9–41. See also C Rhee, L Sumulong, and S Vallee, 'Global and Regional Financial Safety Nets: Lessons from Europe & Asia, in C Rhee and AS Posen (eds), *Responding to Financial Crisis: Lessons from Asia Then, the United States and Europe Now* (2013) 213–246.

[93] See Chapter 8.

scope of this book, about the international legal responsibility of the issuing country of the dominant currency and its central bank.[94]

International legal status issues

The international legal status of these regional financial arrangements differ. The Latin American Reserve Fund and the AMF are both international organizations established by treaty. Consequently, they are subjects of international law and have the rights, privileges and immunities that go with that status—at least in the signatory states.

The fact that these institutions are regional in scope and so are established by a treaty signed by a small group of states raises the issue of their status in non-signatory states. The Arab Monetary Fund (AMF or Fund) had a role in establishing an important precedent regarding the status of international organizations in non- member states.[95] The Fund sought to sue its former executive director in an English court. The issue before the court was to decide whether, given that the United Kingdom was neither a member of the AMF nor had taken action to recognize it under the International Organizations Act, a UK statute, the AMF had standing to sue in English courts. Ultimately, the court decided that if the entity was incorporated under the law of a foreign state, it could be recognized under principles of comity by the English courts and would have standing to sue. However, if it was only an international organization created by treaty then unless the UK government was a member of the organization so that its treaty had been ratified pursuant to UK domestic law or it had been recognized as an international organization under the applicable UK domestic law, the AMF would not have standing to sue. Since the UK government had not taken any action in domestic law to recognize the AMF and the AMF was only created by an international treaty to which the UK was not party, it did not have standing to sue in English courts. This decision resulted in the former executive director evading liability for allegedly embezzling funds from the AMF.

94 For more information on this issue, see D Bradlow and SK Park, 'A Global Leviathan Emerges: The Federal Reserve, COVID-19, and International Law' (2020) 114 American Journal of International Law 1–10 <https://repository.up.ac.za/bitstream/handle/2263/79509/Bradlow_Global_2020.pdf?sequence=1&isAllowed=y> (accessed 29 June 2022).

95 *The Arab Monetary Fund v Hashim & Ors* [1997] EWCA Civ 1298 (21 March 1997).

The international legal status of the CMIM and the CRA is more complicated. The CMIM is established by international agreements between the ministries of finance and the central banks of the ASEAN + 3 states. However, they have established the CMIM as a series of swap arrangements rather than as an organization. Consequently, the CMIM itself has no international status. However, the AMRO has been established by treaty among the member states and so has been established as an international organization. It therefore has the privileges, rights, and immunities of such an international organization.

The CRA has followed the model of the CMIMThe arrangements for the CRA include an umbrella agreement between the participating states. This agreement merely commits the states to establish inter-central bank swap lines between their central banks. Separately, the central banks have entered into an inter-central bank swap agreement that implements the treaty provisions. However, since the central banks are agencies of each of their states and not sovereign states, these agreements do not have the status of an international treaty. They also do not create any new legal persons.

Conclusion

It is clear from this chapter that the universe of international financial institutions has expanded dramatically since the Bretton Woods conference and the establishment of the IMF and the World Bank. The international financial institutions that were created subsequent to their establishment have either been modelled on them or have learned from their experiences. In fact, some of the later IFIs have sought to improve on the examples of the Bretton Woods institutions. In particular, they have sought to be more responsive to the needs of those member states that actually use their services and to be more inclusive in their governance arrangements. Nevertheless, they have not strayed far from the basic model. This is even more true in international legal terms than in operational terms.

8
The Challenges Facing the International Financial Institutions

In addition to being the concluding chapter for this book, this chapter considers those challenges that the international financial institutions (IFIs) are facing and which international law can help address.

The focus on the chapter is on the World Bank Group (World Bank) and the International Monetary Fund (IMF), which will be referred to collectively as the IFIs. It should be noted, however, that some of the challenges and the international legal developments discussed in this chapter are also likely to also apply, *mutatis mutandis*, to the regional development banks and regional financial arrangements.

The chapter will begin by explaining how the context in which the IFIs are having to conduct their operations has changed. A comprehensive discussion of these changes is beyond the scope of this book. Thus, the chapter will focus on those aspects of the global context that are most significant from an international legal perspective. Thereafter it will describe in more detail the specific challenges confronting the IFIs that have international legal implications. The final section of the chapter will discuss what international law can contribute to the IFIs' efforts to address these challenges.

The changing global context

It is indisputable that the global context in which the IFIs must operate today is different in many ways from that which existed when they were established in 1944. For example, the dramatic developments in transport, technology, communications, and in production processes that have taken place over the past seventy years have all profoundly changed the structure of the global economy and the way in which it functions.[1] There have also been substantial shifts in the balance of international economic power since that time. At the end of the Second World War, the United States accounted for 50 per cent of the global economy and for 80 per cent of all foreign exchange reserves.[2] In 2022, the United States accounted for about 24 per cent of the global economy in nominal terms and about 59 per cent of global foreign exchange reserves.[3] China, the second largest economy in nominal terms in 2022, accounted for about 15 per cent of global GDP. Measured in purchasing power parity terms, China is now the largest economy in the world.[4]

These developments have profoundly affected the context in which the IFIs operate.[5] They have influenced the concerns of their member states and the types of issues about which they are likely to seek IFI advice. They also have affected the sorts of projects and programmes that the IFIs fund.[6] Finally, they are also affecting the balance of political power in the world and the role that the IFIs can play in global economic governance.

However, not all the economic and political changes that have occurred over the past seventy years have had international legal implications for the IFIs. For example, they have not changed the international legal status of the IFIs as subjects of international law. In addition, while they have raised questions about the scope of the immunities of the IFIs and their international responsibilities, they have not, in fact, led to substantial changes in their immunities or international responsibilities.[7] In some cases they have

[1] See, eg, R Baldwin, *The Great Convergence: Information Technology and the New Globalization* (Harvard University Press 2016).

[2] See, eg, 'A Short History of the US Economy Since World War II', The Wilson Center, available at <https://medium.com/the-worlds-economy-and-the-economys-world/a-short-history-of-americas-economy-since-world-war-ii-37293cdb640> (accessed 11 November 2022).

[3] See, eg, S Arslanalp, B Eichengreen, and C Simpson-Bell, *The Stealth Erosion of Dollar Dominance* (March 2022) IMF Working Paper. WP/22/58.

[4] These figures are from the World Population Review and are available at <https://worldpopulationreview.com/countries/by-gdp> (accessed 11 November 2022).

[5] See G Gereffi, 'The Global Economy: Organization, Governance, and Development' (2005) 2 The Handbook of Economic Sociology 160–182.

[6] See generally, D Kapur, P Lewis, and R Webb, *The World Bank: Its First Half Century, vol. 1 & 2 Perspectives* (The Brookings Institution Press 1997); ES Mason and RE Asher, *The World Bank since Bretton Woods* (The Brookings Institute Press 1973); JM Boughton, *Back Matter, IMF and the Force of History* (IMF 2014) 1–44; MG de Vries, *The IMF in a Changing World, 1945-85* (IMF 1986).

[7] See, eg, B Hollander, 'Jam v. International Finance Corporation: The End of Absolute International Organizational Sovereign Immunity and the Argument for a Functional Immunity Regime' (2020) 35 Maryland Journal of International Law 202; RSJ Martha, 'International Financial Institutions and Claims of Private Parties: Immunity Obliges' (2012) 3 World Bank Legal Review 93.

contributed to changes in the interpretations of the Articles of Agreement of these institutions, but they have not necessitated substantially amending their Articles.[8]

There are however three developments in the global political economy that both have impacted the context in which IFIs operation and have international legal significance. The first is that the identity of the key actors on the international stage has changed. The second relates to the changes in the functioning of the international financial system. The third is the growing attention to the environmental and social impacts of economic activity. They are each discussed in more detail below.

The changes in identity of key actors in global economic governance

At the end of the Second World War there were ninety-nine sovereign states in the world and large parts of Africa and Asia were subject to colonial rule.[9] The leading international institution during the inter-war years, the League of Nations, was no longer functional. Within a short period, new international organizations, including the IFIs, were established and began working in their member states. As this book has discussed, the IFIs were innovations in global economic governance and, when they opened for business the actual role that they would play in global economic affairs was still uncertain. In fact, when they opened for business, only thirty-nine of the ninety-nine sovereign states had joined the institutions.[10] In addition, the United States enjoyed overwhelming power and influence in the global economy and in the new international organizations.

[8] See, eg, IFI Shihata, *The World Bank Legal Papers* (Martinus Nijhoff 2000) 1–45.

[9] CR Butcher and RD Griffiths, 'States and Their International Relations Since 1816: Introducing Version 2 of the International System(s) Dataset (ISD)' (2020) 46 International Interactions 291–308.

[10] IMF/IBRD Board of Governors Inaugural Meeting Report (8 May 1946) <https://archivescatalog.imf.org/Details/archive/110024924> (accessed 6 June 2022). On the history of IFIs, see, for example, E Helleiner, *Forgotten Foundations of Bretton Woods: International Development and the Making of the Postwar Order* (Cornell University Press 2014) 1–100; Kapur, Lewis, and Webb, *The World Bank* (n 6) 16–73; B Steil, *The Battle of Bretton Woods: John Maynard Keynes, Harry Dexter White, and the Making of a New World Order* (Princeton University Press 2014) 10–55; Boughton, *Back Matter* (n 6); MG de Vries, *The IMF in a Changing World* (n 6).

The situation today is very different. There are 191 internationally recognized sovereign states, and another fifteen whose sovereignty is contested.[11] Almost all the internationally recognized sovereign states—193 states are members of the United Nations—are members of the IFIs.[12] The status of the IFIs as important international actors in the global economy is well established. However, their global influence has been weakened by the rise of new actors in the global economy, who have sufficient economic power and/or political influence that they are, in fact, active participants in global economic governance. These new actors include transnational financial institutions many of which are privately owned, transnational corporations, and civil society organizations. In addition, old actors in global economic governance, particularly central banks, have gained new influence.[13]

The rise of these new actors is one factor undermining the capacity of sovereign states to control their own economies and, together with the IFIs, to manage the global economy. For example, the role and influence of the United States in global economic governance, while still powerful, is no longer unchallenged. In addition to the growing influence of non-state actors, rising powers like China and India are increasing able to challenge the United States and its allies.[14] These developments have functional implications for the IFIs.

As discussed in earlier chapters,[15] the increase in IFI membership has changed the focus of their operations. In the case of the World Bank, its founding members expected the Bank's first priority to be financing reconstruction in its war-ravaged European member states.[16] This did not prove to be necessary and it shifted its focus to financing physical infrastructure projects in its developing country member states. This was seen as the most efficient way to promote development in these countries. However, as discussed in Chapter 5, over time the Bank's view of development evolved and

[11] 'World Population Review Sovereign Nation' (2022) <https://worldpopulationreview.com/country-rankings/sovereign-natio> (accessed 6 June 2022).

[12] The IMF has 190 member states. IMF List of Members <https://www.imf.org/external/np/sec/memdir/memdate.htm> and The World Bank Group has 189 member states. WBG Member Countries <https://www.worldbank.org/en/about/leadership/members> (accessed 6 June 2022).

[13] See D Bradlow and SK Park, 'A Global Leviathan Emerges: The Federal Reserve, COVID-19, and International Law' (2020) 114 American Journal of International Law.

[14] The creation of the G20 to replace the G7 as the premier forum for global economic governance is a consequence of these changes in the arrangements for global economic governance. See G20, 'About the G20' <https://g20.org/about-the-g20/> (accessed 29 June 2022).

[15] See Chapters 5 and 6.

[16] WBG History <https://www.worldbank.org/en/about/history> (accessed 6 June 2022).

the range of projects and programmes that it was willing to fund expanded, and so did the range of issues that the Bank considered in making its financing decisions. In particular, the Bank began to pay more attention to the governance of its member states and to the environmental and social impacts of its operations.[17]

In the case of the IMF, the initial focus was on promoting and managing the par value monetary system established at Bretton Woods and in which all IMF member states were expected to participate. Its focus and the nature of its operations necessarily changed when the par value system ended in 1971.[18] One consequence of this event was that the rich countries, with limited exceptions such as the United Kingdom in 1976[19] and some of the members of the European Union in 2011,[20] no longer needed to use the financial facilities of the IMF. Consequently, they were able to avoid having to pay close attention to the advice that flowed from its surveillance missions. This, in turn, pushed the IMF to become relatively more interested in the monetary and fiscal challenges faced by its developing member states. These states have become the predominant consumers of its services.

These consumer countries because of their histories and relatively weak governance institutions had different needs from those that the participants at Bretton Woods imagined would have to be address by the IFIs.[21] These states face monetary and fiscal challenges and development financing needs that have intertwined economic, social, cultural, political, institutional, and environmental dimensions. They therefore need support that is multidimensional rather than the relatively narrow technocratic economic and financial support that was originally envisaged by the creators of the IFIs.[22] As a result, the IFIs have been pushed to develop expertise in a broader range of issues and to discuss a wider range of issues with their member states than their founders imagined would be necessary. They have

[17] See Chapter 5.

[18] See Chapter 6.

[19] See K Burk and A Cairncross, *Goodbye Great Britain: The 1976 IMF Crisis* (Yale University Press 1992).

[20] See 'The Eurozone in Crisis', Council of Foreign Relations (2015). <https://www.cfr.org/backgrounder/eurozone-crisis> (accessed 11 November 2022).

[21] See Chapters 5 and 6.

[22] There is an extensive literature on this point. See, eg, MM Muhumed and SA Gaas, 'The World Bank and IMF in Developing Countries: Helping or Hindering?' (2016) 28(4) World 237–249 and G Bird and P Mosley, 'The Role of the IMF in Developing Countries' in D Vines and CL Gilbert (eds), *The IMF and its Critics* (CUP 2004); FJ Carvalho, 'The Changing Role and Strategies of the IMF and the Perspectives for the Emerging Countries' (2022) 20 Brazilian Journal of Political Economy 3–18.

also been pushed to condition their financing on a more complex set of conditionalities than was originally anticipated.

These differences in the needs of member states have affected the IFI's relations with their member states. They have pushed the institutions to directly interact with a more diverse group of state and non-state actors in their member states than their founders anticipated. In other words, the growth in the IFI membership has had qualitative as well as quantitative impacts on the institutions.

Another implication, albeit unintended, of the changes in IFI membership is that the power relations among the member states of the IFIs has changed. As indicated above, the United States, *de facto*, dominated the IFIs in their early years. In fact, the United States, based on its overwhelming economic and political dominance and the relative weakness of the leading European states after the end of the Second World War, was able to effectively control the IFIs even though it did not have *de jure* control of them.[23] As noted in Chapter 2, the other protagonist in the Cold War, the Soviet Union, did not join the IFIs and so was not a factor in how they functioned in their early years.

One indication of the original dominance of the United States in the IFIs is its influence on the IFIs' operational policies and practices, their decisions on how to allocate their resources, their policies towards their member countries, and their relations with the United Nations and the other specialized agencies.[24] They therefore also influenced how they addressed the international legal questions that they confronted. These included the legal nature of their basic transactions, their international legal status and privileges and immunities, their relations with their member states, and their policies towards their employees. These characteristics of the IFIs have not materially altered over time.[25]

While the United States and the European countries continue to have the dominant voice in the IFIs, the relative balance of power in the global economy has shifted. New powers have arisen. The most obvious of these is

[23] IMF History <https://www.imf.org/external/about/history.htm> (accessed 6 June 2022). Also see Boughton, *Back Matter* (n 6); MG de Vries, The IMF in a Changing World (n 6).

[24] MJ Wolff, 'Failure of the International Monetary Fund & World Bank to Achieve Integral Development: A Critical Historical Assessment of Bretton Woods Institutions Policies, Structures & Governance' (2013) 41 Syracuse Journal of International Law & Commerce 71; G Ranis, 'The Evolution of Development Thinking: Theory and Policy' in F Bourguignon and B Pleskovic (eds), *Lessons of Experience* (World Bank and OUP 2005) 120–165; T Oatley and J Yackee, 'American Interests and IMF Lending' (2004) 41(3) International Politics 415–429.

[25] See Chapters 5 and 6.

China, which is now, in purchasing power parity terms, the largest economy in the world, the largest trading nation and one of the largest holders of US debt.[26] Other rising economic powers include India, Indonesia, Brazil, and Turkey. The result is that power in the world is more diffuse and it is harder for any particular country to impose its views on the global system. It is also harder to reach agreement on key issues in global governance.

The rise of these emerging powers has implications for the governance arrangements in the IFIs. In principle, their voice and votes in the IFIs should increase both absolutely and relative to those countries which were the dominant powers at the time of the Bretton Woods conference. In fact, the votes of some countries in the Global South, like China, India, Brazil, Turkey, and Indonesia, have increased but they have not grown commensurately with their growing role in the global economy.[27] The result is that European countries still have a disproportionately large voice and vote in the IFIs. This is leading to tensions in the governance of the IFIs and is complicating decision making about their operational policies.

The changes in the international financial system

As discussed in Chapter 2, the IFIs were designed to overcome the problems that the world had experienced after the collapse of the gold standard and the rise of protectionism in international trade. The architects of the Bretton Woods system sought to avoid a repeat of these problems by creating a monetary system that promoted unrestricted payments for the current transactions that were needed to support the growth of international trade. Consequently, they stipulated in the IMF's Articles of Agreement that the members would commit to maintaining free current account

[26] In 2021, the gross domestic product (GDP) of China amounted to around US$18 trillion, in purchasing power parity. See Gross Domestic Product (GDP) of China 1985–2027 <https://www.statista.com/statistics/263770/gross-domestic-product-gdp-of-china/#:~:text=In%202021%2C%20the%20gross%20domestic,reached%20around%2012%2C359%20U.S.%20dollars> (accessed 6 June 2022).

[27] IMF Quota <https://www.imf.org/en/About/Factsheets/Sheets/2016/07/14/12/21/IMF-Quotas#:~:text=On%20February%207%2C%202020%2C%20the,for%20the%2016th%20Review>. For World Bank Capital Increase, see MA Weiss, '2018 World Bank Capital Increase Proposal' (14 December 2018) CRS In Focus 1–2; World Bank Group Press Release, 'World Bank Group Shareholders Endorse Transformative Capital Package' (21 April 2018) <https://www.worldbank.org/en/news/press-release/2018/04/21/world-bank-group-shareholders-endorse-transformative-capital-package> (accessed 6 June 2022).

transactions.[28] At the same time, they recognized that countries, in order to promote their own economic development, may wish to impose some restrictions on foreign investment. They, therefore, provided that the management of capital flows would be left to the discretion of their member states, provided they did not use this discretion to create barriers to payments for current transactions.[29] This division between current and capital flows was respectful of the sovereign's prerogatives to manage its own development process and the role of foreign investors in this process.

The IFIs were also created in a context in which finance was largely national in scope.[30] Companies and governments tended to raise the finance they needed in their domestic markets. Their primary need for foreign exchange was to fund their international trade. Moreover, they understood that the technology used to support cross-border transactions was slow and relatively inefficient. At that time, the communications needed to settle their transactions could take days or even weeks. In addition, they would often be dealing with counterparties about whom they knew relatively little. As a result, these transactions were costly, cumbersome, and only really feasible when the transactions were large enough to justify the cost. It was, therefore, relatively easy for states to exercise control over cross-border financial transactions.

Furthermore, the essentially national character of finance and the novelty of the IFIs, led their architects to be cautious in empowering them to intervene in the domestic affairs of their member states. One way in which they limited their ability to do so was that IFIs were established as specialized economic institutions.[31] Their founders understood this to mean that, in deciding whether or not to extend financing to a member state, the IFIs would only consider relevant economic and financial issues. The IFIs were not expected to take non-economic or social and political considerations into account in their transactions. In the case of the World Bank this meant that it would focus on such issues as whether the member state's

[28] IMF Articles, Article VIII.

[29] IMF Articles, Article VI.

[30] See Chapter 2.

[31] The IMF is one of the UN specialized agencies. See Agreement Between the United Nations and the International Monetary Fund, 17 September 1947, entered into force 15 November 1947 in 'IMF, Selected Documents Relating to the Fund, the United Nations, and other International Organizations' in IMF, *Selected Decisions and Selected Documents of the International Monetary Fund* (IMF 1998) 695–701 <https://www.elibrary.imf.org/view/book/9781451971149/sc03.xml> (accessed 29 June 2022). See also The United Nations System Principal Organs <http://www.un.org/aboutun/chart_en.pdf> (accessed 9 June 2022); L Perinbam, 'The World Bank and the United Nations' (1966) 3(4) Finance & Development 292.

proposed use of the financing was consistent with its purposes, as stipulated in Article I of its Articles of Agreement, and whether the borrower would be able to repay the Bank according to the terms on which the financing was provided.[32] In the case of the IMF, this meant that it would consider if the member state needed financing to deal with a balance of payments problem and if the policies it was proposing to adopt to deal with its payments problem was likely to enable it to return the financing to the IMF in a timely manner.[33] Both institutions treated the social, political, cultural, and environmental aspects of these operations as matters within the sovereign prerogatives of the member state. In order to emphasize their respect for these prerogatives, they stipulated in their Articles that they would be non-political in their decision-making and activities.[34]

The current environment is very different. The international financial system has become global. This means, firstly, that corporations and sovereigns can now raise financing both in their home jurisdictions and externally on international markets in foreign currencies. For example, there is now a large market in Eurodollars, which are US dollars held in deposit outside the jurisdiction of the United States.[35]

Second, private financial institutions operate on a global scale.[36] This means that their decisions about to whom to extend finance, in what form and on what terms are premised on there being effectively one global financial system and global economy in which all sovereign and corporate borrowers compete for financing. However, these private financial institutions are creatures of domestic law.[37] This means that they are subjects of particular national jurisdictions and are supervised by national regulatory authorities. This disjuncture between the scale of their operations and the

32 IBRD Articles, Art I and III, Section (3) and (5).

33 IMF Articles, Art I and V, Section 3(a).

34 IMF Articles, Art V, Section (2) and (3); IBRD Articles, Art IV Section 10 See also Chapters 5 and 6.

35 See M Goodfriend, 'Eurodollars' (1981) 67 FRB Richmond Economic Review 12–18 and CR Schenk, 'The Origins of the Eurodollar Market in London: 1955–1963' (1998) 35 Explorations in Economic History 221–238.

36 RM Levich, *International Financial Markets* (2001) 10–55. See also MD Bordo, 'The Globalization of International Financial Markets: What Can History Teach Us?' in L Auernheimer (ed), *International Financial Markets: The Challenge of Globalization* (University of Chicago Press 2003) 29–78; and J Madura, *International Financial Management* (Cengage 2020) 61–101.

37 See M King, 'Governor of the Bank of England Speech' (25 October 2010) *Banking: From Bagehot to Basel and Back Again*, The Second Bagehot Lecture Buttonwood Gathering, 1–14 <https://www.bis.org/review/r101028a.pdf> (accessed 9 June 2022). King noted that banks live globally but die nationally.

national character of their legal capacities creates opportunities for regulatory arbitrage and the need for international coordination between national financial regulatory authorities.[38]

These regulatory arbitrage opportunities have been enhanced by developments in information and communications technology. They enable financial institutions to move their resources from one jurisdiction to another with a click on their computers. Moreover, they can do so much more rapidly than regulators can alter regulations. Consequently, financial institutions and their wealthy clients, in principle, are able to evade unwelcome regulations in any jurisdiction.[39]

It should also be noted that these technological developments have accelerated the globalization of finance. They lead to transactions and activities that promote the cross-border integration of national financial markets. This in turn means that each of the integrating national markets are becoming more vulnerable to developments in other national markets.[40]

Unfortunately, this process of globalization does not impact all states equally. Consequently, not all national financial systems are being equally integrated into the global market. It is only those markets that are viewed as attractive and systemically relevant.[41] Small poor countries are not being incorporated into the global market to the same extent as rich countries and the larger developing countries. Similarly, small and medium size businesses do not have comparable access to the global financial market as large transnational corporations.

Third, the globalization of finance has expanded the range of options available to both investors and borrowers with sufficient resources.[42]

[38] See T Büthe and W Mattli, 'International Standards and Standard-Setting Bodies' in D Coen, W Grant, and G Wilson (eds), *The Oxford Handbook of Business and Government* (OUP 2010) and K Alexander, 'Global Financial Standard Setting, the G10 Committees, and International Economic Law' (2008) 34 Brooklyn Journal of International Law 86.

[39] G Wenxia et al, 'Subsidiary Operations in Offshore Financial Centers and Bank Risk-Taking: International Evidence' (2022) Journal of International Business Studies 1–34; DK Tarullo, *Banking on Basel: The Future of International Financial Regulation* (Peterson Institute for International Economics 2008) 1–42, 259; GJ Benston, 'International Harmonization of Banking Regulations and Cooperation Among National Regulators: An Assessment' (1994) 8 Journal of Financial Services Research 205–225; JP Trachtman, 'Recent Initiatives in International Financial Regulation and Goals of Competitiveness, Effectiveness, Consistency and Cooperation' (1991) 12 Northwestern Journal of International Law & Business 241.

[40] See H Sless, *Merchant Princes and Charlatans or Makers of Money? Decoding Icons of Nineteenth Century British and International Finance* (Palgrave Macmillan 2022) 1–59; SL Schmukler, 'Financial Globalization: Gain and Pain for Developing Countries' (2004) 89 Federal Reserve Bank of Atlanta Economic Review 39–66; K Pilbeam, *International Finance* (Palgrave Macmillan 2013) 257–487.

[41] Pilbeam, ibid.

[42] Pilbeam, ibid.

Individuals, private equity funds, hedge funds, sovereign wealth funds, pension funds, insurance companies, and investment vehicles of all sorts are no longer limited to investing in their own national financial markets. They can choose to place their funds in an internationalized market, in a range of different financial instruments and in a range of currencies. It also has expanded the financing options available to both corporate and sovereign borrowers. Those with access to the international market can now choose to raise funds in a number of different currencies and through a variety of different debt and equity instruments. Those borrowers with fewer resources or viewed as less creditworthy have fewer options. In the case of poorer sovereigns, this means that they may become more dependent on official sources of funds, like the IFIs.

Fourth, these developments have resulted in markets that are more liquid. This means that those investors and borrowers with access to these markets have more options. But it also means that there are many international investors who, for both financial and legal reasons, are nervous investors and are likely to sell their foreign investments at the first sign of problems. This is particularly the case with their riskier investments, which tend to include those in both sovereign and private borrowers in developing countries. Consequently, for these borrowers, this new world of finance is a mixed blessing. They face a world of inherent unpredictability regarding the sustainability of their access to global financial markets at affordable rates. There is also an increased risk that their creditors will not be forthcoming in the event that they experience payment difficulties.[43]

Changing approaches to the management of environmental and social issues

A third important development since the establishment of the IFIs, as discussed in Chapter 5, is that the relatively sharp distinction between the economic and financial aspects of transactions and their environmental and social aspects has broken down. This initially occurred in large extractive and infrastructure projects which have substantial environmental and social impacts.[44] The scale of their negative social and environmental impacts

[43] MD Levi, *International Finance* (Routledge 2005) 3, 402–424.

[44] DL Stone and C Wright, *The World Bank and Governance: A Decade of Reform and Reaction* (Routledge 2006) 2–50, 70. See also D Bradlow, 'Differing Conceptions of Development and the Content of International Development Law' (2005) South African

led those who were being adversely affected by these projects to look for ways to hold both the project sponsors and their funders responsible for the harm their projects caused. Over time, this resulted in demands for the project sponsors and their funders to account for the impacts in their planning and implementation of the project. These demands were supported by developments in international environmental and human rights law. The result is that today both the project sponsor and, in many cases, their financiers are expected to do *ex ante* impact assessments of the social and environmental impacts of these projects. Moreover, they are expected to incorporate these impacts into their project planning and to take the appropriate steps to either eliminate or mitigate any harms that their projects might cause.[45]

It should be noted that to date the responsibility of the IFIs for doing such impact studies has been limited to the World Bank and the multilateral development banks. The IMF has been largely exempted from this responsibility. However, the need for the IMF to do comparable studies is likely to become more pressing. The reason is that the IMF has acknowledged that environmental issues like climate change and social issues like inequality have macroeconomic relevance and so need to be incorporated into its work.[46] One interesting indicator of the IMF's move in this direction is that in July 2022, it adopted a strategy for mainstreaming gender in its core operations.[47] These changes in its operations mean, ultimately, that the IMF will need to develop some means for assessing the environmental and social impact of its policy advice and financing conditionalities on the macroeconomies of its member states.

Journal of Human Rights 1–34. See also World Commission on Dams and Development: A New Framework for Decision-Making Report 2000; and D Moore, J Dore, and D Gyawali, 'The World Commission on Dams + 10: Revisiting the Large Dam Controversy' (2010) 3(2) Water Alternatives 3–13.

[45] World Bank Group, World Bank Environmental and Social Framework 2018. <https://www.worldbank.org/en/projects-operations/environmental-and-social-framework> (accessed 22 June 2023).

[46] K Georgieva and R Weeks-Brown, 'The IMF's Evolving Role Within a Constant Mandate', (2023) 26 Journal of International Economic Law, 17–29. <https://doi.org/10.1093/jiel/jgac064>; IMF, How to Operationalize Inequality Issues in Country Work IMF Policy Papers 2018; and N Taconet, A Mejean, and C Guivarch, 'Influence of Climate Change Impacts and Mitigation Costs on Inequality Between Countries' (2020) 160 Climatic Change 15–34. See also a new study from BIS on inequality, LA Pereira da Silva et al, *Inequality Hysteresis and The Effectiveness of Macroeconomic Stabilisation Policies* (BIS 2022) 1–122.

[47] The strategy is available at <https://www.imf.org/en/Publications/Policy-Papers/Issues/2022/07/28/IMF-Strategy-Toward-Mainstreaming-Gender-521344> (accessed 11 November 2022).

Implications for global economic governance

The changes described above have had substantial impacts on the IFIs. First, they mean that they are no longer necessarily the most desirable source of financing for their member states. This is particularly the case with their middle-income member states which are able to raise financing on international financial markets.[48] These financial markets can offer these states access to financing more quickly than the multilateral development banks (MDBs) and with relatively more focused and less onerous conditions, including in regard to environmental and social issues, than the IFIs. The net effect is that the IFIs tend to be driven to focus on low-income and vulnerable countries and those countries facing financial stress.[49]

However, it is important to recognize that the favorable environment for middle income countries may change. Financial markets are fickle. They may pull their financing from these countries whenever they perceive that the country is becoming too risky, when they find more lucrative alternative investments, or when international developments make them more risk averse. When this happens, these middle-income countries are likely to look to the IFIs for their financial support.

The changed financial options for its emerging market member states, in turn, has reduced the IFIs' efficacy as key actors in global economic governance.[50] This, in part, is due to the increased amount of funds available to many states from other sources. However, it is also due to the increasing number of new actors in global economic governance. In particular, partly because of the growing influence of financial markets, the leading central banks have become key actors in global governance, particularly in times of crisis. They are able to relatively quickly offer those central banks that they view as important and friendly access to foreign exchange. These central banks can then make these funds available to banks and financial markets in their jurisdictions. Subject to the constraints of their mandates, they can

[48] See, eg, A de la Torre and SL Schmukler, *Emerging Capital Markets and Globalization: The Latin American Experience* (IBRD 2007) 1–80.

[49] A Mourmouras, 'Conditional Lending Under Altruism' (2004) WP/04/100 *IMF Working Paper* 1–25 and N Brune, G Garrett, and B Kogut, 'The International Monetary Fund and the Global Spread of Privatization' in DR Cameron, G Ranis, and A Zinn (eds), *Globalization and Self-Determination: Is the Nations Under Siege?* (Routledge 2006) 139–164.

[50] Bradlow and Park, 'A Global Leviathan Emerges' (n 13). See M Barr, 'Who's in Charge of Global Finance?' (2014) 45 Georgia Journal of International Law 971, 976–980 and P-H Verdier, 'The Political Economy of International Financial Regulation' (2013) 88 Indiana Law Journal 1405, 1416–1422.

also begin buying financial assets in financial markets, thereby providing price support and liquidity to these markets. In fact, they can move faster and can provide larger sums than the IFIs. As a result, the incentive for other states and non-state actors involved in global economic governance to listen to the IFIs is diminished.

This situation, however, is problematic. The reason is that the leading central banks provide access to their finance on a less uniform and universal basis than would be case with the IFIs. This follows, firstly, from the fact that central banks are creatures of the domestic law of their home states and their mandates are domestic. Consequently, any international support they provide must be consistent with their domestic mandates. The result is that central banks tend to only make their financial support available to those countries they view as important to financial and monetary stability in their own countries.[51] They do not offer it to all similarly situated states, as would be the case with the IMF. This in turn means that the growing role of central banks in global financial governance is exacerbating the inequality in the global financial system. It is accentuating the differences between advanced economies and key emerging markets, on one hand, and the remaining middle-income countries and low-income countries that are not granted access to these facilities, on the other hand.

Finally, the controversies that the IFIs generated because of their insistence that they are specialized financial institutions and are not accountable for the social and environmental impacts of their operations tended to undermine their legitimacy among many of their stakeholders.[52] They also limited the IFIs' efficacy in many of their member states. Their subsequent

[51] Bradlow and Park, 'A Global Leviathan Emerges' (n 13).

[52] D Bradlow, 'The World Bank, the IMF, and Human Rights' (1996) 6 Journal of Transnational Law and Contemporary Problems, 47–90 <https://ssrn.com/abstract=1710636>; N Wahi, 'Human Rights Accountability of the IMF and the World Bank: A Critique of Existing Mechanisms and Articulation of a Theory of Horizontal Accountability' (2005) 12 UC Davis Journal of International Law & Policy 331; E Toussaint, 'The World Bank, the IMF and the Respect of Human rights' (25 October 2020) CADTM; T Pogge, 'Recognized and Violated by International Law: The Human Rights of the Global Poor' (2005) 18 Leiden Journal of International Law 717–745. For studies on structural adjustment, see M.R Abouharb and DL Cingranelli, 'The Human Rights Effects of World Bank Structural Adjustment, 1981–2000' (2006) 50 International Studies Quarterly 233–262; EN Nwagbara, 'The Story of Structural Adjustment Programme in Nigeria from the Perspective of the Organized Labour' (2011) 11Australian Journal of Business and Management Research 30–41; M Petithomme, 'Much Ado About Nothing? The Limited Effects of Structural Adjustment Programmes and the Highly Indebted Poor Countries Initiative on the Reduction of External Debts in Sub-Saharan Africa: An Empirical Analysis' (2013) 7 African Journal of Political Science and International Relations 107–120; and J Zattler, 'The Effects of Structural Adjustment Programmes' (1989) 24 Intereconomics 282–289.

acknowledgement that the economic and the social and environmental aspects of their operations are intertwined and that they have a responsibility to incorporate all these issues into their operations has improved the situation to some extent. In the case of the MDBs, the adverse impact on their credibility and legitimacy has been mitigated by their establishment of independent accountability mechanisms.[53] However, it has not ended these controversies.

In fact, the controversies are unlikely to end in the short to medium term. The reason for this is that their resolution is not within the control of the IFIs. It is widely acknowledged that no-one knows exactly how these environmental and social issues should be incorporated into either macroeconomic policies or into development project or programme planning, implementation, and management.[54] Consequently, the likelihood that the IFIs will continue experiencing controversies in connection with their operations and their operational policies and procedures is high. Moreover, given the IFIs' international prominence, the challenges that they face in this regard, while not unique, results in their responses to these challenges being closely watched. As a result, they are effectively on the cutting edge of developing a new approach to economic policy making and project planning and implementation.[55]

The challenges confronting IFI operations

The international community expects the IFIs to contribute to the international effort to meet the environmental, social, human rights, economic, and financial challenges that it faces. The most prominent of these challenges is climate change. It is clear that the cost of adapting to, mitigating, and managing the loss and damage cause by the impact of climate change is substantial.[56] The IFIs can help their member states meet these costs by providing them with both financial and technical support.

[53] See Chapter 6 for a discussion of these independent accountability mechanisms.

[54] See, eg, D Bradlow, 'Differing Conceptions of Development and the Content of International Development Law' (2005) 21(1) South African Journal on Human Rights. <https://ssrn.com/abstract=788070>.

[55] Sachs J, Kroll C, Lafortune G, Fuller G, Woelm F. *The Decade of Action for the Sustainable Development Goals: Sustainable Development Report 2021* (Cambridge University Press 2021). <https://www.sdgindex.org/reports/sustainable-development-report-2021/> (accessed 22 June 2023).

[56] OA Shobande, 'Is Climate Change a Monetary Phenomenon? Evidence from Time Series Analysis' (2022) 29 International Journal of Sustainable Development & World Ecology

Two aspects of the climate challenge are relevant to the IFIs. The first flows from the fact that climate change is about more than carbon emissions. The impacts of climate change are felt across a range of environmental variables, including water, land, air, and bio-diversity.[57] It also has a broad range of social impacts, including on the health and welfare of individuals and their livelihoods and on the stability and security of communities.[58] Moreover, climate has an impact at both a micro and a macro level and these two sets of impacts interact dynamically. For example, climate change leads to extreme weather events—such as droughts and floods—that can affect the availability of food, the wellbeing of communities, and a country's trading patterns and balance of payments. How communities and individuals react to these developments—for example, whether the communities respond to the weather events by deciding to migrate from their homes—will influence whether the social impact of the extreme weather is transitory or permanent, whether the country as a whole is able to effectively deal with the climate event, and whether the government is able to manage the event and its aftermath in a financially sustainable way. Thus, in order to fully understand the impact of these events and the role that IFIs can play in helping their member states to manage them, the IFIs need to interact with communities, civil society organizations, businesses, and subnational governments so that they have a sense of how they might react, or have reacted in the past, to these events and the policy responses to them.[59]

The World Bank is better positioned to adapt to this challenge than the IMF. The reason is that for many years it has been engaging in these types of interactions with communities and civil society organizations as part of its approach to the environmental and social aspects of its operations. It has formulated extensive and detailed operational policies and procedures to guide its staff.[60] These policies also inform external stakeholders about how

99–111. M Jakob, 'Globalization and Climate Change: State of Knowledge, Emerging Issues, and Policy Implications' (2022) Wiley Interdisciplinary Reviews: Climate Change 771.

[57] RSJ Tol, 'The Economic Impact of Climate in the Long Run' (2022) Climate and Development 3–36; A Bhattacharyya, 'Green Finance for Energy Transition, Climate Action and Sustainable Development: Overview of Concepts, Applications, Implementation and Challenges' (2022) 4(1) Green Finance 1–35.

[58] ibid.

[59] ibid. See S Nanwani, 'SDGs and the Role of International Financial Institutions' in A Pekmezovic, G Walker, and J Walker (eds), *Sustainable Development Goals: Harnessing Business to Achieve the SDGs Through Finance, Technology, and Law Reform* (Wiley 2019) 37–52.

[60] See World Bank Group Operations Manual 2008. See also Operations Policies <https://web.worldbank.org/archive/website00527/WEB/OTHER/TOC1_DEF.HTM?OpenPage> (accessed 9 June 2022).

the World Bank does its work and what they can expect from it. The World Bank's independent accountability mechanisms[61] and its cases have helped the Bank learn valuable lessons about these aspects of its operations.

The IMF will have to change its *modus operandi* in order to effectively incorporate climate into its operations.[62] Since it operates at the macroeconomic level, it has tended to focus its attention on the ministries of finance and central banks in its member states and, outside government, on the financial sector. To be sure, it has made an effort to engage informally with other relevant state and non-state actors in its member states, at least to the extent that it felt this to be necessary and the member state government allowed. However, as it takes a more active interest in the climate issue, will be pushed to develop a more formal and systematic approach to these engagements. This will be necessary so that its own staff understand how they should go about organizing these engagements and incorporating their outcomes into their work. This more formal approach will also help inform outside stakeholders about how they can engage with the IMF staff, how they provide information to the IMF and what sorts of things the IMF is expecting to learn from them. Finally, it will need to think more carefully about what the consequences are if its staff fail to follow these policies and this causes external stakeholders to experience adverse consequences.[63] In this regard, it should learn from the example of the MDBs and create its own independent accountability mechanism.

The second challenge that the IFIs must address is encapsulated in the term inequality. It serves as a shorthand expression for a range of social issues. These include general levels of income and wealth inequality within states, as well as inequalities in opportunity, access to services and differences in status that arise because of social exclusions on grounds such as gender, race, ethnicity, disability, and geography that are a feature of all societies. There is evidence showing that the capacity of governments to manage macro-economic shocks can be helped or hampered by the level

[61] The World Bank Accountability Mechanism <https://www.worldbank.org/en/programs/accountability#:~:text=The%20World%20Bank%20Accountability%20Mechanism%20is%20an%20independent%20complaints%20mechanism,a%20World%20Bank%2Dfunded%20project> (accessed 9 June 2022). IFC/MIGA Independent Accountability Mechanism (CAO) Policy 2021 1–36. See also Chapter 5.

[62] IMF Financial Operations 2018 1–196. See also Chapter 6.

[63] Chapter 6. Also see D Bradlow, 'Operational Policies and Procedures and an Ombudsman' in B Carin and A Wood (eds), *Accountability of The International Monetary Fund* (Ashgate Publishing 2005).

of inequality in their society. In addition, how they choose to manage the shock can exacerbate or mitigate the level of inequality in the society.[64]

This underscores the fact that monetary and macroeconomic policy responses can have distributional implications which in turn have consequences for their efficacy and their sustainability. In order to understand these implications, policymakers, including the IMF, will need to understand how proposed policies will affect these different communities and population groups and how they will react to these impacts. This once again highlights the need for more formal and systematic engagements with these population groups.

It is obvious that, while the IFIs cannot avoid them, both the climate and the inequality issues are complex and controversial. There is therefore room for disagreement about how they should be addressed and resolved. This complicates the role of the IFIs but it also makes the need for clear procedures for addressing these issues more urgent.

A third challenge that will require IFI engagement is the increasing evidence of breakdowns in global economic governance. It is no longer the case that the IFIs have the capacity and the legitimacy to play decisive leadership roles in global economic governance. Their authority is increasingly being challenged. They cannot effectively make and implement decisions without the support of a range of new actors on the global stage. These actors, which have the power and resources to make the decisions of the IFIs either effective or ineffective, include the world's leading central banks, globally significant financial institutions, leading transnational corporations, regional groupings and organizations, leading philanthropic foundations, and leading civil society organizations.[65]

The relevance of these developments can be seen, for example, in the global response to the Covid pandemic. The most forceful financial response came from the world's leading central banks and from international financial markets.[66] The IFIs moved more slowly and were only able to

[64] IMF Staff Report 'How to Operationalize Inequality Issues in Country Work' IMF Policy Papers (2018). <https://www.imf.org/en/Publications/Policy-Papers/Issues/2018/06/13/pp060118howto-note-on-inequality> (accessed 22 June 2023); and LAP Da Silva et al, 'Inequality Hysteresis and the Effectiveness of Macroeconomic Stabilisation Policies' (Bank for International Settlements, May 2022). <https://www.bis.org/publ/othp50.pdf> (accessed 22 June 2023).

[65] JE Stiglitz, 'Is there a Post-Washington Consensus Consensus?' in N Serra and JE Stiglitz (eds), *The Washington Consensus Reconsidered: Towards a New Global Governance* (OUP 2008) 41–56. See S Babb and A Kentikelenis, 'Markets Everywhere: The Washington Consensus and the Sociology of Global Institutional Change' (2021) 47 Annual Review of Sociology 521–541.

[66] Bradlow and Park, 'A Global Leviathan Emerges' (n 13).

provide relatively limited financial support to their member states.[67] The most powerful states and the IFIs, acting through the G20 were only able to provide low-income countries with limited debt relief and were unable to convince private commercial creditors to provide any debt relief. In addition, some of the eligible states were reluctant to take the debt relief offered by their official creditors because of concern about how credit rating agencies and their private creditors might react to this development.[68]

The above brief description underscores the role that non-state actors play in global economic governance. The IFIs are not insensitive to this development. However, they have not yet developed effective mechanisms for incorporating all of its implications into their decision-making procedures in regard to global economic governance. They have long experience interacting with private financial institutions. They are now developing mechanisms for interacting with other categories of non-state actors.[69] For example, they have established liaison committees with civil society and they invite representatives of civil society to participate in at least some parts of their annual and spring meetings and in other meetings that they may organize. However, they have not yet established effective formal structures to guide and organize these interactions. If they wish to continue playing effective and influential roles in global economic governance, they will need to develop these mechanisms.

In addition to the growing number of actors in global economic governance and the increased tensions between key states in the international system, the growing role of technology and social media in international relations is adversely affecting the efficacy of global economic governance.[70]

[67] World Bank Group, 'The World Bank Group's Response to the COVID-19 (coronavirus) Pandemic' <https://www.worldbank.org/en/who-we-are/news/coronavirus-covid19>; 'IMF Policy Response to COVID-19' <https://www.imf.org/en/Topics/imf-and-covid19/Policy-Responses-to-COVID-19> (accessed 10 June 2022).

[68] World Bank Group, 'Debt Service Suspension Initiative' <https://www.worldbank.org/en/topic/debt/brief/covid-19-debt-service-suspension-initiative>(accessed 18 May 2023); H Fuje, F Ouattara, and A Tiffin, 'Has the DSSI Helped Lower Sovereign Spreads of Participating SSA Countries?' (24 August 2021) IMF African Department.

[69] A Kutay, 'Civil Society, NGOs, and Governance' (2021) NGOs, Civil Society and Structural Changes 85–105; J von Bernstorff, 'New Responses to the Legitimacy Crisis of International Institutions: The Role of "Civil Society" and the Rise of the Principle of Participation of "The Most Affected" in International Institutional Law' (2021) 32 European Journal of International Law 125–157.

[70] X Xu, 'Emerging Economies and the Structural Transformation of Global Economic Governance' (2021) Chinese Perspectives on Global Governance and China 205–245; C Duncombe, 'Twitter and Transformative Diplomacy: Social Media and Iran-US Relations' (2017) 93 International Affairs 545–562; C Hayden, 'Digital Diplomacy', in *The Encyclopedia of Diplomacy* (2018) 1–13.

It is causing divisions between different stakeholder groups, at both the national and international level, to grow. The resulting and rising risk of fragmentation is also weakening both the authority and the legitimacy of governments and the IFIs. It is also undermining their ability to marshal the necessary resources to play a leading role in global economic governance. There is no obvious way in which the IFIs can address this problem. Nevertheless, they need to account for it in their management of their relations with the other actors in global economic governance and in their relations with their member states.

A final issue constraining the role of the IFIs in global economic governance is that there are now new multilateral organizations with aspirations to play a role in global economic governance.[71] These include such new multilateral development banks as the AIIB and NDB and such new international financial arrangements, such as the Chiang Mai Initiative Multilateralization and the Contingent Reserve Arrangement. In addition, existing international organizations, such as the Organization for Economic Cooperation and Development and the United Nations, are beginning to demand more voice in global economic governance.[72] The potential relevance of the latter can be seen in the support that the ambitious sustainable development goals and Agenda 2030 have gained. It can also be seen in the efforts by the UN and its supporters to play a larger role in regard to financing for development, international tax reform, and the reform of the sovereign debt architecture.[73] In addition, it is evident in the role that the UN's convening power plays in regard to such profound challenges as climate change and food security.

[71] See Chapter 7. See also H Wang, 'New Multilateral Development Banks: Opportunities and Challenges for Global Governance' (2017) 8 Global Policy 113–118 and D Elson, '*International Financial Architecture: A View from The Kitchen*' Politca Femina (Spring 2002 issue) <https://economicsofcrisis.typepad.com/readings/elson.pdf> (accessed 22 June 2023).

[72] Asian Infrastructure Investment Bank (AIIB) <https://www.aiib.org/en/index.html>; New Development Bank <https://www.ndb.int/>; Chiang Mai Initiative [Multilateralisation] <https://aric.adb.org/initiative/chiang-mai-initiative>; BRICS Contingent Reserve Arrangement <http://www.treasury.gov.za/brics/crp.aspx>; Organisation for Economic Co-Operation and Development <https://www.oecd.org/about/>; and UN <https://www.un.org/en/> (all accessed 10 June 2022).

[73] K Conca, 'Is There a Role for the UN Security Council on Climate Change?' (2019) 61 Environment: Science and Policy for Sustainable Development 4–15; KA Mingst, MP Karns, and AJ Lyon, *The United Nations in the 21st Century* (Routledge 2018) 1–55; S Brooks and D Lombardi, 'Governing Sovereign Debt Restructuring through Regulatory Standards' (2015) 6 Journal of Globalization and Development 287–318; H Abebe et al, 'The United Nations' Role in International Tax Policy A Research and Policy Brief for the Use of the NGO Committee on Financing for Development' (2012) Milano School of International Affairs 1–58.

In this regard, it should also be noted that the regional financial arrangements and development financing institutions are also a possible check on the discretion of the IFIs in global economic governance. They can provide their participating states with alternative sources of funds to the World Bank and the IMF. These alternate sources offunds can help strengthen some states'bargaining position relative to the IFIs. The UN can also provide some support to these states. While the UN does not have and is unlikely ever to gain the financial power that the IFIs have, the fact that those states that feel excluded or unfairly treated in the IFIs governance arrangements view the UN as an alternate locus for global economic governance decision-making serves to at least somewhat constrain the decision-making discretion of the IFIs.[74] It also raises some issues regarding the IFIs' responsibilities for their decisions and operations.

What role for international law?

The first point to note in delineating a role for international law in helping the IFIs meet these challenges is that international law itself has evolved since the time of the establishment of the IFIs. As discussed in Chapter 4, in 1946, there was no Universal Declaration of Human Rights[75] and no human rights treaties; international environmental law was in a rudimentary state and respect for state sovereignty was close to absolute.[76] In this context, the IFIs were expected to interpret their mandates cautiously and narrowly in order to avoid underming the sovereignty of their member states. In addition, they were expected to limit their decisions and operations to matters within their specialized economic and financial mandates.[77] Pursuant to their Articles and the temper of the time, they were expected to avoid interfering in the domestic political and social affairs of their member states and allowing political considerations to influence their decisions. Moreover, even though their Articles of Agreement were silent on the subject, the IFIs were expected to treat the management of environmental

[74] See discussion in Chapter 5 on the creation of the International Development Agency.

[75] UN Universal Declaration of Human Rights (10 December 1948) (UDHR).

[76] J Dunoff et al, *International Law: Norms, Actors, Process* (Wolters Kluwer 2020) 1–50 and A Anghie, 'Time Present and Time Past: Globalization, International Financial Institutions, and the Third World' (1999) 32 New York University Journal of International Law & Policy 243.

[77] See generally CE Di Leva, 'International Environmental Law, the World Bank and International Financial Institutions' in D Bradlow and D Hunter (eds), *International Financial Institutions and International Law* (Wolters Kluwer 2010) 343–384.

matters as domestic affairs.[78] Consequently, they could only address them to the extent that it could be shown that these issues were directly relevant to achieving their specialized mandates in particular operations.

As discussed throughout this book, the situation today is very different. At least formally human rights are universally recognized as legally binding obligations on states. International environmental law has developed into an important area of international law. In addition, it has become widely recognized that international organizations, including the IFIs, can play a role in making international law.[79] It should also be noted that the one area in which international law has not evolved significantly is in the law governing international financial transactions. This area of activity remains substantially subject to national law.[80] In order to adapt this national law to global markets, the international community has established a number of entities that are either creatures of domestic law or are relatively informal international bodies for addressing common international financial regulatory and transactional issues. These bodies can make proposals, but they only become binding when incorporated into the domestic law of each state[81] or into financial contracts.[82]

These developments suggest that international law can play a constructive role in helping the IFIs meet the challenges that they face and navigate the changing context in which they must operate. In order to identify and understand the contributions that international law can make in this regard, it is useful to look at the contributions specific areas of international law can make. The particular areas on which this chapter focuses are international human rights law, international environmental law, and the law of international organizations.

[78] ibid. See also W Carrington, J DeBuse, and H Lee, 'The Theory of Governance and Accountability' (2008) The University of Iowa Center for International Finance and Development 1–24.

[79] JE Alvarez, *International Organizations as Law-makers* (OUP 2006) 1–45.

[80] See, eg, CJ Brummer, 'How International Financial Law Works (and How it Doesn't)' (2010) 99 Georgetown Law Journal 273–275. See also PR Wood, *Conflict of Laws and International Finance*, vol 6 (Thomson Sweet & Maxwell 2007) 3–11, 358.

[81] K Alexander, 'Global Financial Standard Setting, The G10 Committees, and International Economic Law' (2008) 34 Brooklyn Journal of International Law & Policy 861; E Jones and P Knaack, 'Global Financial Regulation: Shortcomings and Reform Options' (2019) 10 Global Policy 193–206.

[82] AE Stolper and S Dougherty, 'Collective Action Clauses: How the Argentina Litigation Changed the Sovereign Debt Markets' (2017) 12 Capital Markets Law Journal 239–252; R Gray, 'Collective Action Clauses: Theory and Practice' (2003) 35 Georgia Journal of International Law 693.

Before discussing each of these areas, it is important to note that the international legal status of international organizations like the IFIs has not been changed by the broader developments in international law. Their rights and obligations as subjects of international law today are largely the same as they were in 1946. They are still, with some qualifications[83], immune to suit and to the jurisdiction of their member states. Their ability to enter into international agreements with other subjects of international law is unchanged. They are bound by the international agreements that they sign. In addition, they are bound by the relevant principles of customary international law.[84]

International human rights

The first point to note in this regard is that the IFIs are not signatories to international human rights treaties. Consequently, they are not technically obliged to comply with the requirements of these treaties. This does not, however, end the discussion of their human rights responsibilities. The Universal Declaration of Human Rights states that 'every organ of society ... shall strive ... to promote respect for human rights ... and by progressive measures, national and international, to secure their universal and effective recognition and observance'.[85] While the Universal Declaration of Human Rights (UDHR) is non-binding, its universal acceptance and its high moral standing means that it exercises, at a minimum, considerable moral force.[86]

[83] See, for example, Jam v. Int'l Fin. Corp. - 139 S. Ct. 759 (2019) (holding that, pursuant to US law, the IFC has the same qualified immunity as states have under the Foreign Sovereign Immunities Act).

[84] J Klabbers, *An Introduction to International Organizations Law* (CUP 2015) 325–328. See also O de Schutter, 'Human Rights and the Rise of International Organisations: The Logic of Sliding Scales in the Law of International Responsibility' in J Wouters et al (eds), *Accountability for Human Rights Violations by International Organisations* (Intersentia 2010) 51–128. International organizations derive both rights and obligations from customary international law, see N Blokker, 'International Organizations and Customary International Law: Is the International Law Commission Taking International Organizations Seriously?' (2017) 14 International Organizations Law Review1–12.

[85] UDHR available at https://www.un.org/en/about-us/universal-declaration-of-human-rights (accessed on 22 June 2023)

[86] H Hannum 'The Status of the Universal Declaration of Human Rights in National and International Law' (1995) 25 Georgia Journal of International Law & Competition 287; D Bradlow, 'Using a Shield as a Sword: Are International Organizations Abusing Their Immunity?' (2017) 1 Temple International and Comparative Law Journal 45–67. For arguments that the UDHR is a soft law with no binding legal force, see E Heinze, 'Law, Force, and Human Rights: The Search for a Sufficiently Principled Legal Basis for Humanitarian Intervention'

The UDHR is generally, if not specifically, applicable to the IFIs. They qualify as organs of society and so have at least a moral responsibility to promote respect for human rights in their operations. This suggests that they should respect and not undermine the capacity of their member states to protect, respect, and promote human rights. Consequently, the IFIs in their operations and in the conditionalities they attach to their financing should not adversely affect the ability of their member states to protect the human rights of their citizens or to progressively realize these rights.[87]

It is controversial to claim that all the individual rights stipulated in the UDHR and the other international human rights instruments have acquired the status of customary international law.[88] However, it is now widely agreed that at least some rights have acquired such a status. It is important to recognize that to the extent particular human rights assume the status of customary international law principles they become binding obligations on the IFIs.

One area where this is the case is in regard to the right of access to an effective remedy.[89] Thus, it is a binding obligation on all subjects of international law, including the IFIs. It also suggests that other actors, regardless of their international legal status, who are able to exert authority over the lives of human beings have a responsibility to provide access to a remedy to those affected by their actions. The scope of these obligations and responsibilities are beginning to be expressed in evolving international norms and standards. Thus, for example, there is now soft international law establishing the extraterritorial human rights responsibilities of states,[90] and the responsibilities of businesses.[91] The same principle is leading to a small but

(2004) 24 Journal of Conflict Studies 5–32; W Sandholtz, 'Global Constitutionalism', in *Elgar Encyclopedia of Human Rights* (2022).

[87] D Bradlow and D Hunter, 'Conclusion: The Future of International Law and International Financial Institutions' in Bradlow and Hunter, International Financial Institutions (n 77) 387–397; W Vandenhole, 'Emerging Normative Frameworks on Transnational Human Rights Obligations' (2012) 2012/17 EUI Working Paper RSCAS1-33; A Morelli, 'International Financial Institutions and their Human Rights Silent Agenda: A Forward-Looking View on the "Protect, Respect and Remedy" Model in Development Finance' (2020) 36 American University International Law Review 52–75.

[88] See Hannum, 'The Status of the Universal Declaration of Human Rights' (n 84) D Shelton, 'International Human Rights Law: Principled, Double, or Absent Standards' (2007) 25(2) Law and Inequality 467.

[89] Bradlow, 'Using a Shield as a Sword' (n 86).

[90] M Gibney et al, *The Routledge Handbook on Extraterritorial Human Rights Obligations* (Routledge 2022).

[91] Guiding Principles on Business and Human Rights: Implementing the United Nations 'Protect, Respect and Remedy' Framework (2011) [ST/]HR/PUB/11/4 <https://digitallibrary.un.org/record/720245?ln=en> (accessed 29 June 2022).

growing body of precedents discussing the human rights impacts of the operations of international organizations. For example, it has been recognized in regard to the peacekeeping operations of the United Nations[92] and in regard to its use of sanctions.[93] The ICJ has also suggestd that the UN has a responsibility to protect its staff, even from their own governments.[94]

The IFIs have been slow to fully recognize the applicability of this customary international law principle to their operations outside of the employment area. The IMF and WBG have both created administrative tribunals to provide a remedy in employment cases.[95] They also include an arbitration clause in their agreements with contractors. However, they provide other possible claimants, particularly those lacking contractual privity, with very limited remedies. As discussed, the World Bank has created two independent accountability mechanisms—one for the IFC and MIGA[96] and one for the IBRD and IDA.[97] However, these mechanisms are limited to conducting investigations and making findings. They do not have the authority to award claimants a remedy for their harm.[98] In the case of the IMF, it does not provide access of any forum or form of remedy for those who claim they have been harmed by its operations but lack contractual privity with the IMF.[99]

92 UN Mission in Bosnia and Herzegovina <https://peacekeeping.un.org/en/mission/past/unmibh/background.html> (accessed 13 June 2022).

93 See *Yassin Abdullah Kadi v Council of the European Union & Commission of the European Communities* [2005] ECR II-3649. See also *Ahmadou Sadio Diallo, Guinea v Democratic Republic of the Congo*, ICJ GL No 103 (Official Case No): ICGJ 52 (ICJ 2007); *Georges v United Nations*, No. 15-455 (2d Cir. 2016); .

94 Applicability of Article IV, Section 22, of the Convention on Privileges and Immunities of the United Nation (*Mazilu Case*), 1989 ICJ 177 & Difference Relating to Immunity from Legal Process of a Special Rapporteur of the Commission on Human Rights (*Cumaraswamy Case*), Advisory Opinion, 1999 ICJ 62.

95 World Bank Administrative Tribunal <https://tribunal.worldbank.org/> and IMF Administrative Tribunal <https://www.imf.org/external/imfat/index.htm> (accessed 13 June 2022).

96 IFC/MIGA Compliance Advisor Ombudsman <https://www.cao-ombudsman.org/> (accessed 13 June 2022).

97 The World Bank Accountability Mechanism <https://www.worldbank.org/en/programs/accountability> and World Bank Inspection Panel <https://www.inspectionpanel.org/> (both accessed 13 June 2022).

98 A notable exception is that World Bank provided a remedy to the victims of gender-based violence following an Inspection Panel report indicating that the World Bank had failed to act in compliance with its operational policies in a roads project in Uganda. See Republic of Uganda Transport Sector Development Project – Additional Financing (P121097) Investigation Report, 4 August 2016 <https://www.inspectionpanel.org/sites/www.inspectionpanel.org/files/ip/PanelCases/98-Inspection%20Panel%20Investigation%20Report.pdf> (accessed 30 June 2022).

99 *Polak v IMF* (2009) 657 F Supp 2d 116 (DDC 2009).

It is important to note in this regard, that the jurisprudence in a number of jurisdictions is beginning to address this gap in international organizational compliance with the customary international law. Courts in these jurisdictions have ruled that international organizations can lose their immunity if they do not provide claimants with access to a remedy equivalent to what would be available to them under the law of the relevant jurisdiction.[100] This development risks exposing the IFIs to contradictory rulings in different member states and potentially to substantial liability in some member states.

One way the IFIs can mitigate this risk is to improve their compliance with the customary international law requirement that they provide claimants with access to an effective remedy. A number of multilateral development banks have already created independent accountability mechanisms, but not all IFIs have done so. The most prominent exception is the IMF. Moreover, most of the existing accountability mechanisms lack the full authority to provide complainants with a remedy for the harm that the mechanism finds they have suffered because of the acts of the MDB.

Th issue of an effective remedy is particularly pertinent because, as discussed above, the IFIs need to engage more actively with external stakeholders in order to effectively deal with the new issues and challenges that they are facing. It is not clear that they can credibly and effectively take on a more active role in regard to such issues as climate and inequality if those who are affected by their decisions and actions are unable to hold them accountable for the consequences of their decisions and actions, particularly if they cause harm. Consequently, if they wish to preserve the necessary immunity that their functions require, the IFIs should offer those whom they harm access to some form of effective remedy. It, therefore, would be prudent for them to be proactive and to establish their own mechanisms for providing access to an effective remedy to those who claim they have been harmed by the IFIs. These mechanisms can offer adversely affected communities a right of redress but without undermining either the sovereignty of their member states or the immunity the IFIs need to fulfil their mandates.

[100] *Waite and Kennedy v Germany*, App No 26083/94, 30 EHRR 261 (2000); *Beer and Regan v Germany*, App. No. 28934/94, 33 EHRR 3 (2001); *Golder v United Kingdom*, App No 4451/70, 1 EHRR 524 (1979–1980) & *Stichting Mothers of Srebrenica and Others v The Netherlands* App No 65542/12 (11 June 2013). See also EC Okeke, 'Chapter 2: The Tension between the Jurisdictional Immunity of International Organizations and the Right of Access to Court' in P Quayle (ed), *The Role of International Administrative Law at International Organizations AIIB Yearbook of International Law* vol 3 (Brill 2020) 26–48.

A necessary corollary to this is that the IFIs will need to ensure that they have sufficiently detailed and clear operational policies and procedures that both their staff and their external stakeholders understand what they can expect in the operations of the IFIs and when the organization might incur responsibility for its actions.

Another way in which human rights law affect the operations of the IFIs is through their incorporation either directly or indirectly into their own operating policies and practices. As discussed in Chapter 5, an example of where the World Bank directly addresses human rights issues in its policies is in its policy on indigenous people,[101] in which they recognize the right of indigenous people to free, prior informed consent.[102] Interestingly, in many circumstances they limit the right to free, prior informed consultation.[103] An example of where it has incorporated human rights indirectly is in its policies on involuntary resettlement[104] and protection of physical cultural properties.[105] In both cases, the World Bank may not explicitly mention human rights but the issues addressed in the policies are clearly human rights issues.

It is also clear that, as subjects of international law required to respect human rights and as organs of society required to promote understanding of human rights, it would be unacceptable for the IFIs to directly contradict human rights law in their operational policies and practices. Moreover, a failure to interpret and apply these policies in a way that is consistent with applicable human rights law would expose them to considerable reputational risks. This follows from the fact that, even though these internal policies are at most soft international law and are only directly applicable to the management and staff of the IFIs, they do create external expectations about the standards applicable to IFI conduct. They therefore

[101] 'The World Bank and Indigenous Peoples Policy and Program Initiatives' <https://web.worldbank.org/archive/website00524/WEB/PDF/IPPOLICY.PDF> (accessed 13 June 2022) and Program Initiative World Bank Inspection Panel (2016) Indigenous Peoples 1–44.

[102] Article 10, UN Declaration on the Rights of Indigenous People, UNGA Res, A/61/L.67 and Ad 1 (13 September 2007) available at <https://documents-dds-ny.un.org/doc/UNDOC/GEN/N06/512/07/PDF/N0651207.pdf?OpenElement> (accessed 11 November 2022_.

[103] See, eg, IFC, Overview of Performance Standard 7: Indigenous People, IFC Performance Standards on Environmental and Social Sustainability, available at <https://www.ifc.org/wps/wcm/connect/3274df05-7597-4cd3-83d9-2aca293e69ab/PS7_English_2012.pdf?MOD=AJPERES&CVID=jiVQI.D> (accessed 11 November 2022).

[104] 'World Bank Group Operational Manual on Involuntary Settlement 2001' (updated April 2013) <http://web.worldbank.org/archive/website01541/WEB/0__C-561.HTM> (accessed 13 June 2022).

[105] World Bank Operational Policy on Physical Cultural Resources <http://web.worldbank.org/archive/website01541/WEB/0__-1678.HTM> (accessed 13 June 2022).

also raise expectations about Bank responsibility for non-compliance with these standards.

It is clear from the above that international human rights can help the IFIs meet the challenges that such global problems such as climate change and inequality pose.

International environmental law

As discussed above, while the IFIs may not be signatories to international environmental treaties, they are obliged to respect the obligations that their member states have assumed in signing these treaties and that arise from any applicable customary international law.[106] In addition, the IFIs have their own duty to comply with applicable customary international law principles. The IFIs currently do comply with these requirements. This is evident, for example, from the fact that the World Bank's environmental policies require it to respect their borrowing member state's obligations pursuant to the international environmental treaties to which the state is party.[107] They also require the Bank to comply with specific international environmental standards such as those dealing with pollution.[108] The World Bank's respect for international environmental law is also evident

[106] D Bradlow and D Hunter, 'Hard and Soft International Law and their Contribution to Social Change: The Lessons Learned' in D Bradlow and D Hunter (eds), *Advocating Social Change Through International Law: Exploring the Choice Between Hard and Soft International Law, (Brill, 2020)* World . Ibrahim FI Shihata, 'The World Bank's Contribution to the Progressive Development of International Environmental Law', in IFI Shihata, *The World Bank in a Changing World* (Brill 2000) 487–516 and F MacKay, 'The Draft World Bank Operational Policy 4.10 on Indigenous Peoples: Progress or More of the Same?' (2005) 22 Arizona Journal of International Law & Competition 65. The IMF operational policies does not mention international environmental law treaties, see IMF Financial Operations 2018 available at https://www.imf.org/en/Publications/SPROLLs/IMF-Financial-Operations (accessed on 22 June 2023).

[107] WBG, World Bank Environmental and Social Framework 2018 available at: https://www.worldbank.org/en/projects-operations/environmental-and-social-framework (accessd 22 June 2023).

[108] See World Bank Group, 'Environmental and Social Standard 3: Resource Efficiency and Pollution Prevention and Management' in WBG Environmental and Social Framework (2017) 39–43. <https://www.worldbank.org/en/projects-operations/environmental-and-social-framework> (accessd on 22 June 2023); World Bank Group, Pollution Management and Environmental Health: Annual Report (2020) <http://documents.worldbank.org/curated/en/876611640299872666/Pollution-Management-and-Environmental-Health-Annual-Report-2020>; International Organization for Standardization – Environmental management systems ISO 14001:2015 <https://www.iso.org/obp/ui/#iso:std:iso:14001:ed-3:v1:en> (accessed 4 July 2022).

in its incorporation of the requirement for *ex ante* impact assessments into its operational policies.[109] As a result, the Bank acknowledges that it has a responsibility to carefully assess the impact of its actions before it acts. It follows from this acknowledgement that external stakeholders are entitled to expect the World Bank to comply with best practice in regard to these assessments.[110]

The IMF has acknowledged that it has responsibilities in regard to climate change. However, it has not yet made clear how it will ensure that its operations and activities in this area will comply with international environmental law. Based on the experience of the World Bank and other international financial institutions, it will have to develop clear operational policies and procedures to guide its staff and management in their work in this area and to inform outside stakeholders about what they can expect from the IMF in this regard. As explained above, even though it is not a project lender, its engagement with these new issues should result in it having to create some form of independent accountability mechanism to deal with cases of non-compliance with these operational policies and procedures. This will be an essential learning tool, as well as compliance mechanism, for the IMF.

The applicability of international environmental law to the work of the IFIs, either directly or through their member states, should help the IFIs to more effectively deal with such challenges as climate change in their decision-making and their operations.

[109] World Bank Operational Policies <https://web.worldbank.org/archive/website00527/WEB/OTHER/TOC1_DEF.HTM?OpenPage> (accessed 13 June 2022). See also World Bank and Nordic Trust Fund, 'Study on Human Rights Impact Assessments' (2013) <https://documents1.worldbank.org/curated/en/834611524474505865/pdf/125557-WP-PUBLIC-HRIA-Web.pdf> (accessed 22 June 2023).

[110] Convention on Access to Information, Public Participation in Decision-Making and Access to Justice in Environmental Matters, 25 June 1998 (2161 UNTS 447) entered into force 30 October 2001 <https://treaties.un.org/Pages/ViewDetails.aspx?src=IND&mtdsg_no=XXVII-13&chapter=27>. See also Regional Agreement on Access to Information, Public Participation and Justice in Environmental Matters in Latin America and the Caribbean 4 March 2018 (CN196.2018/UN Reg No I- 56654) entered into force 22 April 2021 <https://treaties.un.org/pages/ViewDetails.aspx?src=TREATY&mtdsg_no=XXVII-18&chapter=27&clang=_en> (accessed 1 July 2022).

IFIs as international lawmakers

It should be recognized that the growing applicability of international human rights and international environmental law, even if in the form of soft international law standards, has implications for the general responsibilities of the IFIs. The first implication is in regard to the relationship between the IFIs and their member states. This follows from the fact that the new environmental and human rights standards necessarily imply that the IFIs should assume a more extensive, if not intrusive, engagement with their member states and their residents. This engagement will need to include direct interactions with a range of non-state actors. The expanded range and depth of the IFI's engagement with its member state means that it will necessarily interact with, if not be seen as interfering with, the sovereign's exclusive domestic prerogatives. This suggests that the IFIs will need to modify their views of the scope of exclusive sovereign prerogatives. They will also need to develop the procedures and mechanisms that can help them manage their new engagement with their member states. Failure to do so will expose them to the risk of being either insufficiently respectful of their member states' sovereignty or of being insufficiently attentive to their own responsibilities.[111]

Second, the IFIs will need to accept that they are becoming makers of international law.[112] This follows from the fact that as they accept their international legal responsibilities in regard to such areas of international law as international human rights and environment, they will have to decide how these legal principles apply to them. They will also have to decide how they should interpret their own policies in light of their own human rights and environmental responsibilities when implementing them in their operations. In doing so, they will establish precedents and practices and will develop their own 'jurisprudence' on how these areas of law apply in their areas of operation.[113] Their precedents will also be relevant to other

[111] D Bradlow, 'The Reform of the Governance of the IFIs: A Critical Assessment' (2012) 3 World Bank Legal Review 37; D Bradlow and C Grossman, 'Limited Mandates and Intertwined Problems: A New Challenge for the World Bank and the IMF' (1995) 17 Human Rights Q 411.

[112] Alvarez, *International Organizations as Law-makers* (n 79).

[113] D Bradlow and AN Fourie, 'Independent Accountability Mechanisms at International and Regional Development Banks' in T Hale and D Held (eds), *Handbook of Transnational Governance: Institutions and Innovations* (Wiley 2011) 122–137; D Bradlow and AN Fourie, 'The Operational Policies of the World Bank and the International Finance Corporation Creating Law-Making and Law-Governed Institutions' (2013) 10 International Law Organization Law Review 3–80; D Bradlow and M Chapman 'Public Participation and the Private Sector: The Role of Multilateral Development Banks in the Evolution of International Legal Standards' (2011) 4 Erasmus Law Review 92–122; EB Weiss, HK Jacobson, and L Gasser,

state and non-state actors, such as transnational corporations and central banks, that are engaged in comparable activities. Moreover, given the nature of their operations, the IFIs may be dealing with issues that are of first impression. In this sense the IFIs will be helping to make the law in regard to both substantive international legal issues and to questions about the responsibilities of international organizations and their officials.

In the case of the IMF, these developments could also begin developing our understanding of the obligations and responsibilities under international law of actors operating at the macroeconomic level. In this way, the IMF could contribute to developing greater clarity and understanding about the respective obligations and responsibilities of states, international financial institutions, and other entities involved in the governance of macroeconomies at the national and global level and about the interactions between the macroeconomy, environment, and human rights.

One additional area where international law will be relevant to the evolving operations of the IFIs is in regard to the institutional arrangements for global economic governance.[114] As indicated above, while the IFIs remain key actors, they are no longer necessarily the primary actors in managing global economic crises. In addition to the growing role of central banks and financial markets in this area, the role of the IFIs in global economic governance is being complemented by informal international groupings such as the G20, the international standard setting bodies,[115] and various interest-based groupings of non-state actors, such as the B20, L20 and the T20.[116] Currently, these various actors are incorporated ad hoc into the arrangements for global economic governance. However, as their number and influence grow, their roles may become more formal and systemic. As a consequence, the role of the IFIs may change. In the future, they may be limited to a supporting role, albeit one with significant convening

Engaging Countries: Strengthening Compliance with International Environmental Accords (Global Environmental Accord: Strategies for Sustainability and Institutional Innovation) (MIT Press 1998) 1–120; and EB Weiss, *Establishing Norms in a Kaleidoscopic World* (Brill 2020) 10–94.

[114] P Quayle and X Gao, 'Introduction: Good Governance and Modern International Financial Institutions', in P Quayle (ed), *Good Governance and Modern International Financial Institutions* AIIB Yearbook of International Law (Brill 2018) 1–15; E Suzuki, 'Global Governance and International Financial Institutions' (2011) 19 Asia Pacific Law Review 13–34.

[115] See generally CJ Brummer, *Soft Law and the Global Financial System: Rule-making in the 21st Century* (2nd edn, CUP 2015) for an overview of the financial international standard setting bodies.

[116] Business20, Labour20, and Think20. See University of Toronto, G20 Information Centre <http://www.g20.utoronto.ca/> (accessed 13 June 2022).

and advisory power. In this regard, their role may be more similar to that of the UN in international relations, international human rights and international environmental affairs. In order for them to play this new role effectively, they will need to ensure that their global economic governance decision making procedures conform to the general principles of good governance, such as transparency, participation, reasoned decision-making, and accountability. Both hard and soft international legal standards may help the IFIs and the international community navigate these changes in ways that do not undermine international financial stability.

Conclusion

This chapter has demonstrated that, even if somewhat diminished, the role of the IFIs as important actors in global economic governance and in helping their member states manage the changing dynamics of the international financial system is now well established. Nevertheless, their role has evolved substantially from the time of their establishment. Moreover, it needs to continue evolving if they are to remain credible and legitimate actors in global economic governance. International law on its own cannot help the IFIs overcome the demanding challenges they face in an everchanging global political economy. However, it can help them manage these challenges and avoid the pitfalls that they will face as they navigate this ongoing evolution in their roles in international finance and global economic governance.

Index

For the benefit of digital users, indexed terms that span two pages (e.g., 52–53) may, on occasion, appear on only one of those pages.